The Year 2000 Computer Crisis: An Investor's Survival Guide

by

Tony Keyes

"The Year 2000 Computer Crisis: An Investor's Survival Guide"
is available from:

Amazon.com—The World's Largest Bookstore (800) 201-7575
http://www.amazon.com

Cover design: Sean Martin Graphics
Text editing: Gramarians Inc.
Type setting: Right Angle Graphics
Back cover photo: Dawn Keyes
Printed by: Edwards Brothers Printing

Library of Congress Cataloguing-in-Publications Data

Keyes, Tony, 1952 –
The Year 2000 Computer Crisis:
An Investor's Survival Guide — by Tony Keyes

ISBN - 0-9658939-0-1 (paper)

Dedication

This book is dedicated to my family. We have all struggled very hard to get through the 6 months I devoted to researching and writing this book. It has been difficult for us all. However, I always felt supported and loved, and I could never have accomplished so much without their willingness to share me with this labor of love and personal achievement. They have given me a wonderful gift. Thank you Dawn, JT, Tim, and Acadia.

It is my wish that the fact I was able to write the book at all represent a message of hope and encouragement to any readers who are living through the challenges of Attention Deficit Disorder and Learning Disabilities. Help is available to us all through work with a professional psychotherapist and, potentially, through the aid of pharmaceuticals prescribed by a psychopharmacologist.

I would also like to send a special thank you to Dr. Marc Hafkin, my coach, cheering section and friend, for his caring support and guidance over the years. It has changed my life.

Biography

Mr. Keyes has spent nearly 20 years working in the information systems industry. He has held executive management positions with companies such as GTE, Applitek, Netrix Corporation and StrataCom Corporation, which was recently acquired by Cisco Systems.

As host of the "Y2K Investor" radio program originating from Washington, DC, Mr. Keyes brings his industry and business experience to bear on the vexing problem of Y2K. He speaks widely on the topic of the year 2000 problem and maintains a web site at: http://www.y2kinvestor.com.

Contents

Chapter 2 — Defensive Investments With Offensive Returns

Chapter 3 — 2000 Thoughts

Chapter 4 — Other Steps You Can Take

Appendix I — Government Documents

Appendix II — Clippings From The Press

Appendix III — Interviews from "The Y2K Investor" Radio Program

Introduction

It was at my favorite breakfast place over 2 years ago that my longtime friend Ed Meagher first told me about the "Millennium Bug." I thought he was nuts. While he went on about the size and implications of the problem, I kept thinking he was just caught up in the hype. Over and over I found myself saying, "yeah, right". "There's no way," I protested, "*THEY* would let this or that happen. Some smart computer geek will come up with some software that will solve the problem. After all, if we can put a man on the moon, we can certainly deal with this stupid little problem."

Yet, Ed is a pretty conservative guy and is not the type to carry a banner for some goofy cause. He remained resolute and, in so doing, got me thinking.

For some time after that breakfast I found that I kept reflecting on this supposed problem, wondering what the implications would be if it were real. Then Ed sent me a white paper written by a gentleman named Capers Jones of Software Productivity Research Inc. The paper outlined the case for a pending catastrophe. Using well-documented facts, Jones drove home his point by describing what he called the "Y2K Problem" (for Year (2)Two (K)Thousand).

I began to do my own independent research and was amazed at what I found. Even though a fairly large group of individuals, including prominent officials, were aware of this huge problem early on, nobody had done anything meaningful about it.

Soon it became clear to me that the reasons we hadn't heard of this problem sooner were rooted in simple, human nature. In fact, it will be the same human foibles that will prevent our solving the problem on time. Everyone who could have brought this to our attention, or devoted resources within their company or organization to solve the problem on time, was afraid of the personal cost. These perceived losses ran the gamut from embarrassment and job security to money, prestige, and power. We have treated this problem just like we have treated many others. Since its consequences are so unpleasant, we first tried to ignore it, hoping it would go away on its own. We've minimized it, maintaining that it really isn't that big a deal and, besides, it's years until the turn of the century. We have behaved the very same way in regard to our natural resources and the environment.

It's not so hard to understand, really. Its nothing more than plain old procrastination. As individuals, we do it with our time and our personal relationships, living as though we had an infinite number of tomorrows. This is nothing more than "denial" of an unpleasant, inconvenient situation. In fact it all makes sense to me now, whereas before I just couldn't accept that something so big could go unaddressed for so long. Think of it. In our fast-paced, highly competitive business environment, the focus is constantly directed to increasing revenues and profits. And given the punishment Wall Street has meted out for disappointing quarterly results, the decision horizon is very near-term.

In the government, the result is the same although the reasons are slightly different. Budget dollars are very tight and they are more often than not directed toward high-profile, politically sensitive programs—if not important politically to taxpayers, then important politically to politicians.

As you read this book, I imagine that you will be highly skeptical at first. That's natural. In fact, it's healthy. But don't let it stop there. If nothing else, try to accept that the subject and threat are serious. Don't write it off. The stakes are too high. If you find yourself having too much difficulty with what I am saying, spend some time in the Appendix. There you will find compelling evidence that this problem is not only real and expensive but also poses a vital threat to our assets and our very way of life.

I will have succeeded if my work here can accomplish the following:

- ✦ Move you, the reader, to take Y2K seriously and to take action to educate yourself
- ✦ Consult with your professional investment advisor regarding your portfolio's Y2K readiness
- ✦ Collect hard copies of all your personal, family records and keep them in a safe place
- ✦ Write your elected, political representatives and let them know how you feel about Y2K. Tell them you expect leadership on this front.
- ✦ Write the Boards of Directors of the companies in your portfolio
- ✦ Write the manager of the mutual funds in which you are invested
- ✦ Prepare for the worst — work and hope for the best.

Chapter 1

The Millennium Bug

Innocent decisions made at the dawn of the computer industry are destined to have a dramatic effect on society and the global financial markets over the next 3 years. This book will explain why and will show you how to protect yourself against the bear market that will ensue, taking you step by step through the process of putting together a portfolio that will protect your assets and position you to reap major returns.

The mother of all procrastinations

In the interest of efficiency, the designers of the world's early computer software programs used just two digits to express the year in a program's date field (i.e., 12/31/99). They never expected, however, that this practice would survive for decades and be incorporated into the vast majority of the world's computer systems. The problem, you see, is that when New Year's Day arrives in the year 2000, computers won't be able to distinguish the year 2000 from 1900.

Since date calculations are designed to compare numbers, often subtracting smaller numbers from larger numbers, by default 00 will always be recognized as the smaller number. If left untouched, these systems at best will stop functioning completely and "crash." At worst they will begin to generate bad data, causing potentially catastrophic results. Had government and industry been working on this for several years, there would be no problem. However, most organizations still have not initiated serious projects to take care of the problem and, for some, it's already too late to finish on time, according to the Gartner Group, a Stamford, Connecticut, information technology consulting firm.

The Gartner group maintains that 20 to 30% of today's businesses will fail.

It is the Gartner Group's contention that less than 70 percent of Information Systems (IS) organizations will have fixed the problem in *mission critical applications.* Based on this projection, the Gartner Group maintains that 20 to 30 percent of today's businesses will fail. Small- and medium-sized businesses that are undercapitalized will find themselves in an untenable situation. If they spend the money required to fix the problem, they'll go out of business, and if they don't fix the problem, they'll still go out of business.

"No problem for me, I don't have a computer"

Our entire civilized world is hugely dependent on computers. Everything from managing your savings account and the digital thermostat in your home to the elevator in your office building and air traffic control systems is controlled by computers. They all are potentially vulnerable to failure if their underlying software is not modified to incorporate an eight-digit date field *(mmddyyyy or ddmmyyyy or any other eight-digit sequence)*. So, even if you don't personally own a computer, this problem will have an enormous impact on your day-to-day life.

In June 1996, the Congressional Research Service provided both the House and Senate with a memorandum covering the various consequences of failing to adequately address the problem at the federal level. Here are some potential glitches that were cited in the report:

- ✦ Miscalculation by the Social Security Administration of the ages of citizens, causing payments to be sent to people who are not eligible for benefits while ending or not beginning payments to those who are eligible;
- ✦ Miscalculation by the Internal Revenue Service of the standard deduction on income tax returns for persons over age 65, creating incorrect records of revenues and payments due;
- ✦ Malfunctioning of certain Defense Department weapons systems;
- ✦ Generation of erroneous flight schedules by the Federal Aviation Administration's air traffic controllers;
- ✦ Corruption of state and local computer systems, creating false records and causing errors in income and property tax records, payroll, retirement systems, motor vehicle registrations, utilities regulations, and a breakdown of some public transportation systems;
- ✦ Creation of erroneous records by securities firms and insurance companies; and
- ✦ False billing by telephone companies, resulting in errors in consumers' bills or lapses in service.

Other examples of what could be disrupted:

- ✦ International Financial Transactions
- ✦ Government Services
  - –Social Security Checks
  - –Welfare Checks
  - –Aid To Dependent Children
  - –VA Checks
  - –Medicare Reimbursement
  - –Medicaid Reimbursement
  - –Tax Collection, Refunds, and Payment Records

- Telephone Systems
- Manufacturing Processes
- Product Distribution Networks
- Inventory Systems
  (including volatile chemicals and drugs)
- Administrative and Payroll Systems
- Bank Vaults
- Security Access Control Systems
- Closed Circuit Television Systems
- Prison Confinement Systems
- Penal System Parole Schedules
- Satellites
- Earth Stations
- Nuclear Power Stations
- Elevators
- FAA Air Traffic Control Systems
- Airline Reservation Systems
- 250 Million PCs

The Mundane:

- Flex-Clocks/Time Recording Systems
- Plant Control systems (e.g. Air Conditioning, robotics)
- Lighting (switching systems)
- Planned Maintenance Systems
- Facilities Management System (AutoCAD)
- Mobile Phones
- Answering Machines
- Voice Mail Systems
- Pagers
- Fax Machines
- Photocopiers
- Postage Machines
- Still Camera Databacks
- Inventory Control Systems

- ✦ Computer-Based Training (CBT) Systems
- ✦ Electronically controlled Clocks/Watches
- ✦ Scientific Calculators
- ✦ Pre-printed Forms (19__)

In spite of what you might hear, the problem doesn't necessarily extend to your household appliances. Large mainframe and desktop computer systems could crash and cause havoc, but most of the embedded systems that are increasingly important in supporting our lives and livelihoods —— in cars, pagers, cellular phones, kitchen appliances, faxes, printers, and hundreds of other applications —— may only cause minor inconveniences. Yet, sorting this all out, and making certain we have done a good job of determining which ones are minor and which are major will be time consuming and costly.

"I think the President should declare this is a national emergency".
— Retired Air Force General, Thomas McInerney

The same is not true for the military, however. The Department of Defense has over 9,300 systems, comprising over 112,000 programs, according to the Honorable Emmet Paige, Jr. Paige is the Chief Information Officer for DoD. In testimony before Congressman Steven Horn's (R.-Calif.) Year 2000 subcommittee, Paige said that the current estimate of over $900 million to fix the Defense Department's problem was likely to go up as more data came in. It is interesting to note that the two top officials in the military with responsibility for IS retired in May 1997.

In an article appearing in *Computerworld*, Robert L. Scheier, Gary H. Anthes, and Allan E. Alter recounted two real life, battlefield situations in their article entitled "Year 2000 May Ambush Military." In one of the anecdotes they shared, it seems that during a routine exercise a submarine commander watched "horrified as a torpedo he launched veers off course and races back toward his submarine." Also quoted in the same article was retired Air Force General Thomas McInerney, who said, "I think the president should declare this a national emergency," His concern comes from first-hand knowledge of the potential disaster a software glitch could trigger.

In the same article, Robert Charette, who wrote code for the Naval Underwater Warfare Center, was quoted as saying, "Will they[the military] be able to find every single date problem? Of course not." He conjectured that, instead, defense officials "are going to cross their fingers and run with it. I will not be surprised if something real bad happens."

This is, of course, the most sophisticated, up-to-date military organization on the planet. What about those countries that are using our second-hand equipment and systems they have nursed along for over 50 years?

Also quoted was Bryce Ragland, author of "The Year 2000 Problem Solver", McGraw-Hill, who heads a Year 2000 team at the Air Force Software Technology Support Center located at Hill Air Force Base, Utah. "There's a real risk that some wacko in another country might decide to launch an attack against the U.S. a few seconds after midnight just to see if our defenses can handle it."

Military systems will be the thorniest to correct. Much of what our military has to address lies embedded in hardware, made specifically for that application, coming from a production line that was shut down long ago. Furthermore, much of the software used in military applications was purposely ad hoc and arcane, in order to frustrate hackers and saboteurs. As a result, the Mitre Corporation, a government think tank, estimates the cost to convert these systems will range from \$1⁺ to \$8⁺ per line of code.

Of course, many failures/problems stemming from Y2K will fall into the "annoying but harmless" category. For instance, credit card companies are discovering that the cards with an expiration date of 2000 are being rejected by thousands of point-of-sale terminals . First USA recalled all cards that had expiration dates in the next century. Late last year it was reported that VISA was informing its processing providers that their systems must be able to accept cards with expiration dates past 2000 by April 1st or experience penalties of \$167,000 per month until their systems are updated.

"But we have nearly 3 years before the turn of the century"

We won't have to wait until 2000 for some systems to have problems. In fact, state motor vehicle departments, insurance companies, and even high schools and colleges are finding that referencing dates beyond 1999 in their databases is triggering bizarre results. Students are shown to have graduated 99 years ago, 5-year driver's licenses have already expired, and insurance actuary tables search for rates based on someone being -50 years old.

Banks began patching systems years ago because they couldn't manage their long-term loans, and utilities were forced to begin work on their systems in 1991 because of their inability to process dates beyond the turn of the century.

"So what is this all going to cost"?

Casper Weinberger, former Secretary of Defense under President Reagan, made the following observation in an editorial appearing in the July 19, 1996, issue of *Forbes* Magazine: "Surely, you say, this is not such a big thing—simply adjust the software programs. But it's the scale of the problem that makes this a nightmare. Computer systems are collections of individual programs, and a medium-size corporation with average computing capability has about 8,000 software programs. The man-hours required for even a well-planned, coordinated repair program of such a company are vast, with an estimated cost of $4 million."

The Gartner Group estimates the global repair costs for the Year 2000 problem to be in the range of $300 to $600 billion.

The Gartner Group has estimated the cost of rectifying this problem worldwide at somewhere between $300 billion and $600 billion." Capers Jones, Chairman of Software Productivity Research, believes a more all-inclusive figure would be $1.5 trillion. In the current version of his very thoroughly researched white paper, entitled, "The Economic Impact of the Year 2000 Problem" (the full text can be found on his website: http://www.spr.com), he has raised the cost in large part because of the snake pit of litigation that will be triggered by the Year 2000 problem.

JP Morgan's William Rubin recently released an update to a report he wrote last summer. In it this most recent report entitled, "The Year 2000 Problem, Its Worse Than We Thought", he raises his estimate from $200 billion world-wide to closer to the $600 billion estimated by the Gartner Group. He also radically changed his position on where these dollars would come from. Initially, Mr. Rubin indicated that spending over and above existing IT budgets would only amount to about 0.38%, however, in the more recent report, he indicates that JP Morgan's analysis shows incremental spending to be 39.84%. A huge change, which underscores our position regarding a major threat to corporate profits. The report also sites data from the Standish Group International, Inc., 1996, which forecasts only 27% of large Y2K system integration projects will be successful, 33% will be late or over budget and a whopping 40% will fail.

"Why don't they just change the dates? What's the big deal?"

For the most part, fixing this problem is not a significant technical challenge. It is, however, enormously labor intensive due to its systemic nature and the exhaustive testing that must take place on mission critical systems. Large corporations and government agencies have thousands of programs, many of which are insufficiently documented. In fact, some aren't even known to exist! Deeply embedded code, representing ad hoc subroutines and other incidental functionality, have been slowly added over the years without any defining documentation. The first task, then, is to identify all of the code in use. If "source" (the original documentation for the software) doesn't exist, it will have to be regenerated.

Another perspective on the scope of the problem comes from Robin Guenier, Executive Director of Task Force 2000, a private sector organization dedicated to raising awareness of Y2K throughout the United Kingdom. Mr. Guenier submits that the total cost for remediation of the Year 2000 problem in the U.K. will be 31 billion British pounds (about $50 billion, U.S.). He informed Ian Taylor, Minister of Science and Technology during the John Major administration, that it will take every one of the 300,000 software programmers residing in the U.K. working exclusively on the Y2K problem, in order to have a shot at completing the work on time.

Many of these veteran programs, modified countless times over the years, have worked so well they haven't been touched in years. Oh, it's true that "Charley," the resident computer guru, may remember some of them, but these key individuals are hopelessly overbooked and, in many cases, have moved on to other fields, have retired, or are even dead. After all, this problem is over 30 years old, meaning that the vast majority of programmers who will work to solve the problem weren't even born when it all began.

"What do they do, when they do it?"

There are several techniques used to address the problem, when remediation is chosen as the course of action. I have identified four below, but there are arguably more, in that there are variations on the approaches I have identified.

Date-Field Expansion — This by all accounts is the preferred approach, given an infinite amount of time. This involves an actual "re-write" of the code, to expand all date references to an eight digit representation *(i.e. mm/dd/yyyy)*. Purists prefer this approach because it is permanent and allows for incorporation of all nuances, such as leap years and such.

The reason this approach isn't being pursued by organizations just getting started now, is that it takes much longer to complete. Testing is very complex, as you are actually changing the software. Changing the software means the introduction of new bugs. According to Capers Jones, Chairman of Software Productivity Research, under normal circumstances one might expect new errors to be introduced at the rate of less than 10% per line of code, yet under the unique circumstances Y2K represents, it could be higher. The indications are that with the lack of source code documentation, the crush of a finite deadline, junior programmers being used and the vast scale and inter-system dependencies involved in the project, it will be much harder to manage the new bugs to a minimum.

Windowing — This is perhaps the most popular approach. This technique directly addresses the problem that computer systems won't be able to distinguish 1900 from 2000. It is accomplished by establishing a reference date or "pivot" year as it is sometimes called. The pivot year becomes a point of demarcation, where prior dates will be considered to be in the 20XX series and the following years up to '99 will be in the 19XX series. This approach while not requiring a change to the actual code, does present some challenges for system designers and testing. You may require different "pivot" years for different kinds of dates. For instance 1950 might work for credit card charges, but it clearly won't work for birth dates.

Encapsulation — By setting all dates back 28 years in any given program, this approach creates some breathing room for programmers. By using 28 as the set-back, the mechanism preserves the same date/day of the week relationship.

This technique utilizes a I/O (Input/Output) routine which adds or subtracts 28 years from the date contained in the data depending upon whether or not it is headed into the system for processing (Input) or out (Output) of the system for presentation to a screen or report.

Hyperdating — This technique, developed by Delsoft Consulting Incorporated, located in Roswell, Georgia, changes all dates to a new "Hyperdate". All date calculations are conducted using this new Hyperdate and the result is either changed to an eight digit date if there is a requirement to present the information to a screen or report, or back to a six digit date if it will be added or returned to the database. The company has a patent pending for this invention which converts six digit dates into another six digit number which can uniquely represent all relevant years. The system software requires very little in the way of modification.

"There's more?"

If this all weren't enough of a problem, the Year 2000 happens to be a leap year. This further complicates otherwise straightforward solutions.

Worldwide, it is estimated that there are some 300 billion lines of code at issue. Using an alternative analysis, Capers Jones defined the problem in "function points" and reached a similar conclusion.

To make matters worse, in some program languages like COBOL, which is used in the software of many mainframe computers (large, centralized computers with powerful processing capability and vast information storage resources), programmers invented their own "code" words and phrases to represent date operations or fields. This presents a problem for the specialized tools that have been developed to search the code automatically. These software agents use artificial intelligence to find date fields and correct them as they go. They can speed up the process dramatically, but only when the target pieces of code can be identified up front. Since many programs are undocumented, the identification doesn't always work. In all cases, projects involve time-consuming preparation and testing.

The cost of bringing systems into compliance can be overwhelming for the average, medium-size company. One that has 5,000 to 10,000 programs might have to spend \$3–\$4 million of unbudgeted funds to fix the problem.

"Wait a minute, if this is such a big deal, why haven't I heard of it before?"

Don't feel bad, you're not alone. There are many studies that have been undertaken recently that indicate you have company. As recently as February 1997, in testimony before the House Subcommittee on Government Management, Information and Technology, chaired by Congressman Steven Horn, the Chief Information Officer for the Department of Transportation, Michael Huerta, admitted that he had not heard of the problem until August 1996. Prudential had been working on its problem for an entire year by then, and the FAA is still only in the assessment phase. The dire situation was corroborated recently by a study conducted by Computer Intelligence, which found that 42 percent of companies polled hadn't any plans to address the Year 2000 problem.

It's even worse overseas, according to Neil Winton of Reuters, who quoted experts in a May 13 report, who stated that: "most small and medium sized British companies are still unaware that the millennium computer bug threatens their survival." He went on to say that, "...Although most bigger British companies are aware of the bug, more that 90 percent have yet to complete an internal audit of their information technology systems."

Cap Gemini, a major systems integrator based in France, with U.S. operations out of New York, conducted a survey of Fortune 500 executives and found that less than 13 percent had implemented plans to deal with Y2K and only 18 percent had developed a plan of action. The survey also indicated that a significant percentage of the companies polled planned to use outsourcing services to deal with the problem.

The reason that executives are in the dark on this issue might be because the Information Systems Manager has been afraid to tell the boss about the problem, concerned he himself might be blamed. Who wants to be the one to tell the CFO that anything spent to fix this problem will bring no return on investment? The only "return" is staying in business after the turn of the century. Yet, even if the CFO and CEO of a public company are aware of the problem, Wall Street judges performance quarterly, and the cost of fixing this problem and the resulting hit to profits would, in many cases, be disastrous for the company's stock price.

Big bucks are at stake for large financial institutions, insurance companies, and agencies of the federal government. It is not uncommon for these enormous enclaves of computer systems and data storage to have hundreds of millions of lines of code. With estimates to repair running more than $1 per line of code, this amounts to billions of dollars. It's important to note that calculations are based on current costs of labor and resources. As time begins to run short, prices will rise dramatically. It's not as if there are legions of programmers just waiting to get to work. In fact, the Meta Group recently found that COBOL programmers in New York were being offered an astounding $120,000 per year. The Chief Information Officer for a large financial services company lamented to me in an interview last year that he had lost one of his programmers to a vendor organization. He told me that they offered his programmer $150,000 per year, when he was currently paying only $53,000.

The dominant programming language at issue is COBOL. It has been out of vogue for decades, yet it still is the workhorse used in a vast majority of the world's mainframe computers. According to Capers Jones, there are approximately 550,000 COBOL programmers in the United States. Mr. Jones estimates the scope of the COBOL problem to be approximately 12,000,000 applications. Because of the processing power required, most of these applications can only be modified and tested off-line when the systems aren't in normal use. That usually means weekends, as large jobs are often done overnight. As of this writing, there are only 88 more weekends until testing should begin and only 140 weekends until 01/01/2000. Since most experts suggest at least a year of testing and debugging prior to implementation, those programmers will be working every weekend from now until well after the new century's first days.

To cope with this shortage of personnel, some companies have resorted to offering bounties to their employees for referring a qualified programmer.

In early 1996, Congressman Horn led the Subcommittee in conducting hearings into the nature and scope of the problem. These hearings, held in April and May of 1996, featured representative experts from industry and government.

One such expert, Peter de Jager, a consultant who has been attempting to raise public consciousness about the serious nature of this problem, identified several unique characteristics of the Year 2000 threat in his testimony before Congress on May 14, 1996.

- ✦ The deadline is real, immovable, and cannot be missed.
- ✦ Those active have found this to be the most complex project they've ever attempted.
- ✦ There are unique, non-technical obstacles in our path.
- ✦ The IS community suffers under a delusion of infallible confidence, despite a proven track record of no greater than 14 percent [on time delivery of software development projects]. *Phrase in brackets is mine.*
- ✦ The sense of urgency required to complete this task on time is absent.

"For many it's already too late," his testimony continued. "There are less than 140 weekends [less than 90 at this writing] left before December 31st, 1998 [September 30, 1998, for the federal government's fiscal year-end]. You should be completed by then, so that you can allocate all of 1999 to test the hundreds of thousands of error prone changes you've introduced into your systems."

After the subcommittee's initial hearings in April 1996, a joint, congressional oversight letter was sent to the heads of each executive department and 10 additional agencies. The letter asked for a detailed response to 13 questions. What the subcommittee got back was disappointing. Of the 24 organizations that received the letter, only nine could say they had a plan for addressing the problem. Others, like the Department of Transportation, the Department of Energy (responsible for oversight of the nation's nuclear reactors), the Department of Labor, and the Federal Emergency Management Association, had never even heard of the problem.

To make a point, the subcommittee issued "grades" to the responding agencies. The four just mentioned above received "F's"; 10 others got "D's", three got"C's", two got "B's", and five got "A's".

As recently as March of this year, NASIRE (National Association of State Information Resource Executives) conducted a Y2K status survey of all 50 states. Here's what they found:

- ✦ 6 States have not reported any progress
- ✦ 22 States are still in the planning stage
- ✦ 22 States are in the implementation/testing phase

It's interesting to note that the current estimate for the cost to convert the systems of all 50 states ($2.5 billion) is approximately what OMB has said it will cost the federal government ($2.3 billion) to make the required changes.

Intuitively that feels off base. One would of course assume the federal government's expense would be much higher than the states. Congressman Horn certainly agrees. It is his opinion that the costs for the federal government will run more in the range of $10 to $20 billion.

"How could two little digits have such an impact?"

These conditions represent an enormous threat to our worldwide economy. Even if we don't suffer the worst of potential scenarios, a sobering chill is likely to run through the veins of Wall Street's most ardent Bulls. Coming at a time when the market is thought to be so vulnerable to a sudden downturn anyway, investors' defensive moves could trigger a precipitous drop all the major indexes. Senator Daniel Patrick Moynihan has taken the problem quite seriously. In a letter to the President, dated July 1996, he suggested that the President may wish to turn to the military to take command of the problem. He also submitted legislation (a copy is provided in the appendix), that would impanel a commission responsible for studying the problem further and providing direction. While the bill has been read on the Senate floor, no action has been taken at this time.

The global economy is at risk. This is not just a U.S. problem. In fact, the United States is leading the world in addressing the problem. In Europe, efforts are further complicated by the transition under way to the common currency. Germany has the added challenge of moving its capital during the peak of the problem.

Asia, on the other hand, has other problems. In Japan, there are cultural barriers preventing this problem from getting the proper attention. In Japan, it is unthinkable for a mid-level IS manager to go to his boss and say there is a problem of this magnitude in the systems for which he is responsible. As a result, only 10 percent of Japanese businesses had even a vague awareness of the problem, when polled recently. Hong Kong represents another unique environment. According to a survey conducted by the Hong Kong Monetary Authority, almost half of Hong Kong's banks have not yet prepared for potential computer malfunctions at the arrival of the year 2000. Hong Kong has grown to be a huge financial center for the Pacific Rim, yet officials have delayed initiating aggressive plans to fix the problem in light of the uncertainty surrounding China's resumption of control this year. A survey conducted recently showed that only 50% of Hong Kong banks had even begun to assess their exposure.

Here at home, the threat to our financial institutions has gotten the attention of two senior legislators. Representative John Dingell, from the state of Michigan, called on the Securities and Exchange Commission to speed up work to address the problem. He cited possible scenarios that could develop if the problem is not solved in time — clearing and settling of stock trades by brokerages would be jeopardized, trades might not be credited to the right investors, and liquidity could come into question if trades were not posted on time. It's not hard to imagine what would happen if investors become worried about these possibilities.

Senator Alfonse M. D'Amato, chairman of the Senate Banking Committee, has focused his attention on the Federal Reserve and other regulators of our financial institutions. Troubled by the answers he received when he queried the authority's officials, he demanded details of their plans. D'Amato said recently, "The agencies lacked an aggressive plan to deal adequately with the problem." Backing up Senator D'Amato's position are data coming out of a study recently conducted by Killen & Associates.

They determined that banks are facing a threat to their survival greater than anything since the Great Depression because of having to deal with the Euro (dollar) conversion, the Year 2000 software conversion, and the creation of the electronic payments/electronic commerce infrastructure. If that doesn't make investors nervous, then perhaps an article that appeared in London's *Sunday Business* newspaper on April 27, 1997, will give them pause. In it, Rachel Oldreyd reported that several of the largest banks in London refused to guarantee their customers that their accounts would be unaffected by the Year 2000 problem.

When asked about the Senator's concerns, Federal Reserve spokesperson Joe Coyne was quoted as saying he had "no comment." The written response to Senator D'Amato's request for further information is expected in early May.

It is difficult to know what event will trigger the first reaction in the market. If the Dow reacts with a 700-point drop, as it did recently to "signs" of rising inflation, just imagine what will happen when Wall Street internalizes the significance of the Y2K threat. In a recent memorandum authored by Morgan Stanley's Scott Slayton, he said his analysts believe a potential "catalyst" to ignite investor interest in the Year 2000 problem could be an earnings shortfall in a large, publicly held company that is caused by unbudgeted spending to fix the Y2K problem. It's coming. . . In the Appendix, you'll find a section detailing the 19 percent drop in earnings posted by New Zealand Telecom, all of which was directly related to Y2K.

On the other hand, it could be something like the conditions written about by Alan Cane and featured in the *Financial Times* of London on May 2, 1997. Mr. Cane reported that major telecommunications operators have warned that it could be impossible to telephone some countries. Just think of it. If a country can't make or receive calls, it's out of the economy. The presumption is, of course, that these are Third World countries that have been buying used IBM equipment, which won't work after the Year 2000 because IBM no longer supports the operating system.

You'll want to have your game plan in place before this happens. To do that, you have to act NOW! Later in this book I'll cover a number of different strategies that will help you protect your assets and, in fact, prosper when the meltdown begins.

All of the right elements are coming together to create a very unique opportunity for the informed investor. Never before has such an enormous market developed virtually overnight. Imagine the effect of a $600 billion market breaking on the economic scene like a tidal wave. There are companies in business today that will be awash in a sea of business so enormous and profitable, it will dwarf anything in their previous experience. Some of the companies are public and will see their market capitalization grow 10-fold overnight. As an investor, you'll want to be sure to participate in this boom market. A later section of the book profiles many of the top players in this arena.

It's only a disaster if you didn't know it was coming

Imagine it's 1926, on a sunny, late fall morning. As usual, you stop at the front door to pick up the paper. On this October morning, however, you look down at the front page in disbelief. "New York Stock Exchange Collapses In Binge of Panic Selling," the banner screams. You read on about the bank runs, suicides, and business failures that ran like a flash flood through the canyons of Wall Street. You're wondering how you could possibly have missed all this, when you notice the date, October 29,1929. 1929!

This book will be like reading that newspaper of long ago, yet it's not history we're talking about. It's the future. And it's true! It just hasn't happened yet. Imagine knowing in 1926 all the details of what transpired in the fall of 1929. Think of the disaster you could have avoided, and now think of the money you could have made. While the majority of investors suffered devastating losses in the crash, for some, it was like shooting fish in a barrel. They were a fortunate few, to be sure, but they had the funds to spend during the recovery on assets at fire-sale prices.

You hold just such an opportunity in your very hands. This book will detail for a select group of individuals the drama that will unfold over the next 3 years. The story will be hard to believe. And perhaps only a few of you will have the vision and fortitude to act. Yet, it is just this skepticism that is creating a window of opportunity for investors to get in at discount prices.

"Ridiculous," you scoff. This market has defied gravity for years. True, but the man in the story above could easily have spoken the same words in 1926. In fact, read what was said in 1929:

Wisdom from 19..?

> *"Democracy has found its way into finance, we have become a nation of investors."*

"Stock prices have reached what looks like a permanently high plateau." Sound familiar? Some have called this the bull market that will never end. Others have postulated that the business cycles that regularly led to inflation are a thing of the past.

"We believe that the investor who purchases securities at this time may do so with the utmost confidence." Analysts and

fund managers in their late 20s and early 30s, sages that they are, have been telling us that there is nothing on the horizon that could threaten this market.

"Democracy has found its way into finance, we have become a nation of investors." In the 20s, an enormous percentage of the population "played" the market. From grannies to garbagemen, they all had a piece of the action. Today, we are witness to billions of "baby boomer" dollars that pour into the market every month. In January 1997, $24 billion was invested in mutual funds alone. In a crisis, these dollars will pour out at an even faster pace. Not like the 9 percent "breather" the market took in April 1997, but rather a smoke trailing nosedive of greater than 30 percent.

"Nothing matters as long as stocks keep going up. The market is now its own law." Don't you believe for one moment that this market is invulnerable. In fact, a growing number of analysts are now saying it's likely we'll see a correction of at least 20 percent this year, and that has nothing to do with Y2K. Alan Greenspan warned us last year that investors had driven the market up with "irrational exuberance." That, mind you, was back before the Dow hit 6000!

Joseph P. Kennedy, father of the late president, was one of the big winners in 1929. He sold out his entire position just weeks before the crash. When chided for the money he left on the table, his reply was: "Only a fool holds out for the top dollar."

Traditionally, Wall Street has never been comfortable with the market's ability to sustain a Price to Earnings (P/E) ratio in excess of 16. We crossed that watermark last year, when the Dow reached 7300. I'm nervous.

Today's investors just can't comprehend the depths to which a bear market can sink. The "crash" of 1987 was essentially limited to the stock market. The economy wasn't devastated, the unemployment rate didn't skyrocket into double digits. One would do well to heed the words of John Kenneth Galbraith in his comments on the markets of the 30s: "The singular feature of the great crash of 1929 was that the worst continued to worsen." In fact, Susan E. Kuhn and Amy R. Kover observed in their article entitled, "Will A Bear Market Wreck Your Retirement Plans?", which appeared in the August 19, 1996, issue of *Fortune* Magazine, "The fiercest bear markets maul investors repeatedly: They're characterized by a series of rallies that fail. For instance, while the Crash of 1929 gets all the publicity, the subsequent decline of 1930 to 1932, a sickening 70% slide, was the most devastating drop on record and wiped out more wealth. Similarly, a 22% decline in stock prices in 1966 foreshadowed a 37% drop between 1968 and 1970, and a 48% catastrophe in 1973 and 1974."

While "bears" might seem like a thing of the past, we have had 14 since 1950, with an average decline in stock prices of 24 percent and an average recovery period of 13 months.

Imagine even a minor mistake made by the U.S. Treasury, which electronically sends and receives over $1,400,000,000,000 every year.

Even for those who are wisely predicting a correction, the crash won't come from anything they're expecting or even thinking about. That, in fact, is the problem. The IS industry faces a total catastrophe, the likes of which our generation has never experienced. After all, for anyone under 60, global catastrophes are a thing of the past. According to a study conducted by the Equitable, a large, life insurance provider, the average baby-boomer earning

$50,000 or more a year is 43 years old, owns $180,000 in financial assets, and plans to retire with $1,000,000. And they'll make it, provided the average return over the next 20 years is about 10 percent. But what if that is threatened? Do you really believe these future millionaire retirees are going to stand by and let the government roll the dice with their retirement? I don't think so. The exit doors are going to look pretty small when the piper is paid. When the bottom falls out, it will come as quite a shock and it's all going to be the result of two little digits.

Imagine if even a minor mistake were made by the U.S. Treasury, which electronically sends and receives over $1,400,000,000,000 every year. In fact, suppose for a moment that the investor community only had a reasonable *fear* that there could be a problem. It's very easy to imagine a blue-collar worker, distrustful of big business to begin with, withdrawing his savings in December 1999. What's to lose? If everything is OK, he might reason, I'll just put it back when things settle down. It would break the banks if only two out of 100 depositors adopted that thinking.

It would be one thing if it were just a U.S. problem. It's not. It involves virtually every business and government agency worldwide. In the United States alone, it is estimated it will cost the Fortune 500 companies an average of $25,000,000 each. The government will have to spend anywhere from $2.3 billion to $30 billion, depending on the source. Congressman Horn recently told a meeting of the Information Technology Association of America's Public Policy Summit, that he believes the number will be much higher than the OMB's estimate, in the range of $10 billion to $20 billion. Any estimate within that range is significant when one considers that the entire federal Information Technology (IT) budget is only $30 billion per year, most of which goes to salaries, charges for telephone lines, and ongoing maintenance.

What's more, there isn't sufficient time left for many private sector organizations and agencies of the federal government. During a February 24, 1997, hearing before the Horn Subcommittee, a representative of the General Accounting Office (GAO) warned that some of the government's computers will stop working in the Year 2000 because agencies will not be able to finish reprogramming their equipment to understand years that do not begin with "19."

Joe Willemsen, Director of Information Resources Management at GAO, said, "There is a high probability there will be some failures." He urged the nation's agency heads to focus efforts on critical systems such as air traffic control, Medicare, and defense. Some see the writing on the wall. Neil Munro, staff writer at *Washington Technology Online*, in an article appearing in the May 8, 1997, edition, quotes Cynthia Warner, Year 2000 Program Manager at the General Services Administration. According to Munro, Warner said top federal managers "are terrified by" [the Year 2000 problem]. They're planning to retire before it hits, if they can."

Y2K 'flattens' the tax system

GAO has warned that government agencies don't have the management experience or technical know-how to solve a problem of this magnitude. Congressman Horn agrees. He has said that, "Federal agencies can't come to grips with their Y2K problems because the government just isn't managed very well." There's tangible evidence to support Congressman Horn's opinion. Earlier this year the IRS announced the outcome of a $4 billion project to update the agency's aging computer systems. In spite of all the money it spent, and the years of effort expended, the IRS decided to scrap the program. Now the agency is saying that it will only cost $129 million to convert the 19,000 applications in 300 to 500 systems spread across the country. Twice burned?

Maybe we will have a flat tax after all. One has to wonder.

Body blows to the economy

Chase Manhattan Bank recently announced that they plan to spend $250 million on Year 2000 renovations. In fact just a handful of the companies that have made their Year 2000 budgets public add up to over $1 billion. Extrapolate that to entire Fortune 1000. We're talking very big numbers here. Numbers that will inevitably impact the bottom line. So, if the market takes a dive on just the "fear" that interest rates will rise 1/4 percent, think what it will do in reaction to a $150 billion hit to corporate profits across the Fortune 1000. Let's put that into perspective. Standard & Poors pegged 1996 U.S. corporate profits at $650 billion. If we assume that an average of $50 billion is spent by "for profit" companies on Y2K annually, that represents 7.7 percent! One could argue, however, that not all $150 billion of the estimated cost for Y2K will be incremental. Most companies will try to manage the expense into existing budgets. True. What will that mean, though, to the non-Y2K segments of the IT industry? Dollars will be shifted away from computers, networking products, software, and services. The combined revenues of computers, peripherals, software, and services in 1996 was $322 billion. Again, let's say that 75 percent of annual Y2K expenses are diverted from this market segment. That would mean $37 billion — or more than 10 percent — would be drained away from the industry! For high-flying companies like Fore Systems, Dell Computers, Hewlett Packard, Ascend, and Intel, a 10 percent drop in sales would spell big trouble for their share prices. Now one can begin to see the impact Y2K could have on our domestic economy.

Come down from that ledge now—it's not necessarily going to be that bad for you personally.

Before you reach for your industrial-strength anti-depressants, consider this: Do the necessary research and convince yourself that the scenario I'm painting is real. Imagine your potential returns if you do rearrange your portfolio to hedge against the Y2K onslaught. The picture is dark, but only if you fail to take steps to create your own silver lining.

Chase Manhattan Bank has said that it is spending $250 million on Year 2000 renovations.

For the uninformed, the Year 2000 problem will represent the harbinger of financial ruin. It won't only impact investors, but every corner of society. In '29, they had heavy industry on which to build a recovery. Over the last 60 some years, we have dismantled much of the industrial base and replaced it with automated systems that are now threatened themselves. The crash of 1929 will pale in comparison to the "crash of the century." For it will be our very infrastructure that has been undermined. No terrorist bomb, no hacker's virus could ever begin to do the damage we have brought upon ourselves with the Millennium Bug.

Y2K is a threat to all electronic assets and personal records. This isn't something that will only be felt by some pocket protected geek in the computer room; every single one of us will undergo an enormous upheaval. I mean everyone. Some might think that the poor in the "third World" will get by unaffected, yet that isn't necessarily true. Charitable organizations will be hit hard by the problem. Their systems are generally older than those in the "for profit" world, and all international relief is of course managed by computers. It will be very tough for these organizations to foot the Y2K bill. Something will have to give, and its likely to be funds dedicated for the relief efforts.

No terrorist bomb, no hacker's virus could ever begin to do the damage we have brought upon ourselves with the Millennium Bug.

Government officials and the captains of industry have been either unaware of the problem or in deep denial. Let's face it, would you want to be the guy who stands in the vector of the CEO's gaze as you tell him that he has only two choices:

1) Spend $50 million for starters, it just might be enough, and I'll get most of the systems updated by the end of the century. Oh, and by the way, you get nothing in return except the right to be in business on January 2, 2000.

2) Plan on closing your doors on New Year's Eve 1999 because our systems will malfunction and no one will do business with us.

Huge returns will be realized by courageous investors who overcome their skepticism and act in anticipation of the coming market reversals. Precious metals will skyrocket as investors run to safety. If you get there first, you'll realize the fantastic appreciation that takes place when supply far outpaces demand. Gold is currently trading under $350 an ounce, yet, in January 1980, it ran well over $800 per ounce. Silver, however, has shown the most leverage. Costing less per ounce, silver, which is trading today under $5 per ounce, hit a high of $50 during the same period.

The Fortune 1000 will suffer enormous hits to the bottom line as the combination of a slowing economy, the cost of fixing the Year 2000 problem, and the litigation it triggers bleed companies of earnings.

Layoffs will be rampant as companies attempt to trim their expenses in order to offset these unanticipated costs. Unemployment will rise dramatically and the economy will drown in a dismal depression. Deflation will drive the value of some commodities downward. Interest rates will drop, making bonds purchased at today's rates worth a fortune. Then the big bang will come with the new century. An already weakened economy will suffer terribly as commerce is further undermined by the loss of computer-supported international trade.

Litigation will represent a majority share of the year 2000 tab

Many industry observers are now predicting litigation costs surrounding the Year 2000 problem will exceed the cost of fixing the problem! Steven Horn's congressional committee heard experts testify that over $1 trillion will be spent sorting out who is responsible for the "costs" of the Year 2000 problem. Is it the customer, the system integrator, or the manufacturer? Obviously, manufacturers will fight with everything they have, because a decision against them could very well mean the end. Shareholders are likely to hold directors and officers responsible for any harm the company experiences because they failed in their fiduciary responsibility to aggressively address this problem. Consumers, harmed by products impaired by Y2K failures, will sue manufacturers. Ultimately, insurance companies will sue each other in order to escape exposure via their underwriting agreements.

The Vicious Circle of Y2K Litigation

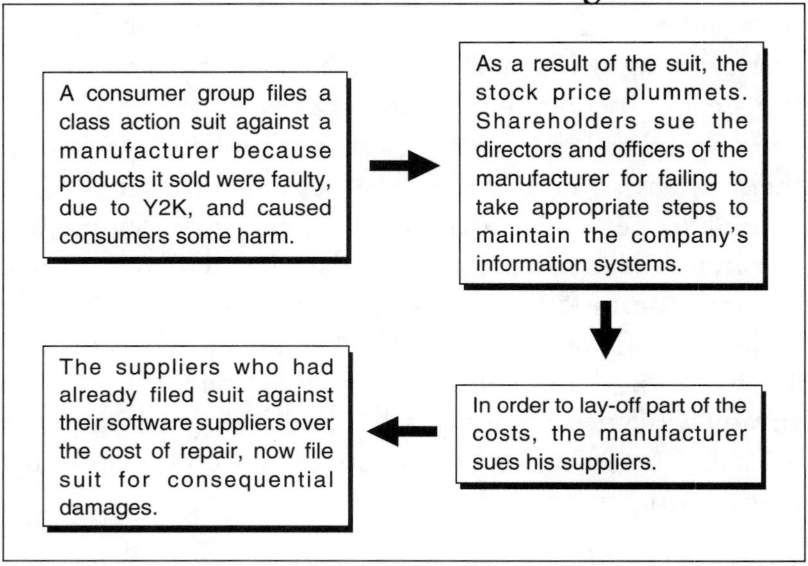

A consumer group files a class action suit against a manufacturer because products it sold were faulty, due to Y2K, and caused consumers some harm.

→

As a result of the suit, the stock price plummets. Shareholders sue the directors and officers of the manufacturer for failing to take appropriate steps to maintain the company's information systems.

↓

In order to lay-off part of the costs, the manufacturer sues his suppliers.

←

The suppliers who had already filed suit against their software suppliers over the cost of repair, now file suit for consequential damages.

Public companies have tried to ignore or cover up their Y2K exposure. Roger Lowenstein reported in the *Wall Street Journal* on July 25, 1996, that; "Companies are afraid that admitting to knowledge of a problem now could arm potential future plaintiffs if something goes wrong." References made now to "bugs" or "viruses" could haunt them later. Not surprising when you consider that officers and directors could be personally accountable to shareholders. Imagine if computer errors cost customers time, money, or even their lives! Or what if computer snafus disrupted the company's ability to conduct business, impacting revenues and profits? Customers and shareholders would be jamming the courts. In fact, public companies that are sued must in turn sue their suppliers, not only to off-lay expenses but also because the officers and directors have a fiduciary responsibility to pursue legal remedies for the company.

In March 1997 the Horn subcommittee heard from various witnesses in regard to the ramifications of the Year 2000 problem for society and the economy. What they were told is sobering. Ann Cofou, Managing Director of Giga Year 2000 Relevance Service, said during her testimony that "legal expenses could easily near or exceed $1 trillion". She added, "It is improbable to believe these immense costs will not adversely affect the economy on a global scale."

Vito Peraino, a lawyer with the California-based firm, Hancock, Rothert & Bunshoft, which specializes in Year 2000 issues, said "There has never been a $300 billion to $600 billion problem that has not attracted significant legal attention." Mr. Peraino knows what he's talking about — he has worked on some of the largest liability claims of all time. When he appeared on my radio program, "The Y2K Investor," he recounted his experience with the Exxon Valdez and other major suits he managed for his client, Lloyd's of London. He said that nothing in his experience even comes close to the scale of the Year 2000 problem.

The broad implications for corporate income taxes

Jeff Jinnett, counsel to LeBoeuf, Lamb, Greene & MacRae, L.L.P., and president of LeBoeuf Computing Technologies. Inc., is an expert in the legal issues surrounding computer hardware and software. He has dealt with the Year 2000 problem in several articles he has written. According to Mr. Jinnett, in his paper entitled "Legal Issues Concerning The Year 2000 "Millennium Bug," "The guiding principles for the preparation by a company of its financial statements are the Generally Accepted Auditing Standards ("GAAS"). One of the GAAP principles promulgated by FASB [Financial and Accounting Standards

Board] is the Statement of Financial Accounting Standards No. 5 ("SFAS 5") ("Accounting for Contingencies"), which provides that contingencies which are reasonably possible, whether or not the amount can be calculated or estimated, must be disclosed in a note to the financial statements."

Lowenstein Sandler, a New Jersey law firm, recently surveyed 10-Ks that had been filed during the last calendar quarter. What they found was quite revealing. Gary Wingens, who specializes in Year 2000 litigation for Lowenstein Sandler, in an interview on "The Y2K Investor," told listeners that, while there were very few specific references to Year 2000 issues in the current round of 10-Ks (SEC mandated annual reports on financial performance), later this year and early next it should pick up considerably. Here is a sampling of what they found:

Chase Manhattan Corporation — "Management has initiated an enterprise-wide program to prepare the Corporation's computer systems and applications for the year 2000. The Corporation expects to incur internal staff costs as well as consulting and other expenses related to infrastructure and facilities enhancements necessary to prepare the systems for the year 2000. Testing and conversion of system applications is expected to cost approximately $200 million to $250 million over the next three years. A significant proportion of these costs are not likely to be incremental costs to the Corporation , but rather will represent the redeployment of existing information technology resources."

Equifax, Inc. — "In 1996, Equifax expensed about one cent per share to modify computer software for compliance with Year 2000 as required by the FASB's Emerging Issues Task Force Issue No. 96-14. Year 2000 expenses will continue to impact results in 1997 (approximately $.04 to $.05 per share) and 1998, as Equifax plans to be Year

2000-compliant in advance of the millennium. The amount and timing of these expenses may vary as current estimates are refined."

Morgan Stanley Group Inc. — "The widespread use of computer programs that rely on two-digit date programs to perform computations and decision-making functions may cause computer systems to malfunction in the year 2000, which could lead to business delays and disruptions in the U.S. and internationally. The Company has been modifying its computer systems to address this issue. However, due to the interdependent nature of the computer systems, the Company may be adversely impacted in the year 2000 depending on whether it or to other entities not affiliated with the Company address this issue successfully".

SFAS 5 defines a "contingency" as an existing condition, situation, or set of circumstances involving uncertainty as to possible gain or loss to an enterprise that will ultimately be resolved when one or more future events occur or fail to occur. SFAS 5 uses three classifications:

A) **Probable** — the future contingent event is likely to occur.

B) **Remote** — there is only a slight chance that the future event will occur.

C) **Reasonably possible** — the chance of the event occurring is more than remote, but less than probable.

SFAS 5 gives as an example of a "loss contingency" the "risk of loss or damage to enterprise property by fire, explosion or other hazards." This definition arguably could include the crippling of an enterprise's computer system by the Millennium Bug.

"Moreover," Mr. Jinnett continues, "if (a) it is 'probable' that the company will not become Year 2000 compliant in time, (b) an asset has been impaired or a liability incurred as of the date of the financial statements, and (c) the amount of the loss can be reasonably estimated, then a charge against earnings for the estimated loss may be required under SFAS 5 and the liability would be reported in the body of the financial statements."

This provision is key, for under its requirements, companies must not only expense their direct costs for fixing the problem, but they also must include the company's potential legal liability to customers and shareholders.

Under the same section of the law, SAS No. 53 notifies auditors that they are responsible for detecting and reporting errors and irregularities. The auditor is responsible for planning each audit to provide reasonable assurance of detecting errors. Some auditors will be in a double bind in regard to certifying a company's Y2K compliance plan. As experts, they are expected to weigh in on the effectiveness of their client's approach and estimated costs associated with addressing Y2K, yet this same information might be used against them in court as they might very well have been the suppliers of the software in the first place. Some speculate that the reason the "Big Six" accounting firms are being so silent on this issue is that, through their consulting practices, they installed many of the systems that are affected.

Further, SFAS 5 holds that any set of circumstances involving uncertainty as to possible gain or loss to an enterprise that will ultimately be resolved when one or more future events occur or fail to occur, would clearly apply to Y2K. The Securities and Exchange Commission also requires under Reg. 303(a) that management must discuss "material events and uncertainties known to management that would cause reported financial information not to be necessarily indicative of future operating results or of future financial condition."

The death knell will start tolling in 1999 when, under SAS No. 59 ("The Auditor's Consideration of an Entity's Ability to Continue as a Going Concern"), auditors will have to state their opinion on the company's ability to remain a going concern for a "reasonable period" not to exceed one year. For some companies, then, the annual reports and 10-Ks they publish in early 1999 may be their epitaphs.

For more information on the legal implications of Y2K, check out the following:

"Legal Issues Concerning The Year 2000 Millennium Bug" — Jeff Jinnett — August 21, 1996 — Copies can be obtained from Mr. Jinnett at the following email address: Jinnett@llgm.com

"Legal Issues Confronting the Federal Government and The State Governments Due to the Year 2000 Millennium Bug Problem" — Jeff Jinnett — November 12, 1996 — Copies can be obtained from Mr. Jinnett at the following email address: Jinnett@llgm.com

"2001: A Legal Odyssey" — Warren S. Reid — Copyright 1996 — Copies can be obtained at: http://www.year2000.com/legal/html

"Words of Warning, Ruling Makes Directors Accountable for Compliance" — Dominic Bencivenga — The New York Law Journal — February 13, 1997

"Companies Beware: Millennium Bug Can Take a Deep Legal Bite, Warns Global Insurance Company" — Business Wire — December 23, 1997 — Based on a press release from Marsh & Mclennan, Incorporated — Contact Jerrold Weitzman for more information at: (212) 345 6253

"The Millennium Bug Will Bite You" — David Loundy — Published by the Chicago Daily Law Bulletin on November 14, 1996 — Copies can also be found at: http://www.leepfrog.com/E-Law/CDLB/Year2000.html

"Y2K Could Cost $1 Trillion in Legal Costs" — Rex Nutting — Published by TechWire Online — March 20, 1997 — Copies can be found at: http://www.techweb.com/wire/news/mar/0320trillion,html,body?

The Gartner Group estimates that up to 50 percent of businesses won't be ready in time and, as a result, there will be 20-30 percent business failures. Imagine what that will do to unemployment and how much money it will take out of the economy. We'll see market consolidation occurring across the board. Some companies will see their Y2K head start as a key differentiator, and will put plans in place to publicize their advantage. This will be particularly true for banks and other financial institutions. BankBoston has appointed Steven McManus as Communications Director to represent its Year 2000 efforts to the public. BankBoston realized early in the game the threat Y2K posed to its business. It was sensitive to the potential anxiety investors might feel as the millennium approaches and wanted them to be reassured that the bank had things under control. With good reason. CS First Boston Vice President Michael Tiernan, in his testimony before Congress in April 1996, said, "If these dates get screwed up, Wall Street Firms' computers will no longer accurately calculate any number of things." Clearing and settlement of transactions could break down. Stocks held electronically and checking accounts could be wiped out. Interest might not be properly credited to accounts. Customers might be denied access to their accounts. Deposits or trades might not be credited to an account, and customers' funds would not be available. "If year 2000 problems are not addressed, the consequences may be catastrophic, from a business and economic perspective," added Tiernan, who is also Chairman of the Securities Industry Association's Year 2000 subcommittee.

Insurance companies have enormous exposure on two fronts. They have their own Y2K problems, which some experts view as the most significant of any individual industry segment, and some might also be awash in claims under their business disruption insurance. Prudential Insurance and its subsidiaries are leaving nothing to chance. Irene Dec, who is responsible for all of the Prudential companies' Y2K efforts, says they have budgeted $100 million for remediation of the problem.

Federal, state, and local governments will feel the effect of Y2K, not only as a result of the impact on their own IT budgets, but also in an unanticipated reduction in tax revenues. The FASB has ruled that costs related to fixing the Y2K problem must be expensed. Therefore, companies will be writing off these costs against their operating revenues over the next 3 years, thereby reducing their tax liability. This was translated into dollars recently by the state of New Jersey. They estimate that the Year 2000 problem will cost them approximately $2 billion in anticipated tax revenues over the next three years. Ouch! Imagine the squeeze on state budgets between the loss of tax revenues and the unanticipated costs associated with Y2K.

Let's take that thought to the federal level now. How many billions of dollars will be lost in federal tax revenues as a result of the "write-offs" from Y2K? Hey Mr. President, won't that blow the "balanced budget" plan?

A Congressional Research report sponsored by Senator Moynihan estimates it will cost $30 billion to bring its antiquated systems into compliance. Congressman Horn says he believes it will be somewhere in the range of $10 to $15 billion to make the required changes, and OMB comes in at $2.3B. Whatever the number, it will represent a significant percentage of the annual IT budget allocated to kind of expenses. The total annual IT budget for the federal government is only $25 billion. The vast majority of any organization's IT budget goes to cover payroll and benefits, another huge expense item is telecommunications. What's left goes to pre-existing maintenance contracts, replacement parts and finally acquisition of new software and hardware. There isn't a lot of flexibility. Certainly not enough to absorb the billions of dollars in question.

The IT industry will feel the pinch too, as dollars that normally would have been spent on new systems are drained off to Y2K projects.

The special threat to Mutual Funds

Fund managers themselves are facing a nightmare of their own. How do they manage their portfolio in anticipation of the Year 2000 problem. Forget about their internal systems for a moment. They are threatened too, but let's just assume they get fixed in time. Fund managers have to contend with the threat Y2K poses to their investments and the overall performance of their portfolio. On the one hand, they will have to divest themselves of:

- Portfolio companies who they believe will not become compliant on time
- Portfolio companies whose industry or marketplace is particularly vulnerable
- Portfolio companies who have a significant number of suppliers or customers who are at risk for being non-compliant.

On the other hand, they will have to augment their portfolios with investments that are likely to flourish in anticipation of the Year 2000 environment. This could mean the following could skyrocket:

- Precious metals
  - Funds
  - Mining stocks
  - bullion
- US government insured bonds
- Real estate that can be used as industrial warehouse space

- The stock of companies who will benefit from the Year 2000 problem.

Where else will these fund managers be able to go with their assets? Surely they will stay in many of their traditional investments, but they will have to diversify with a view toward the Year 2000 problem's impact.

In the not too distant future you will begin seeing mutual funds advertise based upon their funds position on the Year 2000 problem. We have already seen this kind of differentiation based upon the environmental friendliness of funds, and it has just started with mutual funds, such as the Calvert Group touting their "tobacco-free" portfolios.

Your 401K plan could wipe out your retirement nest egg

Many 401K plans provide investors with very few choices when it comes to investment vehicles. Usually, there are several mutual funds to choose from, ranging from high growth/high risk, small cap funds to "Blue Chip" value funds designed for long term growth and stability. There might be some bond funds available, both commercial and municipal. If you are lucky, you'll have the option to choose US government insured certificates of deposit.

However, if your situation is like many others, you'll have a vexing double bind. Do you withdraw your assets from your 401K plan, recognizing that you'll be liable immediately for the taxes deferred under the plan, plus you'll have to pay a penalty for early withdrawal. If you find yourself in this position, and you don't plan to retire for another 10 years, you might as well stay put. History has shown time and time again that equities outperform any other alternative over the long term.

If, however, you will be retiring sooner, you should work closely with your financial advisor on a course of action. If they aren't aware of the Year 2000 problem, you may wish to look for someone who is. At this late date, it is inexcusable for an investment professional to be uniformed on such an important topic. I guarantee you that the senior executives that run his or her company are well aware of the problem. If your broker isn't, attempt to educate them. If they refuse to take the situation seriously, fire them. Your retirement is at stake, and you don't have enough time to waste on another Y2K ostrich.

The Big Picture

One very common mistake is made by most people when they contemplate the impact of the Year 2000 problem. By analyzing a single part, they draw conclusions on the whole. Even experts who should know better are often guilty of over simplifying the solution and minimizing its ramifications because they draw only on their parochial knowledge and experience. This problem is far, far greater than simply the sum of its parts. It is a huge mistake to conclude that simply because one part of the problem might have a solution, that the entire problem must therefore be manageable. It's not.

Anything other than a fully informed, systemic view of they Year 2000 problem will lead to underestimating its dimensions. This threat must be viewed globally with a sensitivity toward the interconnectedness and interdependencies that bind all the world's economies and their underlying information systems together.

Let's attempt to look at the macro level implications of the Year 2000 problem. Keep in mind that any one of these events or conditions, once set in motion, could in fact, trigger one or more of the others.

In anticipation of the Year 2000

- In order to address the budget busting costs of Y2K, commercial and governmental entities divert money from other projects to fund Y2K remediation. High-tech companies whose product revenues suffer as a result of these diversions, experience a drop off in profits. Layoffs begin. The stock market reacts negatively.
- Investor's growing concern for the Y2K vulnerability of companies and mutual funds in which they are invested, begin to bail out. The stock market reacts negatively.
- Insurance companies stop writing policies that insure Director's and Officers of publicly traded companies against shareholder, or product liability suits.
- Large companies such as large manufacturers begin to terminate relationships with suppliers who cannot certify their systems for Year 2000 compliance. If these companies are public, their stock will plummet.
- Portfolio managers of Mutual Funds will begin to scrutinize the companies in which they are invested, divesting those who cannot guarantee investors that they will be Year 2000 compliant, on time.
- Moody's lowers the rating of certain commercial and municipal bonds based upon the issuer's Year 2000 exposure. This can be because the entities internal systems are threatened, the industry within which a company operates is particularly vulnerable or because some external dependency is threatened.

- As they begin to understand the potential threat of Y2K, nervous investors begin to withdraw money from uninsured investments, such brokerage accounts, mutual funds, commercial and municipal bonds. Instead, they begin opening "mattress accounts". The stock and bond markets react negatively. Wide spread withdrawals lead to bank runs.
- Revenues of federal, state and local taxing authorities are significantly diminished as a result of companies writing off the Y2K problem. Some state and local governments flirt with insolvency.

After the Year 2000

- Certain countries are electronically marooned. International telephone carriers stop placing or receiving calls into or out of countries whose telephone systems cannot supply billing information in a Year 2000 compliant format.
- Some public services begin to malfunction or cease to operate. International flights are disrupted as the air traffic control systems of certain countries, including possibly the US are not Year 2000 ready.
- Those small, and regional bank operations that were unable to convert their systems in time are disrupted. Investors are temporarily denied access to their accounts.
- Mission critical systems begin to crash on a widespread basis. Production and distribution are disrupted. Manufacturers are forced to abandon "Just-in-Time" manufacturing. Inventories go up. Cost of goods sold is skewed, further impacting

revenues and profits. Massive layoffs occur. Prices begin to skyrocket as companies scramble to adjust to the scarcity of raw materials and resources.

- Litigation begins as isolated brush fires, but ultimately builds to an international conflagration as liability suits are filed on all fronts of the Year 2000 issue.
- Social order is threatened as state and local law enforcement agencies loose the use of their communications, dispatch and database systems.
- The death rate goes up as medical systems and appliances malfunction in hospitals and long-term care facilities.
- International tensions grow as military operations around the world deal with their known and unknown vulnerabilities.

We will learn of countless other anecdotal threats as time goes on and the end-date draws nearer. As an investor, it is vital to remember two words. Markets move in **ANTICIPATION** of **PERCEIVED** events or circumstances.

Chapter 2

Defensive Investments With Offensive Returns

Where Do You Go With Your Dough?

In a financial crisis, cash is king! True, but it's not quite that simple. Liquidity is the goal, and that is of no use unless your funds will be safe. In a massive, global meltdown, Federal Deposit Insurance Corporation (FDIC)-insured deposits won't guarantee much. The whole concept of the FDIC is to protect investors against the occasional bank or savings and loan that goes bust. They don't keep on hand anywhere near the funds required to cover universal losses to millions of depositors.

How much should you keep in cash or other highly liquid assets? The goal I'm shooting for is 75 percent. I am divesting myself of as much real estate and moving IRA and KEOGH investments into government securities. I might even consider taking the penalty and withdrawing these funds at some point, as these accounts are not insured. None of our brokerage accounts are, for that matter.

"OK, so liquidity is the goal, now where do I go with my dough?" An account with First National Mattress is a bad idea. Its not insured, and you could be putting you and your family at risk if anyone should find out. You'll want to keep some cash on hand, perhaps some of your bullion coins, but it shouldn't be necessary to make either of these moves until some time in 1999. Safe deposit boxes are a good alternative. Yes, bank vaults may have some difficulty post Y2K in terms of opening on the right schedule, but they will open or be opened at some point and you'll have access to your hard assets.

Markets move in anticipation of perceived events or conditions that will exist in the future.

In the nearer term, I would carefully consider your choice of a banking institution. Small banks are definitely at risk. They don't usually have the resources that a large, multinational bank would have, and the cost to repair does not scale linearly with size. A small- to medium-sized bank must maintain systems that provide all of the functionality of a major bank.

You are looking for an institution that can withstand the trauma of a crash prior to the Year 2000. I don't, at this point in time, have confidence in any institution after the Year 2000. So I am only speaking of deposits you maintain in accounts prior to the turn of the century. Timing will be everything, however, if you choose to leave your money in your account during 1998 and 1999. Remember, markets anticipate bad news. If there is going to be a bank run, it won't take until January 4th, the first business day after the holiday, for the fur to start flying.

Look carefully at your prospective bank's annual report. You are looking for an institution that has a relatively low loan to deposit ratio. Banks that have a large percentage of deposits invested via loans to corporations and individuals, are much more vulnerable in a downturn or crash.

You also want a bank that has invested here in the United States. Avoid banks that have a high ratio of international deposits. Eurodollars will get killed in a global crash, and your bank will be left holding the bag. You'll hear later that we will actually be buying "puts" on Eurodollars.

If there is going to be a bank run, it won't take until January 4th, the first business day after the holiday, for the fur to start flying.

S&Ls are also high risk. They have your money invested in the highly illiquid real estate market. In a post-crash depression, they'll have a really difficult time foreclosing on properties and selling them for anything close to their investment.

I intend to jump earlier rather than later. Sure, you'll forgo some interest earnings, but big deal. I'd much rather give up 6 percent or so and be certain my principal remains intact. If we once again return to 1929, those skeptical types who stayed out of the market and kept their money "under the mattress" were able to watch the entire collapse unscathed. In fact, when the dust settled and deflation was at its peak, their buying power was increased many times over. In 1929, people were selling new cars in the street for $100. People were desperate to raise cash.

Staying liquid and holding your funds in a "safe" institution or mechanism will allow you the opportunity to protect yourself against a post-crash period of currency devaluation. In the years after the crash of 1929, some currencies managed to hold up for some period of time after the bottom fell out for the United States. The U.K., for instance, was one of the last major currencies to drift down. They could only hold out so long before it became so expensive to buy products produced in the U.K., that they had no choice but to let their currency find its "own level" in the world economy. However, smart money moved around the globe, finding stable currencies like stepping stones across a creek.

Say you started by holding Austrian currency. In anticipation of instability, you exchanged it for Swiss Francs, a historically stable currency. Then, judging that the U.S. dollar has probably hit bottom, you bought dollars. In the summer and fall of 1931, both Germany and Britain went off the gold standard.

Then Franklin Delano Roosevelt became president, and his "New Deal" was certain to drive up inflation as millions of government dollars were dumped into the economy. With the threat of devaluation on the horizon, Swiss Francs still look good, and a move back might make sense. Switzerland was one of the few countries that held fast to the gold standard. Years later, as tensions grew in Switzerland due to rising unemployment, and the Swiss economy was strangled by its inability to compete in a world market, you could once again buy U.S. dollars, which had stabilized by 1935. Just before the start of the war, the recovery had begun in the United States and your "value" was intact.

This scenario wouldn't repeat itself in the exact same way today. Now we have sophisticated communications systems and intricate interdependencies from one country to another. Where it might have taken months or years for the dominoes to fall in the early 30s, today it might only take days or weeks. So, unless you are able to devote full time to your investments, are highly sophisticated, and can sustain high risk, you'll want something more secure, like precious metals.

Precious Metals

For years, financial experts have recommended gold as an excellent way to add diversity to your portfolio. Why?

Because the price of this "hard asset" generally moves contrary to other "paper assets" such as stocks and bonds. That will never be more true than in the coming electronic asset crisis. Precious metals may move up marginally in the wake of the first wave correction, as investors internalize the impact of Y2K costs on corporate profits, but the huge moves will come later. Once investors begin to appreciate the threat to everything they hold electronically, precious metals will skyrocket. In hard financial times, this has always been true. In fact, over the long run, gold has an excellent track record in maintaining its purchasing power relative to other financial assets.

While gold is the well-known favorite, silver is the better investment from the standpoint of utility and leverage. When gold moves up it takes silver with it, but just as a lower priced stock tends to make moves on a higher percentage basis than higher priced stock, so silver tends to move non-linearly to gold.

There are any number of ways of investing in precious metals. One can invest in precious metals futures, mining stocks, bullion, coins, or even jewelry (although there is an aesthetic mark-up on jewelry). Some of these make more sense now, and some will be better investments later. Here, at the threshold of the crisis window, any of the aforementioned vehicles makes sense; however, the most leverage can be had through precious metals futures. While one can hold the futures contracts directly, the more conservative approach is to acquire options on precious metals futures contracts. Here's the reasoning. While holding the contract directly provides better returns overall and appreciates dramatically on smaller moves, it also means exposure to margin calls during the potentially volatile, early threshold of the crisis period. Therefore, buying calls on futures contracts, while representing a greater risk to your principal and requiring bigger moves to be profitable, is the better choice in a panicky market. In day-to-day investing, it's unlikely that you could predict a move significant enough to make money buying options on precious metals futures. However, the Y2K market provides a unique driver for prices to climb steadily over the next several years. We're anticipating extraordinary moves. Silver could double, triple, quadruple or simply soar weightlessly. Remember, silver was trading at over $50 dollars per ounce in January 1980. At this writing, it is less than $5 per ounce.

Let's speculate for a moment. Let's say you buy the December 1998 calls at a strike price of $5.00. At today's quotation, a $12,500 dollar investment would buy 10 contracts. Since each contract represents your right to buy 5,000 ounces of silver at a pre-agreed-upon price of $5.00, you make $500 for every penny silver increases in price. So, if silver were to double, you'd make $250,000!

Remember now, we're talking about a global loss of confidence in electronic assets. So it's not unreasonable to see silver approach its all-time high of $41 per ounce, achieved in 1980. By the way, if silver did move that high, your options would be worth $4,000,000. I don't know about you, but that floats my boat! To make my point about the leverage in silver, gold was trading at a high that approached $900 per ounce in 1980.

By acquiring contracts with expiration dates inside of the century rollover, your electronically recorded investment is not threatened. In fact, one could actually take delivery on the metal! That, however, creates some other challenges. Safe deposit boxes are reasonable for gold; however, silver is another matter. It's far more cumbersome, and therefore for large amounts, it would make more sense to use a repository.

Mining stocks are another way to speculate on the future value of precious metals. Just as buying calls represents a leveraged investment in the future value of silver, so too does an investment in the stocks of mining concerns. Right now silver is only marginally above its cost to produce. However, if the metal takes off, so will your stock.

There are several ways to invest in precious metals

- ✦ Owning individual mining stocks
- ✦ Precious metals mutual funds
- ✦ Precious metal bullion
- ✦ Jewelry

Mining Stocks

Just as with equities in any industry, winning by picking individual issues takes a great deal of research. One must analyze the company's track record, management team, and market strategy. One then has to map this data to the Y2K opportunity and decide if it's a good fit. If you have the time and desire (I don't), fare thee well. If you are like me, however, you'll go with a mutual fund. Mutual funds make sense in your Y2K strategy, because if the market takes off as we believe it will, almost any fund will benefit. That's not necessarily true for all individual mining stocks.

Precious Metals Mutual Funds

For the very reason common stock mutual funds make sense for any investor, the same principle makes them a prudent investment in your Y2K portfolio. There are a number of funds, some offered by the large, reputable fund families. Here are a few:

Fund	Assets $M's	Telephone Number
Fidelity Select Precious Metals & Mining	258.8	800 544 8888
Fidelity Select American Gold	354.8	800 544 8888
American Century Global Gold	433.5	800 331 8331
Franklin Gold	349.3	800 342 5236
Invesco Strategic Gold	229.6	800 525 8085
Keystone Precious Metal Holdings	169.9	800 343 2898
Midas	200.7	800 400 6432
Oppenheimer Gold & Specialty Minerals	151	800 525 7048
Scudder Gold	184.3	800 225 2470
United Services Gold Shares	153.3	800 873 8637
United Services Gold World	225.5	800 873 8637
Van Eck Gold/Resources	138	800 826 1115
Van Eck International Investment Gold	450.9	800 826 1115
Vanguard Specialty Gold & Precious Metals	496.5	800 662 7447

Precious Metals, Bullion Coins

Coins are another great way to invest in precious metals. After all, if the global financial transaction system breaks down, we're going to have to spend this stuff. It's going to be somewhat difficult to buy milk and eggs with a 50-lb. ingot of gold.

Coins are minted around the world. One well-known source is South Africa, with its Krugerrand; however, the all-time favorite is the American Gold Eagle. Canada's Gold Maple Leaf is also popular and has some practical benefit, in that it comes in sizes down to 1/20th of an ounce. Again, if we have civil unrest, failure of the banking system, and a crisis in commerce and infrastructure, we may need something we can spend. These smaller coins make some practical sense in that regard. I hate thinking about such circumstances.

The following mints all produce bullion coins:

- Australian Mint (gold Kangaroo coins, platinum Koala coins, silver Kookaburra coins)
- Austrian Mint (gold Philharmonic coins)
- British Royal Mint (gold or platinum Britannia coins)
- Royal Canadian Mint (gold, platinum, or silver Maple Leaf coins)
- South African Mint (gold Krugerrand coins)
- U.S. Mint (American Eagle coins in gold or silver)

American Eagle, Gold and Silver Bullion Coins

These congressionally authorized bullion coins contain their stated weight in gold and silver and are available worldwide. Their price fluctuates with the market price of gold and silver. To be placed on the Mint's customer mailing list, call: (202) 283-COIN.

Another way to participate in precious metals, and leverage your capital while doing so, is to use a program, such as one offered by The Monex Companies, which finances up to 80 percent of your investment. I work with Jeff Gaynor. He can be reached at: 800 949-GOLD. The company also maintains a website at: http://www.monex.com

Remember, though, silver is my favorite. It is more cumbersome. $10,000 worth of silver bullion coins is about the size of three large shoeboxes and weighs nearly 100 lbs, while a similar amount of gold can be held easily in the palm of your hand. Silver's lower price per ounce, however, makes it more practical as legal tender, and that will give you much better leverage.

Commodities

Not all commodities will be a good bet in the squeeze period following a crash. In a depression, construction and mass production virtually come to a standstill because there are no buyers for goods produced. The secondary market is flooded with merchandise people are trying desperately to liquidate for cash. All this adds up to weakness in commodities. Yet, those who work the commodities market as a regular component of their overall investment strategy, know that its neither strength nor weakness that makes a good market in commodities. It is rather, predictable cycles.

Yu-Dee Chang, President of Assett Management Corporation in Potomac, Maryland helped me understand this concept. In fact, Yu-Dee has invested a significant amount of time to educate me. I very much appreciate that.

He has developed a highly effective model with which he can predict the ebbs and tides of commodity prices. The system works for the value of indexes as well. With his system, it doesn't matter which way the market is moving, its only important that you know where it is headed. There is an equal opportunity to make money on the way up or down.

He and I have put together a precious metals strategy for the coming Y2K environment. We also bought "puts" on the NYSE index.

For further information about the "TED" spread (explained in an upcoming section), precious metals options or futures and options on the major indexes, you can reach Yu-Dee at (301) 840-8999.

Jewelry

Jewelry is perhaps the least desirable method of investing in precious metals. The first criterion for making an investment decision on a piece of jewelry (after you have established its purity and fair market value with a reputable dealer) is the fact that you like it and would enjoy wearing the piece. After all, the reason we pay more per ounce for jewelry is the aesthetic value of its design. Here again, though, if gold leaps to historic highs, it could be hard to make a mistake. Anecdotally, according to Susan E. Kuhn and Amy R. Kover, gold, Chinese ceramics, and stamps outperformed the overall market during the period between 1968 and 1979. For my part, I'll stick with the gold, thank you.

Since diamonds are not required to any large extent by industry, their value is established solely on the basis of their quality and supply and demand driven by subjective valuation. On this basis, diamonds are perhaps a good investment in a healthy economy. They are certainly not liquid and depend entirely on a market with discretionary funds for luxury.

Real Estate

As I mentioned before, I am divesting myself of all real estate holdings except for my self-sustaining hideout. I'm still adjusting to this kind of thinking. Gary North, editor of the *Remnant Review,* has stacked all his chips on 00. He has bought property in a remote region of northwest Arkansas. He chose that part of the country for its comfortable distance from large urban areas and the fact that many properties have natural gas wells right on the land.

I know it's difficult to think of letting go of your vacation dream house, but in a post-crash depression, interest rates will hit rock bottom as the Federal Reserve attempts to stimulate activity. With your cash in hand, you'll be able to pick up beach front property for a song and secure a loan at a ridiculously low rate of interest.

My wife and I recently went through this gut wrenching experience ourselves. We had two beautiful, six bedroom homes on the Outer Banks of North Carolina. We closed on the sale of one in June of this year and have buyers interested in the other. These weren't just "rentals".

We really treated them as our homes. The one we just sold, was the site of a Keyes family reunion this past spring, and the other, our dream home holds a steady gaze out over Currituck sound. It will be very hard to let that one go. But we will.

On the positive side, real estate that can be used for industrial warehouse space should shoot up in value. As companies have to abandon their newly instituted "Just In Time" manufacturing practices, they will have to beef up inventories, reacquiring warehouse capacity they only recently abandoned.

A Word About Insurance

Your insurance policy is only as good as the company that wrote it. With whole life, variable life, annuities, and other products, some portion of your premium is held by the insurance carrier, which invests it to make a profit on the returns and be able to pay you premiums when the insured event or casualty occurs. And even though insurance companies have time-tested, conservative portfolios, their assets (your money) are not federally insured.

I carry only term insurance. My strategy is to keep the difference in premiums between the two programs, invest it, and keep 100 percent of the return. Those excess premiums, by the way, could be invested in some of the companies and vehicles mentioned earlier.

Buy Bonds

Asset allocation should include a suite of bonds. You should take possession of any bonds you hold prior to January 1, 2000. Keep them in a safe deposit box. They could come in real handy.

- AAA-rated bonds of cash-rich corporations
- Treasury Bills (T-Bills)

- ✦ U.S. Government 30-Year Long Bond
- ✦ Tax Free Municipal Bonds — Municipalities with a budget surplus
- ✦ Foreign Bonds

The TED Spread

In times of economic crisis, the value of uninsured bonds such as Eurobonds are depressed, while U.S. government bonds (T-Bills), backed by "The Full Faith and Credit of the United States Government," go up in value. T-Bills are the safest investment in the world. It is virtually impossible that the U.S. government would default on its obligations. In fact, the government could just print money to pay off its bond holders, if need be. But the safety of T-Bills can be undermined by the electronic system used by your financial institution to track ownership. Your best bet is to hold the certificates physically. All things being equal, in a global depression, the U.S. dollar will continue to be the most favored currency in the world. For that reason, our interest rates will always be lower than those offered on any other bond representing higher risk.

There is a way to play this differential between uninsured bonds (Eurobonds) and T-Bills. This strategy is called the "TED Spread". The "T" is from Treasury, and the "ED" comes from the EuroDollar. The strategy involves buying T-Bills and writing "puts" on Eurodollars. The T-Bills act as security for your margin on the puts. Under normal circumstances, Eurodollars pay 20 percent more interest than T-Bills. So, if T-Bills are paying 5 percent, then Eurodollars are likely to be paying 6 percent. When the Y2K economic crisis hits, rates on both bonds will go up, but the differential between the two will widen. You'll be able to sell your Eurodollars at a profit while also realizing a gain in the value of your T-Bills.

Stocks

I am already out of the general equities market. The only stocks I own at this time are Y2K related. The Year 2000 problem will kill the stock market. Annual reports are already coming in that foretell of significant charges against earnings.

If you intend to keep your current equities, you would be well advised to write the Board of Directors of each company, requesting a detailed discussion of what it is doing to prepare for the Year 2000. What you get back can help you decide whether to hold onto your investment.

Here is a sample letter you might send to the board of a company in which you have invested:

> *To the Board of Directors*
> *The Very Big, Quarterly-Driven Corporation:*
>
> As I am sure you are aware by now, the Year 2000 problem threatens to disrupt computer operations worldwide. Systems affected are mainframe computers, as well as any software, written in any language running on any platform, including embedded microprocessors that run digital devices. This means that many computers will fail to process year 2000 dates correctly, and factory, office, and environmental control systems will also be affected.
>
> This is a highly controversial subject as it is portrayed in the press; however, research will reveal that the problem is serious, expensive, and represents a significant threat to business continuity.
>
> Beyond the direct costs experienced by The Very Big, Quarterly-Driven Corporation, the company could also be adversely impacted by any company with which it communicates electronically. If the company's suppliers and customers

haven't upgraded their systems compatibly, the manufacturing supply chain could be interrupted and receivables may balloon. Government agencies to which the company is accountable or dependent on may not have their systems ready in time, and this ,too, could have an impact.

General market conditions arising out of the Year 2000 problem must also be considered. Some companies will suffer a tremendous expense to fix their problem. To blunt the devastation such unexpected expenses would have on the bottom line, companies will decide to rob funding from other IT projects, thereby impacting revenues for an industry that underpins our economy's performance. All of this will take place on a global scale.

The company must also assess its legal exposure as it relates to the problem. Y2K-related damages suffered by your customers could represent a significant liability in the coming years. Unless the company moves quickly to instill confidence in the marketplace that its systems will be ready, revenues and share prices may suffer as customers and investors move to companies that are perceived as representing less risk.

As a shareholder, I would like to receive a written discussion of the company's plans to deal effectively with the Year 2000 problem. Please include the status and schedule for the completed implementation of all aspects of the company's strategy.

As an investor, I need to know that senior management at The Very Big, Quarterly Driven Corporation has devoted the appropriate resources and funding required to deal effectively with the problem, and that the Board is monitoring progress on a regular basis.

Sincerely,
A concerned shareholder

Who Ya' Gonna' Call

There are a growing number of companies that are in business, at least in part, to solve the Year 2000 problem. These cover a range from "pure plays" such as Viasoft Inc. (VIAS) to broad-based system integrators such as Computer Sciences Corporation (CSC).

The solution involves a process with very clear milestones. One such process is Gartner Group's INSPECT process or Data Dimensions' Ardes 2k. Initially, an organization needs to take an inventory of the various programs it has in operation. Once these have all been identified, an analysis is required to determine the extent to which the code is date-sensitive.

A project plan is then developed so that all of the code is examined, modified, and tested individually and systematically. The result should be that 100 percent of the date references are modified and that the code works correctly with all other systems with which it interacts.

The Millennium Bug Exterminators

In the late summer of 1996, I received some email from a Michael Tantleff in Santa Barbara, California. He had visited my web site, thought we probably had a lot in common and wanted see if I might want to work together on a joint site. We hit it off right away.

Michael is a Senior Vice President with Prudential Securities in their Santa Barbara, California office. Since early in 1995, Michael has been totally immersed in the Y2K arena. So much so, he consulted with David Stewart publisher, of the newsletter *The Stewart Report.* Mr. Stewart was credited by Fortune magazine, in their August 1996 issue with having fueled the first launch in Y2K stocks back in March of 1995.

Michael has been an invaluable resource for me in developing my personal portfolio of Y2K stocks. At this writing, my account with Michael is up 186% since the first of the year.

Here are some of his thoughts on Y2K:

> Y2K, the Year 2000, the second millennium, is a much anticipated event. As this inevitable day draws near there will be much fanfare and discussion on the state of our world. Where have we been, where are we going and what will the 20th century bring are some of the questions we will be asking.
>
> Applying these questions to Information Technology, we realize that computers and the internet have brought the world much closer together. We have stood on the shoulders of the microchip in the last half of this century, ushering in information access and productivity on a scale unthinkable just a few decades ago. Unfortunately, the very foundation of our "cyber" world must now be changed. The vision that brought us to this high ground of technological possibilities was, regrettably, myopic. For our reluctance to deal with the Year 2000 problem early on, will now cost us dearly. At first the problem will create many investment opportunities for companies who can effectively compete in the business of repairing old systems. There is, however, a dark side. For while the world will strive at this late date for millennium compliance, we can now only hope for millennium survival. Studies have shown that

while the global cost of Y2K is expected to run to many hundreds of billions of dollars, we have spent a mere pittance so up to now. In 1995, we spent $25 million and in 1996, only $150 million.

Now, I say, we cannot get there from here. (Michael can be reached at 1-800-368-9370).

This section highlights some of the many companies that are viable players in the Y2K market. Y2K represents an unprecedented opportunity for investors. Up to now we have covered many of the negative aspects of the problem, "the dark side" if you will, but now we turn to how investor's can play on the solution side of the equation.

This is an extraordinary situation we're in. I don't ever recall the "overnight" emergence of a $600 billion dollar market. Even if you take the most conservative of estimates, it is still enormous. The following chart provides annual sales figures of other markets, for comparison.

Year 2000 Conversion vs. Other Key Industries

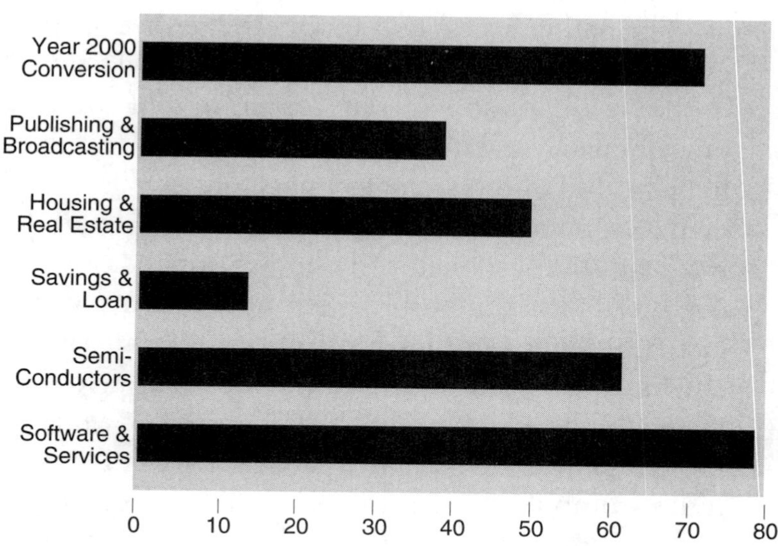

Which phase or phases of the process a particular company's products or services are focused on (discussed below) will have a direct correlation to when it will feel the greatest Y2K impact on revenues and profits. If we break down the full spectrum of Y2K conversion efforts into phases, we can identify at what point in the continuum each company should begin to flourish. This knowledge will help the investor determine at what point a company's share price might begin to make a move upward in anticipation of increased revenues and profits.

The Year 2000 Fix: Life Cycle Phases

Phase I *— Inventory, Assessment, Analysis, and Planning:* 1996 through 1997. Any of this work done in 1998 could conceivably bring with it huge margins. If a company has not completed this phase by the beginning of 1998, it will find itself at the mercy of the market and available resources.

Phase II *— Code Conversion (Peak for Automated Tools):* 1997 through 1999. This business will continue to be strong well after the Year 2000, experts say, as only mission critical systems will have been converted, leaving a large population of programs to be converted post Y2K.

Phase III *— Testing, Debugging:* 1998 through 2000 and beyond. This is turning out to be the "long pole in the tent." There is simply no escaping exhaustive testing for mission critical systems. It is highly labor intensive and requires an organization's users to be directly involved in the design and implementation of the testing. This will be an enormous distraction in 1999 and will result in the diversion of key resources to non-revenue producing activities.

Phase IV *— Implementation Management:* 1998 through 2000+

Viasoft Inc. (NASDAQ Symbol: VIAS)
Expertise = *Phases I, II, III & IV*

Recent Price:	*$54 — June 1997*
30-Day Avg. Vol:	*525,000*
Shares Outstanding:	*17,400,000*
52-Week High:	*$65 1/4*
52-Week Low:	*$14.37*
Market Capitalization:	*$939M*
FY 1996 Revenues:	*$43M*

(An interview from "The Y2K Investor" with Steven D. Whiteman, Chairman & CEO of Viasoft, can be found in Appendix IV.)

Viasoft has had real staying power over the last year. While there has been extreme volatility in many Y2K stocks, Viasoft has been fairly stable. Business Week identified Viasoft as one of their "Top Tech Bets" in the June 16, 1997 issue, page 98.

Viasoft's tool suite is probably the most mature of all the Year 2000 vendors. It has been marketing its products and services to Global 5000 companies since 1983 and has earned an excellent reputation for helping customers understand, manage, and evolve the mission critical software applications that run their businesses. Viasoft maintains product independence and has developed cooperative relationships with many of the industry's leading solution providers. This strategy allows Viasoft to offer the broadest range of products and services, which, in turn, allows its customers to migrate their mission critical applications safely into the future.

The company's Enterprise 2000SM™ for solving the Year 2000 problem is based on Existing Systems Workbench®, an integrated suite of software development tools. Enterprise 2000SM™ divides the date conversion task into three phases:

- Impact 2000™ determines the size, scope, and level of effort that will be required to implement the Year 2000 modifications.
- Plan 2000™ generates a project plan based on project goals. It identifies dependencies of application and data conversion efforts, prepares a detailed work plan, and executes a pilot project.
- Operation 2000™ manages the implementation and testing of the changes made.

Viasoft is also offering its products to the federal government with special discounted pricing. To address the huge federal government market, Viasoft introduced US2000™ on April 1, 1997. Designed as a special program expressly for government clientele, US2000™ makes the company's software and process framework available at rates equivalent to their maintenance-based pricing. Upfront license fees are completely waived.

With the acquisition of R&O Software in December 1996, Viasoft has expanded its ability to address a more comprehensive view of an organization's applications and provide a broader range of solutions. Through the use of R&O's repository technology, Rochade™, it can provide a leading-edge technology infrastructure to manage the vast amounts of information necessary for a comprehensive enterprise-wide inventory.

Viasoft's most recent product announcement was the debut of Bridge 2000™. Bridge 2000™ is an important offering that allows customers to execute a triage strategy without having to change all their application interfaces and test the interoperability of each. The product acts essentially as a gateway: non-compliant data are taken in and changed to an expanded field representation. The data are then passed along to the application where they are processed. The path is then reversed.

To summarize, the product provides the following:

- ✦ Allows you to bridge compliant programs with non-compliant data.
- ✦ Ensures that historical data remain untouched, but keeps the data readily available.
- ✦ Reduces the risk of system disruptions by converting your programs in smaller groups.
- ✦ Protects your business when you exchange data between trading partners that have not yet converted.
- ✦ Minimizes system disruptions.

Viasoft also announced with Keane Inc. that they have jointly developed a comprehensive testing methodology to handle the unique requirements of validating Year 2000 compliance projects. The companies retained industry renowned Year 2000 expert Ian Hayes, principal of consulting firm Clarity Consulting, to assist with the industry's first comprehensive testing methodology specifically designed to handle century compliance projects. The methodology will initially be offered in conjunction with the products and services of the two companies.

Viasoft customers are spread across the finance, insurance, government, telecommunications, manufacturing, and utility industries. Customers have chosen Viasoft to handle their large, complex, mission critical applications that need to be converted, maintained, and enhanced.

On April 24, the company posted third quarter and year-to-date revenues of $23.9 million and $57.7 million, increases from the previous year of 131 percent and 98 percent, respectively. Net income for the third quarter was $3.1 million, or 17 cents per share, an increase of 148 percent over the third quarter of fiscal 1996. The weighted average number of common and common equivalent shares outstanding was 18,337,000 and 17,278,000 for the quarters ended March 31, 1997 and 1996, respectively.

Net income for the nine months ended March 31, 1997, excluding charges related to the R&O acquisition that closed on Dec. 5, 1996, increased 94 percent to $7.5 million, or 41 cents per share, from $3.9 million, or 22 cents per share, for the same period last year. Including the acquisition-related charge of $27.0 million, relating principally to purchased in-process research and development, the net loss per share for the nine months ended was $1.14. The weighted average number of common and common equivalent shares outstanding was 17,149,000 and 17,220,000 for the nine months ended March 31, 1997 and 1996, respectively.

Two of Viasoft's current customers are also their most visible. The Social Security Administration has chosen Viasoft as one of its key partners in converting 33 million lines of code, and The Federal Reserve Bank (as yet unannounced) is also working with Viasoft on its highly sensitive applications. During the most recent quarter, Viasoft announced contracts with U S WEST Communications, Inc., and Credit Suisse First Boston Corporation. According to the company, these contracts are for Year 2000 services, but also have Viasoft providing a broader array of other services as well.

Data Dimensions Inc. (NASDAQ Symbol: DDIM)

Expertise = *Phases I, II, III & IV*

Recent Price:	*$30 — June 1997*
30-Day Avg. Volume:	*359,000*
Shares Outstanding:	*11,382,000*
52-Week High:	*$26 ½*
52-Week Low:	*$6*
Market Capitalization:	*$339*
FY 1996 Revenues:	*$14M*

(An interview from "The Y2K Investor" with Larry Martin, President of Data Dimensions, can be found in Appendix IV.)

Data Dimensions is one of the leading providers of millennium services. Incorporated in 1968, Data Dimensions offers highly advanced, cost-effective, information processing consulting services to help its clientele through the complex date conversion process. It helps plan, prepare, and implement complex, global-scale solutions to technology problems that affect the enterprise at all levels — including its customers and suppliers.

Data Dimension's customers are from the market sectors of banking, finance, insurance, health care, telecommunications, utilities, and the government. Domestically, DDIM has over 30 of the Fortune 500 in its client list, and internationally, it has partnered with other service providers to handle prominent clients in the banking, insurance, and financial communities.

The corporate headquarters are in Bellevue, Washington, with domestic sales and technical support offices strategically placed in major metropolitan centers nationwide. International offices are located in Canada, the British Isles, Scandinavia, Europe, the Middle East, Africa, and the Pacific Rim.

Data Dimensions has an impressive track record. It has massaged over 3 billion lines of code, updated millions of lines of code, and assessed portfolios ranging from 10 to 500 million lines of code for over 150 international clients. It uses an assembly line approach and uses its own factories, when necessary, to support the implementation process.

Data Dimensions is helping European customers convert to a common currency, and is also helping U.S.-based Telco to modify its applications and databases to incorporate changes made necessary by the Telecommunications Reform Act of 1996.

In 1996 Data Dimensions introduced Ardes 2k, a methodology that utilizes an enterprise-wide approach that treats the date-dependent issue as a total business problem. It includes comprehensive processes for diverse issues ranging from legal compliance and organizational awareness to code redesign and testing for final acceptance. The Ardes 2k package effectively integrates guidelines, examples, proprietary tools, project plans, and real world experience into a continuous stream of effort designed to resolve any organization's update procedures. Data Dimensions has made Ardes 2k available to customers on CD-ROM and the Internet via a licensing fee.

Ardes 2k utilizes a Modular Repeatable Process (MRP) that can be customized for individual environments, dynamically scaled to adapt to any size organization, and is configured to measure any and all quantifiable results. The MRP embraces all operating systems, languages, hardware, and software applications. Ardes 2k also incorporates a tools-neutral process bound only by the best automation software available. As a result, cost and training time — both key factors for any organization — are effectively minimized.

CACI Inc. (NASDAQ Symbol: CACI)
Expertise = *Phases I, II, III & IV*

Recent Price:	*$18 June 1997*
30-Day Avg. Volume:	*87,000*
Shares Outstanding:	*11M*
52-Week High:	*$11.375 — $23.62*
Revenues 1996:	*$240M*
Market Capitalization:	*$198M*

CACI is an international information technology corporation with over 30 years of experience in systems integration. The company has approximately 3,400 employees, and fiscal 1996 revenues exceeded $240 million.

Restore 2000 is the company's Year 2000 conversion methodology. It involves a comprehensive three-stage process for information systems: ASSESS, PLAN, and RENOVATE. CACI's approach is tool independent and therefore the company is able to provide solutions that are customized to clients' needs.

CACI is in my portfolio because of its preexisting contracts with the federal government. Even though there are efforts in place to streamline the government's procurement process for obtaining Year 2000 products and services, it will still be far more difficult and time consuming than any commercial process. CACI's contracts will allow it to add the provision of Year 2000 services to many of its contracts, thereby avoiding the highly competitive and time-consuming RFP/Proposal process. Furthermore, CACI was successful recently in getting its Year 2000 services added to the General Services Administration's schedule of prenegotiated contracts. This will allow agencies an even more streamlined process for obtaining services from the company.

CACI's non-Y2K business base is very strong, with $100s of billions of contract dollars in backlog.

CACI, located in Arlington, Virginia, says it will significantly expand its Y2K operations with recent hires and new contracts across multiple state agencies. Michael Guido, formerly with Computer Associates and DBE Software, Inc., has joined the firm as senior vice president. Carole Morton, President of Sterling Software, Inc.'s Information Management Group (IMG), has joined the board of the Year/2000 Journal. Sterling's Information Management Division (IMD) announced that the company's stock was selected for the new de Jager Year 2000 Index on the American Stock Exchange.

CACI's performance in the Y2K market has been anticipated with great interest, however, to date results have been less than stellar. The fact remains, however, that

CACI has been a good performer in the systems integration market, they have a relatively low P/E and they have contract vehicles that could be used for government business. They remain one of my top picks.

Keane Inc. (AMEX Symbol: DDIM)
Expertise = *Phases I, II, III, IV & V*

Recent Price:	*$55 June 1997*
30-Day Avg. Volume:	*174,000*
Shares Outstanding:	*32,853,000*
52-Week High:	*$57.75*
52-Week Low:	*$16.3*
P/E Ratio:	*60*
EPS:	*0.89*
FY 1996 Sales:	*$550M*
Market Capitalization:	*$1.8*

(An Interview from "The Y2K Investor with Brian Keane, Senior Vice President of Keane Inc., can be found in Appendix IV.)

Keane was founded in 1965 and is leveraging its long-standing relationship with a large customer base to rapidly build its Year 2000 business. An IT services company, Keane has been providing outsourcing services to Fortune 1000 companies worldwide.

Keane will provide its customers with services that span all phases we have identified. It has consolidated these into three phases:

Enterprise Planning — Tool-assisted analysis and data gathering to develop an assessment of the existing environment. Identifies constraints; information sources; potential problems; an inventory of systems, languages, and databases; and new application plans.

Strategy Development — Development of a detailed plan prioritizing conversions based on cost, time, and planned application redesigns criteria.

Implementation — Activities driven by Keane's project management methodology and by leveraging all industry-leading toolsets, including Viasoft's Existing Systems Workbench™ and Ernst & Young's Cleopatra®, as applicable.

Keane will also contract for a total application outsourcing solution in which Keane maintains legacy systems for 3 to 5 years while making designated applications century compliant. It will also deliver century-compliance services as a stand-alone offering via its Resolve 2000 solution/process. This will allow the company to use century-compliance services to attract new customers.

Keane reported revenues and earnings for the first quarter ended March 31, 1997, of $141,110,000 (up 33 percent compared with $105,761,000 in the first quarter of 1996) and pretax income for the first quarter of $17,276,000 (up 86 percent from $9,276,000 for the same period last year), while net income was $9,848,000, up 83 percent from $5,380,000 a year ago. Earnings per share rose to $.29 on 33,573,826 shares compared with $.16 on 32,842,000 shares in the first quarter of 1996.

Keane announced in April a testing methodology jointly developed with Viasoft (*see* details under Viasoft's profile).

Olsten Inc. (NYSE Symbol: OLS)
Expertise = *Phases I, II, III, IV & V*
(supplying personnel to Year 2000 projects)

Recent Price:	*$20.25 June 1997*
30-Day Avg. Volume:	*212,000*
Shares Outstanding:	*81,200,000*
52-Week High:	*$31 3/4*
52-Week Low:	*$13.37*
P/E Ratio:	*31*
EPS:	*$0.89*

FY 1996 Sales: *$3400M*
Market Capitalization: *$1.64B*

Olsten Corporation is one of the world's leading providers of staffing services and is North America's largest provider of home health care and related services. It delivers solutions for two of the most important challenges of our time — the need for business to become more productive in a competitive global economy and the equally important need to control health care costs.

Olsten Staffing Services in North America and the staffing operations in Europe and Latin America provide supplemental staffing to business, industry, and government. The Information Technology Services companies in North America and Europe, led by IMI Systems, Inc., provide services for the design, development, and maintenance of information systems.

Olsten Health Services in North America provides network services and caregivers for home health care and institutions, as well as home infusion and other therapies. Olsten Health Management provides management services to hospital-based home health agencies. These admittedly don't have anything to do with the Year 2000; however, it's a high-growth industry in which Olsten is a leader.

Olsten delivers services on three continents and employs approximately 650,000 people serving some 575,000 client/patient accounts annually. The international headquarters are located in Melville, New York.

In the company's press release reporting first quarter earnings, the following appeared:

"We are pleased with the progress we have made in the first quarter in both Staffing Services and Health Services," said Frank N. Liguori, Olsten Chairman and Chief Executive Officer. "Revenues increased 24 percent to $951 million, while systemwide sales rose 21 percent to $1.1 billion.

Net income, before a 1996 non-recurring charge related to Quantum Health Resources, Inc., declined 22 percent to $19.2 million, or $ .24 per share."

The consolidated financial statements of the company have been restated for the first quarter of 1996 to reflect the 1996 acquisitions of Quantum and CoCounsel, Inc. Certain reclassifications have been made to conform Quantum's and CoCounsel's results to the company's presentation.

"Good growth was also reported by our Information Technology Services and professional services operations," Liguori added. "During the quarter, IMI Systems, Olsten's IT Services company, strengthened its position serving the telecommunications industry with the acquisition of VISTECH, Inc. Also, our professional services division, led by CoCounsel and Olsten Financial Staffing Services, experienced good growth during the quarter."

Olsten stands to benefit greatly from the tremendous staffing requirements presented by the Year 2000 market. Another staffing provider to watch for is Robert Haft Inc. (RHI).

Strategia Inc. (NASDAQ OTC BB — STGI)

Expertise = *Phases I, II, III, IV & V*
(heavy emphasis on phases IV & V)

Recent Price:	*$14 June 1997*
30-Day Avg. Volume:	*Not Available*
Shares Outstanding:	*4,025,000 (estimated)*
52-Week High:	*Not Available*
52-Week Low:	*Not Available*
P/E Ratio:	*Not Material*
EPS:	*0.00*
Revenues for 1996:	*$9.4M*
Market Capitalization:	*$13.6M*

In March the company completed the secondary public offering of its common stock. The company received subscriptions for more 1.35 million shares at $7 per share. The company netted $8.75 million, which Strategia President Richard Smith said he expected to exceed the company's budgeted capital requirements for the next 12 months. The company has applied to have the common stock listed on the Nasdaq SmallCap Market under the symbol "STGI" following completion of this offering.

Strategia Corporation provides disaster recovery, consulting , information processing, outsourcing, and millennium services to users of large-scale computer systems in North America and Europe. Founded in 1984, the company has specialized in assisting business organizations and government agencies to prepare for and avert the consequences of unknown, unplanned interruptions. The company has provided services to 200 companies to date.

Strategia has focused its attention on the users of (Honeywell) Bull computer systems, but has recently added IBM users as a target market.

Zitel Corporation (NASDAQ Symbol: ZITL)
Expertise = *Phase II*
(while the company does participate in other phases, conversion should be the biggest contributor to revenues and earnings)

Recent Price:	*$20 June 1997*
30-Day Avg. Volume:	*1.1M*
Shares Outstanding:	*15,264,000*
52-Week High:	*$72.87*
52-Week Low:	*$5*
P/E Ratio:	*272.3*
EPS:	*0.07*
Revenue for 1996:	*$23M*

(revenue for the first half of FY 1997 was $8.3M, down from $15.7M during the first half of FY 1996)
Market Capitalization: $30M

Zitel has tested the blood pressure extremes of its shareholders many times over the last 12 months. Last year the stock ran up to $72 and change on rumors that George Soros held a position in the stock. When the rumors were dispelled, we saw the stock drop from the $70s to the $40s in one day. Then again more recently the company's stock reflected investor nervousness about the unexplained departure of the President of Matridigm and the rumor that there was a problem with Matridigm's conversion tool.

Zitel Corporation specializes in the design, manufacture, and marketing of high-performance, mission critical storage subsystems for enterprise-wide applications, which include relational database, batch, and on-line transaction processing. Its claim to the Year 2000 market is via its 35 percent stake in Matridigm, a conversion tool vendor. Additionally, the company's Solutions Services Division is a certified reseller of Matridigm's Year 2000 compliance products and services. Zitel also develops and markets single-system and multi-system performance measurement and modeling software used on a variety of UNIX and proprietary platforms to measure the performance of client/server environments. Zitel products are offered through systems integrators, value-added resellers and distributors, original equipment manufacturers, as well as directly to end users.

Zitel reported operating results for the second quarter of fiscal 1997 ended March 31, 1997. Revenue for the second quarter of fiscal 1997 totaled $2,772,000, compared with $5,460,000 for the comparable quarter of the prior year, primarily as a result of lower royalties from IBM. The net loss for the second quarter of fiscal 1997 was $1,914,000, or $.13 per share, versus net income of

$984,000, or $.06 per share, in the comparable fiscal 1996 quarter. Results for the quarter reflected a tax benefit of $1,077,000 resulting from the recognition of deferred tax assets in accordance with SFAS No. 109 ("Accounting for Income Taxes"), versus a tax provision of $659,000 for the second quarter of the prior year. Weighted average shares outstanding in the second quarter of fiscal 1997 were 15,234,000 compared with 15,562,000 for the second quarter of fiscal 1996.

While Zitel and its more stable cousin, BRC Holdings are still on my top picks list, its getting down to a case of "show me the money". If Matridigm rings the bell as many expect, Zitel and BRCP will enjoy huge returns from their arrangement with the company. Yet, if something concrete isn't announced before the end of the summer — I'm out.

Comdisco (NYSE Symbol: CDO)

Recent Price:	*$37 June 1997*
30-Day Avg. Volume:	*187,000*
Shares Outstanding:	*48,705,000*
52-Week High:	*$38.5*
52-Week Low:	*$22.62*
P/E Ratio:	*16.8*
EPS:	*$2.17*
Revenues for FY 1996:	*$2.431*
Market Capitalization:	*$1.77B*

Comdisco is the largest independent lessor and remarketer of high-technology equipment and provider of business continuity services, supplying solutions for reducing technology cost and risk to more that 8,000 customers worldwide. Based in Rosemont, Illinois, the company posted 1996 revenues of $2.4 billion and assets of $5.6 billion. The company is traded on the New York and Chicago Stock Exchanges.

From more than 100 locations around the world, Comdisco helps businesses acquire, manage, and protect their high-tech equipment. Services include equipment leasing, refurbishing, and remarketing; business continuity; consulting; technology integration; asset management software tools; and more.

The company has entered the Year 2000 services market through its disaster recovery division. It announced a relationship with Viasoft last year. The two will jointly develop a testing guide that supports both the application- and system- level software testing requirements associated with a Year 2000 conversion. The guide will leverage the companies' respective strengths in those areas, and is targeted for completion by the first quarter of 1997. As part of this relationship, Viasoft will be actively participating in Comdisco's Millennium Testing Services (MTS) program. This program allows each participant to co-market services and create opportunities to work closely with Comdisco and other MTS team members.

The testing aspect of the Year 2000 market opportunity represents more than 50 percent of the effort and expense of any given project.. It also carries with it the highest soft costs in that it is a huge diversion of user's attention. In addition to using the testing guide themselves, organizations may choose to work directly with Comdisco or Viasoft to address their system- and application-level testing requirements. Comdisco's MTS offers companies a test bed environment in which to learn the precise impact that the Year 2000 will impose on their computing system software. By duplicating their system structures in one of Comdisco's controlled testing facilities, organizations can identify program code areas vulnerable to the date change. Participation in Comdisco's MTS Team is open to third-party Year 2000 solution providers.

Comdisco announced results of the quarter that ended March 31, 1997. The company reported net earnings of $31 million, or $.58 per common share, compared with $26 million, or $.49 per common share, for the year earlier period. The company also reported revenues of $690 million for the second quarter of fiscal 1997, an increase of 19 percent, compared with $581 million for the prior year period.

Other revenue for the quarter increased by $25 million as a result of a litigation settlement. Other costs reflect a $25 million addition to the equipment valuation allowance for the quarter.

For the six months ended March 31, 1997, the company reported net earnings of $59 million, or $1.13 per common share, up 18 percent on a per share basis compared with $51 million, or $.96 per common share, for the prior year period. Total revenue was up 19 percent to $1.3 billion, compared with $1.1 billion for the prior year period.

Comdisco will be a winner in the Year 2000 marketplace. The question is how big. They are a solid pick for my top 10.

Computer Horizons Corp. (NASDAQ Symbol: CHRZ)

Recent Price:	*$38 June 1997 (post 3 for 2 split)*
30-Day Avg. Volume:	*207,000*
Shares Outstanding:	*24,130,000*
52-Week High:	*$39.10*
52-Week Low:	*$9.9*
P/E Ratio:	*54.6*
EPS:	*$0.70*
Revenues for 1996:	*$234M*
Market Capitalization:	*$915.8M*

Founded in 1969, Computer Horizons is a diversified information technology services company offering a variety of solutions to its Fortune 500 clients through an international network of 45 offices and subsidiary organizations.

The company helps its clients with advanced technology solutions in the areas of Year 2000 conversions and migrations with its full life cycle solution, Signature 2000™. Computer Horizons also provides solutions in the areas of outsourcing, client/server migration and development, enterprise management design, applications development, and legacy systems maintenance.

Computer Horizons maintains sizable outsourcing facilities in Pompano Beach, Florida, Parsippany, New Jersey, Cincinnati, Ohio, Denver, Colorado, and New Delhi, India, where it conducts domestic and international outsourcing and offshore projects. Headquartered in Mountain Lakes, New Jersey, Computer Horizons has regional headquarters in Detroit, Cincinnati, Toronto, London, and New Delhi, and employs 3,500 people worldwide.

Computer Horizons' staff size and national locations significantly expand its capacity for assembling large numbers of resources required to solve today's complex problems. The company's numerous sites allow projects to be executed at any combination of on-site, off-site or offshore facilities.

Computer Horizons' Signature 2000 is a total life cycle solution to the Year 2000 challenge. The solution consists of five major phases: Discovery, Analysis, Construction, Testing, and Implementation. Computer Horizons' offering integrates methodology, management, a suite of automated analytical and construction software, plus the experience to provide your organization the required decision-making information to plan and implement a Year

2000 solution. The Signature 2000 solution employs a rigorous approach for the implementation of Year 2000 changes.

The company announced a strategic alliance with Price Waterhouse. The two organizations will jointly provide consulting and technology solutions to bring client organizations into the next millennium. Complemented by Computer Horizons' technology assessments and sophisticated tools, Price Waterhouse will develop business assessments, customized strategies, and comprehensive Year 2000 compliance plans. Code correction and conversion services will be provided by Computer Horizons, with Price Waterhouse supplying systems testing and program management.

Computer Horizons also announced that it has been awarded a Year 2000 contract by AT&T Corp., confirming a story that appeared on the Dow Jones newswire on April 7. Under the terms of the agreement, Computer Horizons will assist in providing Year 2000 planning and project management support, as well as perform assessment and code repair. Computer Horizons' work on the project began in December 1996 and is expected to be completed by the end of 1998. Code assessment and repair are conducted at the Computer Horizons Millennium Refurbishment Center in Parsippany.

With these and other contracts that have been announced, underscored by its most recent quarterly results, Computer Horizons has clearly established itself as the chief beneficiary of the Year 2000 market up to now.

If there were such a thing as a sure thing in the Y2K arena, this would be it. The company has a strong track record in their core business, they have real contracts, producing real revenue. All of which has been reflected in the stock price.

Unicomp (NASDAQ Symbol: UCMP)
Expertise = *Phases I, II, III, IV & V*

Recent Price:	*$8.75 June 1997*
30-Day Avg. Volume:	*43,000*
Shares Outstanding:	*7,090,000*
52-Week High:	*$10 1/4*
52-Week Low:	*$3 1/2*
P/E Ratio:	*32.7*
EPS:	*$0.26*
Revenues 1996:	*$22.3*
Market Capitalization:	*$61M*

Unicomp provides information technology services to businesses located primarily in the U.K., and platform-migration software and payment-processing systems to users in North America and Europe. The company's strategy is to emphasize its platform-migration and payment-processing software products and to expand its services business within its existing geographic markets. Unicomp believes this strategy will allow it to expand profit margins and provide its high-quality information technology services to a broad and growing installed base of users of its platform-migration and payment-processing products.

The company has experienced significant growth, with total revenues growing to $22.3 million for fiscal 1996 from $12.2 million for fiscal 1994, a compound annual growth rate of approximately 35 percent. In fiscal 1996, approximately 51 percent of total revenues were derived from the company's maintenance and other information technology services, with more than 80 percent of total revenues attributable to international operations, primarily in Northern Ireland.

Unicomp attacks the Year 2000 problem through its Unibol subsidiary. Unibol is a software tools company specializing in IBM midrange migration products. It offers solutions that provide total support for rehosting IBM System/34, System/36, System/38, and AS/400 applications (there are approximately 400,000 AS/400 systems installed worldwide) on Open Systems. The company's products are available on all leading UNIX platforms and Windows NT Server.

The company recently announced that DHL has contracted Unibol Ltd. to use its UNIBOL GO2000 Toolset in order to provide DHL with a Year 2000 ready set of their core business applications. The value of the contract is around $3 million. The company said, "DHL has an extensive range of core business applications which support their operations world wide. These applications, such as International Billing, Tracking, and Tracing, are vital to this critical time where reliability and speed are key factors. DHL has seen significant expansion in their business over the past 10 years and over this time Unibol has been reliable suppliers of both software products and services to DHL."

Gordon Monro, IT Director for DHL's Europe and Africa Region, said, "I see this agreement as a natural extension of the extremely successful partnership between DHL and Unibol that was forged in 1987 and has provided 10 years of close cooperation and mutual benefit, to both companies. The Year 2000 programme has a very high focus in DHL and once again Unibol will be providing the services that we require to bring this programme to a successful conclusion."

Unicomp has a large customer base worldwide, with over 400 staff and over 50 distributors internationally. All together the company has over 30,000 installations in more than 55 countries. The company licenses its technology to a cross section of industries, including manufacturing, distribution, transportation, public sector, point of sale, and transaction processors.

An Alternative

Not all of us have the time or expertise to do the research and pick the companies in which we should invest. It's just too complex and far reaching a subject. Even with the recommendations I am making, you should always consult your broker before making any investments. Yet your broker may not be familiar with this market opportunity or the players in it.

I believe an excellent alternative to trying to pick individual stocks on your own is to use a system like that offered by John Vazquez of Prudential Securities in Bethesda, Maryland.

John has customized a product offering of Prudential Securities they call "Autoport." Autoport allows an investor to acquire holdings in a number of individual stocks representing a particular investment theme, yet to pay a commission only on a single transaction. John uses Autoport for Y2K, picking the equities to be included based on his personal research and market experience. With John's approach, all his clients have to do is place a single order for a specific dollar amount and John takes care of the rest. If this sounds like it might work for you, give him a call at: (301) 961-0101

Other companies I own, intend to own or have owned and probably will own again:

Alydaar (ALYD) — This tool vendor has garnered a great deal of excitement around their full fledged debut. Under Bob Gruder's direction, they have amassed a significant workforce and are withholding public announcements until they feel they are ready to handle the demand.

Computer Associates (CA) — A software powerhouse. They will enjoy significant business providing Year

2000 solutions for their existing clientele, yet they are so large, its hard to believe that the incremental revenues will have much impact on their bottom line.

Ciber (CIBR) — Viewed as a sleeper, this one is expected to burst upon the scene. We've already seen a strong run up from the doldrums of the past six months. They have a strong story for continued business after the Y2K wave has hit the beach.

Complete Business Systems (CBSL) — Great performance of late. Strong up and comer.

Compuware (CPWR) — While they don't have tools that are specifically designed to address the Year 2000 problem, the general-purpose tools they do offer have applicability to the problem. They have enjoyed healthy growth in their market and should continue to experience above average growth.

Computer Sciences Corporation (CSC) — The company will probably will do significant Y2K business, but its unclear what impact it will have on the company's already large revenue stream. There is some risk that money might be taken from some existing contracts to fund Y2K projects. That would potentially just move money around, not add anything incremental. In fact it could spell disaster for profits, as it would be very difficult to manage expenses effectively when employees are underutilized on existing contracts, yet the company has to hire new employees for Y2K work.

Delsoft Consulting Inc. (DSFT) — Delsoft has developed a proprietary, patent pending technique for changing all system and data dates to a new "Hyperdate". This Hyperdate is only six digits long so it fits into the space already provided for dates. All calculations are conducted on the Hyperdate and then converted either to eight digits if the date needs to be presented to a screen or report, or back to a six digit date if the date is returned or added to a database.

IBM/ISSC (IBM) — As my teenager would say, "Duh…!" As obvious as it may seem, I am wary of "Big Blue". They have an enormous problem of their own and its not clear to me that they can avoid exposure to suits by customers who want to off-lay some of the blame and expense for the Year 2000 problem.

Information Management Resources (IMRS) — This company would be my first choice to replace any company currently on my top "10" list. They have real contracts and have produced significant revenue in the Y2K sector. Many analysts pound the table on this one.

Intersolv (ISLI) — I just don't get this one. By all accounts ISLI should be taking off like gang busters. I have owned this company three times now, and each time it has fizzled. Maybe somebody knows something I don't, but their profile, client base and market position, should add up to a winner.

Micro Focus (MFIGY) — A much ballyhooed tool vendor from the UK. With new management at the helm they are pulling out of a very bad period spanning several years. They had a great first quarter, turning in results that showed 25% growth in revenue. They seem within reach of achieving profits of over $14M in 1997 and $26M in 1998 as forecast by Merrill Lynch.

Platinum Technology (PLAT) — Tool Vendor. Claims Fed Ex as a customer.

Peoplesoft (PSFT) — A powerhouse. Customers talk very favorably about the company's products.

Robert Haft International (RHI)|— RHI is a leader in the field of professional personnel placement services. They should enjoy a strong increase in business through 2001.

SEEC — (SEEC) — Another tool vendor. They moved up quite sharply during June. They recently announced a distribution agreement with IBM.

Sungard (SNDT) — Leader in the disaster recovery business. Shares a Department of Defense contract with CSC worth $6 billion.

ZMAX (ZMAX) — Strong tool vendor that provides services as well. The company attracted a high ranking member of the Cap Gemini management team to serve as president.

Readers should be aware that I am a trader of the issues listed in this section. Therefore, I bought and sold many of these issues for my personal portfolio. Their inclusion here does not necessarily mean that I own them now or are recommending that they be purchased. You should always consult your professional financial advisor before making any changes to your portfolio.

Chapter 3

2000 Thoughts

The following are edited excerpts from contributions I have made to John Westergaard's award winning web page, *"Westergaard Online"* which can be found at the following URL: [http://www.westergaard.8080.com]. Select Y2K Time Bomb from the home page main menu.

I found John's opinions and insights on the Y2K problem back in early 1996. Until then, I thought mine was the only voice predicting an economic catastrophe in the wake of the "millennium time bomb". John has done more than just write about the problem. He has taken direct action.

It was John who first brought this problem to the attention of Senator Moynihan, and helped him write both the letter to the President and draft his Senate Bill 2131 (see the appendix for the full text).

BT Gives Suppliers 18 Months to Get Bug Free

British Telecom has given its 1,800 core suppliers an ultimatum. "Guarantee Y2K compliance, or you're out!" BT is only the first of many major, international concerns that will demand that their suppliers be compliant before the turn of the century. Milli Lewis, BT's Year 2000 Project Manager, believes that they will have their short list of surviving kit suppliers by March.

While publicly held European companies may be able to sweep their pending expulsion under the rug, U.S. companies are legally bound to reveal such major threats to their business (*see* column of January 8, 1997). As the number of major corporate players that demand compliant suppliers grows exponentially, so will demand for Y2K solution resources in the marketplace. Prices will escalate and, eventually, the ante will be too high for some.

Many experts have predicted 20 to 30 percent business failures as a result of Y2K. What will come as a surprise to some, is that these failures won't necessarily come post 1/1/2000. In fact, the death spiral will begin soon for some. Marginal competitors will experience the Y2K challenge as the final blow to their solvency.

Advice: If you intend to maintain your investments in the general equities marketplace, you'd better start asking some tough questions of the boards of directors. If you are going to stand pat in your mutual funds, demand that your fund managers provide written assurance that their portfolio companies have formal, documented plans in place for Y2K compliance.

Finally, the winners will take the high ground as BT has done. For it will not be enough just to be compliant. To survive and prosper, companies of which you are a shareholder must demand compliance from their suppliers.

Business Week, August 12, 1996, "Panic in the Year Zero Zero" — "Firms that spend the necessary money get to stay in business. And some of those are plotting to take advantage of their competitors' possible demise," says [Kevin] Schick [of the Gartner Group]. "We have players looking forward to the great market crash of zero zero," he added. He thinks as firms run out of time to fix their [Year] 2000 problems, they will discontinue certain lines of business or even fail.

P/E Ratio Not a Fair Measure of Y2K Pure Plays

In the many forums, chats, and strings that I frequent, I often run across an investor who is rabid for selling Y2K issues short because of their often "outrageous" price to earnings ratios. It's lunacy, they argue, for a company with no revenues to be valued so highly, often with three-digit P/Es.

Surely they will be right about some companies that will not live up to the expectations the market has set for them. Yet, there are those others that will offset many, many mistakes.

One must suspend the use of traditional criteria when evaluating Y2K players, because this is a market where 95 percent of the opportunity is in the future. It is not so ridiculous for a company like Zitel (owner of 37 percent of Matridigm) to have a market cap of over $600 million and a P/E of 160+, when one considers its near-term opportunity. If Matridigm's product truly can fix a million lines of COBOL per hour with a very high degree of accuracy, then it'll be renting space at Fort Knox. Matridigm proposes to charge $0.50 per line of code. It is not uncommon for a Fortune 1000 company to have 10,000,000 lines of code. That's $5 million bucks for five hours' work. Hmmmmm. Probably a fair amount of profit in that.

Stepping back from the market for a moment to consider its size, it's easy to see why many of these companies will see their stock skyrocket in the very near future. It is estimated that the federal government alone will have a $30 billion tab for correcting the Y2K problem. The government's current annual IT budget is only about $25 billion. Yikes, we're talking about spending 40 percent of the annual IT budget on Y2K over the next several years. That will fuel a lot of start-ups, my friend. From another vantage point, the global market for systems integration is about $33 billion. JP Morgan estimates the U.S. tab for Y2K to be in the neighborhood of $200 billion. Fine companies like CSC, AMS, EDS, and others will be awash in a sea of business. The "Big Six" are already turning down projects.

The business opportunity of Y2K is on a scale, the size of which none of us has had any experience. To attempt to apply the standard, "tried and true" methods of evaluating investments in this market could leave you out in the cold. And short sellers betting against the Y2K boom may have a big surprise as some of these young bucks are able to sustain a spectacular stock price performance.

The Year 2000 Market Opportunity Will Be a Double-Edge Sword for Some

EDS, IBM, CSC, and others may very well experience an enormous bonanza of Y2K-related business over the next several years. IBM in particular will see non-linear sales growth in its ISSC division as well as in mainframe and software sales. ISSC will provide womb to tomb project management, mainframes, and DASD will be sold to provide "off-line" platforms upon which an organization's source code can be worked, since Y2K-related work cannot be accomplished during the day, when the system is in high demand. EDS and CSC will see market demand more than outstrip their capacity to provide support.

Yet, with all of this high margin business laying about their feet, the companies in question are not the "no brainer" plays that they seem. For each also has potential Y2K liabilities for software they have provided (often times written for) their clients over the years. IBM and EDS customers, in particular, may hold them accountable for the non-compliant software products they have provided over the years. Just think of the potential litigation costs IBM potentially faces as a result of Y2K. These legal fees and judgments could far outweigh any incremental business it might enjoy as a result of fixing the problem it may very well have created.

Some By-Products Will be Winners in the Wake of Y2K

The beneficiaries of the Y2K problem won't just be those companies in business to fix the problem. While these are the obvious plays, and some inarguably will do very, very well, there will be niche markets that form in the eddies left by the leading edge of this digital hurricane. Let's take a look at a few from a very high level.

Secondary Market Mainframe Suppliers — One of the challenges of addressing Y2K on mainframes is the fact that one cannot work on the code while the system is in operation. That limits work to weekends, as days are filled with entries, queries, sorts and other jobs that support the real-time work environment. At night, batch files are processed. That leaves weekends. There just aren't going to be enough for some companies. The alternative is to acquire "off-line" processing capability, either by purchasing new hardware or renting duplicate capacity. This should favorably affect the disaster recovery marketplace and suppliers of reconditioned equipment for sale or rent. While mainframe manufacturers might be an obvious play, I remain very concerned about their exposure to litigation over responsibility for Y2K.

Products and Services that Support the Legal Profession — These businesses should feel a rising tide of business. The amount of information that will need to be collected, analyzed, and stored will be without precedent. Practices will need to hire a veritable army of temporary legal and clerical personnel. Tools of the trade should also pick up. Providers of software geared toward litigating attorneys should get a boost.

Is it safe? — Late in the game (say 1999) there just might be a run on "in-home" safes. People who are nervous about having their money in someone else's hands on

1/1/2000 might want to keep some assets at home. While I don't agree with this approach, and I think keeping large sums of money in the home is ill advised, people still will need a fireproof and secure repository for their personal records and valuables. I recommend a safe deposit box. You might have trouble accessing your records and currency on January 1, but such problems should clear up rather quickly after the crash.

Test equipment, mass storage, networking equipment, and project management software should also get a lift from the problem.

Beware Your High Flying — High Tech Investments

During the "*Y2K Investor*" radio broadcast last week, Congressman Steven Horn, co-chairman of the subcommittee that held hearings on Y2K, confirmed the estimated cost for the federal government's Year 2000 repair bill is $30 billion. The actual figure will not be known for some time as the data are still coming in from the various agencies.

The government currently spends $25 billion on information technology. Congressman Horn also reiterated what many have said in regard to Y2K expenses: "No additional funding will be made available." The problem must be addressed within existing budget parameters. Assistant Secretary of Defense Emmett Page said it best, I think, "These expenses must be paid out of hide." Hmmm. Let's see now, if the government has to spend an average of $30 billion per year to fix Y2K (by the way, it won't be a nice neat linear expense), then that means 40 percent of the annual IT budget must be reallocated. Reallocated away from buying new software, computer systems, printers, networks, etc. Do your high-tech portfolio companies do substantial business with the federal government? I bet they do.

Think about it. Sun, Oracle, Motorola, 3Com, Bell Atlantic, and many others do substantial business with the federal government. Some, such as Fore Systems, are disproportionately top heavy in federal business. Companies with this profile are vulnerable to sudden cutbacks in anticipated government business. You should review your portfolio to determine which of your holdings rely on Uncle Sam for a significant portion of their annual sales.

Hold on to others, like Cisco for instance. Cisco does less than 10 percent of its business with the federal government, and any loss there should be made up by increased client/server applications that are implemented to replace the Y2K-riddled mainframes.

The Dow and Nasdaq continue their Icarus-like flight. It's getting warmer. Don't be caught with your shorts down.

Yikes, Talk About Volatility!

Y2K plays are NOT for the weak-hearted investor. You've got to have an iron stomach and the nerve of a bull fighter, as proven by the recent swings in some of the more visible issues. Zitel has literally been all over the map lately. Yesterday (1/15/97) it was down over $3, then closed up over $5. It was only a few weeks ago that Zitel climbed $6 in the morning to a new high of $72+ and in the afternoon dropped back to $42.

We will probably see this kind of behavior for the near term. The sector is intensely speculative, given the controversy over the extent of the problem and the possibility of a potential "silver bullet.". On Monday a bevy of investors believes Matridigm has the "Mother of all Date Changers," but by Friday reality sets in and the stock settles back down.

The sector is a favorite of traders too. Huge short positions are held in some of the high fliers, and some of the most remarkable premiums I've ever seen for calls. I sold Zitel June 45s for over $10 just 2 weeks ago. Another reason the sector has been so volatile is the lack of institutional investors. Fidelity, it was reported last week, has 11 percent of Viasoft, but I am not aware of any other funds that hold large Y2K blocks. George Soros was rumored to own a big piece of Zitel, but when it was revealed he in fact did not, the stock took the aforementioned dive.

This is a market for believers like me. I'm looking out toward summer. These wild swings should disappear and be replaced by wild growth.

Mr. Gore, Are You There? Isn't There Anyone There?

Newsweek Magazine's current issue is dedicated to "Beyond 2000, America in the 21st Century." It was gratifying to see a full page dedicated to Y2K. No caveats, no hedging, just a straightforward article on the problems ahead.

The article concludes with yet another reported warning to the administration. Vice President Gore, surely our most technologically enlightened VEEP, was told once again of the horrors of not addressing Y2K aggressively. This time it was Howard Ruben of Hunter College, who, in a meeting last summer, told Mr. Gore, "Just think about trying to get elected president in 2000 if the government is starting to collapse."

It would appear that our Vice President wishes this would go away. It won't. He may.

How Do You Spell Relief? D-E-N-I-A-L

Mr. Taranto in today's *Wall Street Journal* has a good laugh poking fun at those of us on the lunatic fringe. I have not lost perspective to the extent that I cannot see how we often sound like victims of alien abduction, coming back to spread truth and love.

Yet, all that Mr. Taranto has done is feed the denial of those in "upper management" who read the *WSJ* and are desperate to find some way to avoid this whole mess. It's interesting, really, this perpetuation of denial is actually "packing the charge," making the situation much more explosive when it can no longer be contained.

I wonder how Irene Dec of Prudential or Mike Vertigans of National Westminster Bank would feel about some of Mr. Taranto's statements. I suppose they would be pretty darned embarrassed that they have budgeted to spend over $100,000,000 on this non-problem. Damn those slippery consultants, they got us again.

As for the article that appeared in *The Economist* last summer, they should stick to counting beans, because they don't know beans about the Year 2000 problem.

Diversification is the Key to Success

As I wrote yesterday, this market is highly volatile. Those who rely on income from their investments and can't/shouldn't risk losing their principal, would be well advised to stay away for awhile.

Yet for those of us who wish to dive in on the strength of our conviction, we still must be prudent and diversify our plays. One point I have made in the past is that our Y2K favorites are not at all immune to a general market correction. With the Dow climbing to dizzying heights, this possibility becomes more and more real. In fact, there are a growing number of bears retreating to the forest. Greenspan won't give up so easily either. We have not heard the last from him. He remains concerned with the equities markets and their value to earnings ratio. Stock prices are also adding to inflationary pressures.

Personally, I am hedging my bets against a general correction by buying December 1997 S&P puts. This strategy provides me with downside protection against a general correction as well as participation in the first wave pullback in reaction to Y2K.

I also am buying covered calls on my Y2K plays. With the near-term volatility we're seeing, one can enjoy a nice premium and limit some downside risk. Even though you stand to have your positions called away, if you sell them out of the money, you can still enjoy a nice profit.

Another strategy I have employed is buying LEAPs. These calls out 6 months or more provide you with the opportunity to play, while not tying up so much capital. THIS IS A FAR MORE RISKY APPROACH AS ONE CAN LOSE 100 PERCENT OF THE PRINCIPAL. It's also tough to buy calls and make money on issues that don't experience a significant upturn. We certainly have that potential here in our Y2K plays. I don't buy calls on the high-profile players such as Viasoft or Zitel. It's better to be the seller on these, but I really like calls on companies like American Management Systems (AMSY), CACI (CACI), Keane (KEA), and Olsten (OLS), among others.

Options on silver futures are my favorite play. I've bought contracts on Dec 97 and Aug 98. With silver and gold both in the basement, they should really take off if the market corrects for general or Y2K reasons and zoom non-linearly when the market takes in the threat Y2K poses to electronic assets and the overall economy.

"The bigger they are, the farther they fall."

A Bright New Future/After the End of Life as We Know It

There have been a few postings on the Y2K strings I follow that debate whether or not things will actually be better after the turn of the century. I happen to believe they will.

You might ascertain from my writings that I am a pessimist, who believes that we all might as well pack it in after the stroke of midnight on December 31, 1999. To some extent you would be right, but not in the long view. While I believe there will be tremendous upheaval in the early months/years of the next century, I also believe that the technology will advance at an even faster rate once we have recovered our footing.

Perhaps you are familiar with Alvin and Heidi Toffler's work, "*Future Shock*," "*The Third Wave*," "*Creating a New Civilization*," and others. I spoke with Mr. Toffler recently about the Year 2000 problem. I suggested that Y2K might actually represent a "digital forest fire," if you will. Burning off the final remnants of the "Second Wave" infrastructure, the scorched IT landscape would create a clean slate from which to build new and better systems for those caught in the conflagration, just as a forest fire clears the canopy allowing the sun to reach the saplings on the forest floor.

There will also be tremendous opportunities to invest all of the hard assets you protected against potential loss in the bank runs and computer crashes attendant to the turn of the century. Companies that survive will be that much stronger for having done so; their share prices will be low along with all others, and some will be a great buy. Competition will be scaled back in almost every industry, and both skilled labor and specialized equipment thrown off by dying companies will be available at bargain basement prices.

Don't get me wrong, this period of social and business distress may last quite some time (the post '29 depression did), but just as in the depression, millionaires were made. Why not aspire to be one of them in the post Y2K era?

Simplify, Simplify, Simplify

This philosophy might be appropriate for an artist, but it's deadly for anyone dealing with Y2K. It is human nature to try to make a problem neat and tidy, to package a complex concept so that it can be thought about and expressed in succinct terms. Yet, one can also misuse these tools of logical process when applied to the Year 2000 problem.

Where problem solving or a desire to communicate might be a healthy motivation for simplification, denial, more often than not, is the chief motivator when anyone is attempting to oversimplify the Year 2000 problem. One cannot afford to look at the challenge with a highly parochial perspective. It's not enough to claim victory when one's own systems are compliant. No one individual, company, or government agency is an island. In fact, the larger and more successful we are, the more daunting our Year 2000 challenge.

The issues can be thought of in concentric rings of influence. At the core is our "closed" system of internal operation. Most often this is represented in the individual PC user. However, certain components of a commercial or government operation might function as a closed system. While systems at this level might be isolated functionally and operationally from other systems, it would be a mistake to think that they are safe from more global influences. We'll discuss these later.

The next ring out from center would be local interdependency. Vendors, customers, taxpayers, constituents, and intradepartmental and interdepartmental communications/interoperability fall into this category. We must bring our systems into compliance, but we are dependent on others not only to be compliant, but also to be compatible with our date management scheme. We must also have a defense against the potential for our systems to be "re-infected," for lack of a better term, by systems that have not been fully repaired. This dependency makes us highly vulnerable to things outside of our control. Not everyone will fix their problem in time, not everyone will fix their problem entirely, and not everyone will be totally honest about their status.

The next ring out involves the international community. The United States may do a superhuman job of fixing the problem in time and with no loss of functionality or participants. Yet, if even minor players in the global community fail to make it 100 percent pure and on time, or at least fail to honestly portray their status, we are all at risk. In the IS environment, the world has long been a global village. The breakdown of any one component impacts all others.

Which takes us to the macro level. The outermost ring of the model. Here, we have the sweeping implications of the Year 2000 problem. Here, we find Y2K's influence on the global economy. If the Third World doesn't make it on time, can the economy survive without impact? If major industrial players or a large segment of the mid-range players don't make it on time, can we sustain the loss of their contribution? If the Year 2000 problem is not successfully addressed in all international military systems, will opportunists not take advantage of a lame country's Y2K-induced weaknesses? Will we have the international cooperation and will to sustain the potential for disastrous mistakes, made by systems that have gone awry?

One can easily see that inner rings are impacted by events in outer rings. It is not enough to fix our own desktop PC. We aren't immune if we don't have a computer. This problem must be attacked aggressively and with a high degree of domestic and international cooperation.

The problem is, humanity is not oriented toward taking aggressive action toward a "threat." We need to be impacted, hurt, or damaged. And, if we wait that long, it will be too late.

That's Why Congress Isn't "Commander in Chief"

This week the wire services carried a story recounting the results of the President's Social Security Advisory Panel. In short, there weren't any.

Our political system is not equipped to deal effectively with a looming crisis that hasn't yet caused any pain. The predicted insolvency of the Social Security Administration is not at all unlike the Year 2000 problem. People (voters) are still receiving checks.

Experts agree that we have a threat of gargantuan proportions in Y2K, not confined to our shores, but in fact global. Yet, no one has died, there haven't been massive layoffs, John Doe can still buy milk, gasoline, and cigarettes, so what's the problem?

Even though Y2K is not nearly as politically volatile as Social Security, it still has not benefitted from strong political leadership. Our politicians aren't designed to care about something that hasn't yet happened. Ours is a government that will always be reactive, and only then in response to clear, broad-based pain or anger. Unless, of course, you happen to be a Political Action Committee, then you can generate legislative activity.

Leadership on this matter will have to come from another sector — the private sector. Driven by the forces of the marketplace, we could very well see public relations campaigns launched by forward-thinking companies that have their Y2K problem well in hand. In the very near future, Y2K compliance will be seen as a competitive differentiator. Companies that are ahead of the game won't be shy about proclaiming their supremacy. These companies will buy advertising and sponsor television programs focused on the horrors of Y2K, and how XYZ company has had the vision to address the problem, thereby protecting its customers' interests. It wouldn't surprise me to see a certification program emerge, where successful completion of an audit produces a compliance certificate. A certificate that will be proudly displayed in future advertising.

It won't be altruistic or patriotic leadership, but, as is often the case, it will be effective. What it won't address are the problems of government agencies. Their failure to bring their systems into compliance in time could undermine whatever gains we are able to make in the private sector. Here there is no substitute for strong political leadership. Let's hope someone on Capital Hill sees political advantage in this cause, otherwise we just might be growing food in our backyards and reading by candlelight, just as we did at the last turn of the century.

Small is Beautiful

The obvious Y2K plays may not in fact be the best or certainly the most stable. I try to find niche players that have a going concern that is successful on its own merits, independent of Y2K.

Some of these are Strategia (STGI), Unicomp (Ucmp), CACI (CACI), Keane (KEA), and others. All of these companies are small caps, and therefore present good share price leverage as the market begins to accelerate. This is not a case of whether or not one "search engine" will beat out the other, rather it is an extremely broad market of literally thousands of languages that need to be addressed. COBOL may be the most widespread, but there are others of significance such as JOVIAL and ADA, which are used by the military. Platforms also come in all shapes and sizes, too.

There are huge populations of DEC VAXs, HP X000s, Prime, and Tandem systems, just to name a few.

By the way, in the federal government market, contracts are king. You cannot do business without a contract in place. Generally contracts are awarded through a full and open competition. Procurement takes time, and there is no guarantee you'll win.

CACI is a great play for the federal space. SAIC (Science Applications International Corporation) is another. With existing contracts in place that could be used as vehicles to obtain the vendor's products and services, these companies are strategically positioned to capitalize on the emerging opportunity.

As I mentioned before, the big boys make me nervous. IBM, EDS, CSC, Unisys, and others are potentially targets of customer suits. Claims will be made against these large system providers, alleging that it is their responsibility to bring systems they sold to the government into compliance, with no additional expense. Directors and officers will be cited as having neglected their fiduciary responsibility in not addressing the problem.

Chapter 4

Other Steps You Can Take

Take an Inventory of Your Family Records

Remember, in the event of a global computer meltdown, all electronic records are at risk. To take defensive measures against this possibility, you should consider the following:

- ✦ **Purchase a Fireproof In-home Safe**— Keep copies of original documents in your in-home safe. Keep the originals in a safe deposit box.

Write for the following records for you and your family members:

- ✦ **Birth Certificates** — If you don't already have certified copies.
- ✦ **Adoption Papers** — Your own and or those of your children.
- ✦ **Immunization Records** — These are often handwritten records held by your doctor, but it wouldn't hurt to have copies.
- ✦ **Medical Records** — History of illnesses, treatment, etc. could be useful in securing reimbursement from your insurance carrier after the year 2000.
- ✦ **Academic Records** — Go back as far as practical to obtain copies of grades and other scholastic and academic achievements.
- ✦ **Military Records** — Make certain you have up-to-date records of your service and discharge.

- **Social Security** — Write for your Social Security Statement.

Set Up a File of Financial Records

Your best evidence that you have assets on deposit will be your records, which reflect a longstanding pattern of activity. If, for instance, you habitually make deposits to your savings account, infrequently, if ever, making withdrawals, you'll have a much better case if you can prove it with hard-copy records.

- **IRS Tax Returns** — Make certain you have at least 3 years running.
- **Bank Statements** — Start saving them now and keep them through the year 2000.
- **Brokerage Account Statements** — Save the monthly statements and the individual confirmation notices. Prior to January 1, 2000, make certain you have either liquidated your accounts or have taken possession of the stock, bond, etc., certificates.
- **Canceled Checks**|— Three years running.
- **Maintenance Records on Your Automobiles**|— Keep the full history for as long as you own the car.
- **Credit Card Statements** — Three years running .
- **Insurance Policies** — Health, Life, Casualty, Automobile, Liability, etc. — Make certain you keep them up to date and file expired policies in order to substantiate a pattern of coverage.
- **Passport** — Get a new one, if you don't have one already, for every member of the family.
- **Wills** — Keep a hard copy at home and in a safe deposit box.
- **Deeds, Title Insurance Policies**|— Make certain you have all of these records in a safe deposit box.

Summary

I know it's a pretty grim prediction I'm making, yet it doesn't necessarily have to be so. There might not be time for everyone, everywhere, to get 100 percent of their systems converted in time, yet there is hope. If our government would take aggressive leadership on the global stage, setting the example for all other nations and their leaders, we could be the source of solutions to the problem and not just another nation of victims.

Vice President Al Gore, a natural for the role, could take the lead by calling for an international Y2K Congress to establish standards. As the nation with the greatest head start on the problem, we could share our experience and lessons learned so that others who follow behind don't have to suffer the same mistakes. I would be an appropriate role for the technology founders who basically exported the problem to the rest of the world.

A coming together of this kind would allow us to make decisions as a global community, in regard to what international systems must be preserved at all costs. We could establish defense protocols in order to minimize or eliminate any accidents or incidents that might arise as the century turns over, and steps could be taken to ensure the public health.

If you take action on your investments, don't neglect to take action with your elected officials. Write your governor, congressional representatives, and senators. Let your local city and county officials know of your concerns. Demand that the board of directors for any company in which you are invested is taking the appropriate action.

We have all benefitted greatly from computers over the last several decades. We will continue to benefit long into the future. This isn't a problem with the technology, but with the humans that manage it. Even though we will all suffer due to the Year 2000 problem, we have all benefitted greatly from computer technology. So let's all be a part of the solution in some way.

More Information on the Year 2000 Problem can be found at:

Comlinks.com — Comlinks web page, the only full service Year 2000 information service online, provides a number of excellent papers and articles from the press that deal with all aspects of the Year 2000 problem.

Comlinks founder, Alan Simpson, has been working tirelessly to raise attention to the year 2000 problem. He has accomplished much. You can find them online at: http://www.comlinks.com

Appendix I

Government Documents

Union Calendar No. 464
104th Congress, 2nd Session
House Report 104-857

Year 2000 Computer Software Conversion: Summary Of Oversight Findings and Recommendations

Sixteenth Report–by the Committee On Government Reform And Oversight

September 27, 1996. Committed to the Committee of the Whole House on the State of the Union and ordered to be printed, Mr. Clinger, from the Committee on Government Reform and Oversight, submitted the following:

Sixteenth Report

On September 24, 1996, the Committee on Government Reform and Oversight approved and adopted a report entitled "Year 2000 Computer Software Conversion: Summary of Oversight Findings and Recommendations." The chairman was directed to transmit a copy to the Speaker of the House.

I. Summary

A. Background

After midnight, December 31, 1999, computer systems throughout the world are at risk of failing. Computers may confuse the year 2000 with the year 1900 on January 1, 2000, and go backward in time instead of forward when the new century begins. The severity of the problem was raised when Congress was told that if businesses and governments continue to ignore this issue, disruption of routine business operations and the inability of the Federal Government to deliver services to the American public could result.

According to a Congressional Research Service memorandum dated April 12, 1996, "Many people initially doubted the seriousness of this problem, assuming that a technical fix will be developed. Others suspect that the software services industry may be attempting to overstate the problem to sell their products and services. Most agencies and businesses, however, have come to believe that the problem is real, that it will cost billions of dollars to fix, and that it must be fixed by January 1, 2000, to avoid a flood of erroneous automatic transactions." The memorandum further suggests that it may already be too late to correct the problem in all of the Nation's computers, and that large corporations and Government agencies should focus on only their highest priority systems.(1)

The Committee on Government Reform and Oversight is deeply concerned that many Federal Government departments and agencies are not moving with necessary dispatch to address the year 2000 computer problem. Without greater urgency, those agencies risk being unable to provide services or perform functions that they are charged by law with performing. Senior agency management must take aggressive action if these problems are to be avoided.

B. Jurisdiction

The Committee on Government Reform and Oversight (the "committee") has primary legislative and oversight jurisdiction withrespect to the "overall economy, efficiency and management of Government operations and activities, including Federalprocurement." It also has primary oversight responsibility to "review and study, on a continuing basis, the operation of Government activities at all levels with a view to determining their economy and efficiency."(2) In addition to its other oversight responsibilities:

[T]he Committee on Government Reform and Oversight may at any time conduct investigations of any matter without regard to the provisions . . . conferring jurisdiction over such matter upon another standing committee. The committee's findings and recommendations in any such investigation shall be made available to the other standing committee or committees having jurisdiction over the matter involved. . .(3)

Pursuant to this authority, the Subcommittee on Government Management, Information, and Technology (the "subcommittee") convened an oversight hearing on April 16, 1996 to examine whether January 1, 2000, is the date for a potential computer disaster (4) . Currently, computers which use two-digit date fields will fail to recognize the entry of the next millennium on January 1, 2000. If left unchanged, a global computer virus could result. The subcommittee reviewed Federal agency management of this potentially disastrous computer problem.

The subcommittee's jurisdiction centers on the Federal Government's operations. Consequently, although the year

2000 problem affects both public and private organizations, the subcommittee has focused its attention on the preparedness of Federal Government departments and agencies.

II. Findings

A. Proceedings of the Subcommittee

On April 16, 1996, Subcommittee Chairman Stephen Horn convened a hearing of the Subcommittee on Government Management, Information, and Technology to collect the facts on the steps Federal agencies are taking to prevent a possible computer disaster. Among the questions he raised were whether agencies are taking the necessary actions to identify where the problem lies and whether they are providing the necessary human and capital resources to correct the problem.

In her opening statement, the subcommittee's ranking minority member, Representative Maloney noted: "The cost of failure is high_systems that deliver services to individuals will not work, and those services will not be delivered. Checks will not arrive on time. Planes will be grounded, and ports will be closed."

As noted by subcommittee member Representative Tom Davis (R-VA), "think for a moment how dates play a part in each one of our lives and how the failure of a computer system or computer scanner to recognize and understand a date can affect us. Our driver's license may prematurely expire and the Social Security Administration may recognize 25-year-olds as 75-year-olds, without conversion that is needed for the year 2000."(5) And as pointed out by Representative Peter Blute, "this is a very important issue_an economic issue for the entire country."(6)

A number of examples were received by the subcommittee of incidences that could occur if industry and government continue to ignore this issue. In fact everything from unexpected expiration of drivers' licenses to the erroneous dates for final mortgage payments could occur if two-digit date fields remain unable to recognize the year 2000. Knowing this information technology project has a fixed date for completion, January 1, 2000, Subcommittee Chairman Horn asked hearing witness, Kevin Schick of the Gartner Group, the estimated cost of fixing this problem. Mr. Schick provided recent estimates as high as $600 billion worldwide, half of which would be in the United States and $30 billion for the Federal Government. In accordance with Congress' responsibility to better understand what steps Federal agencies are taking to ensure a minimalization of risk and cost to the American taxpayer, Subcommittee Chairman Horn then queried Schick of his knowledge regarding the administration's and, in particular, the Office of Management and Budget's current efforts to convey the urgency of this problem. Mr. Schick responded "there is no sense of urgency . . . We [the Gartner Group] are not interested in creating a sensational story here about the year 2000. We don't want to panic. That does nobody any good . . . Yet, if [Federal agencies] are not already well into this project by October of 1997, [the Federal Government] will be doing a disservice to the very constituents that depend on [it] to prevent something like this from happening to them. . . ."(7)

To further understand the impact of this issue on the Nation's businesses and State and local governments, Representative Constance Morella, chairwoman of the Subcommittee on Technology of the Committee on Science, called for a joint hearing with the Subcommittee on

Government Management, Information, and Technology, to review the impact on personal computers, State governments and Federal agencies. During the hearing held on September 10, 1996, Larry Olson, Deputy Secretary for Information Technology for the Commonwealth of Pennsylvania, presented Pennsylvania's plan of action. As noted by Olson, the key to success of the plan is senior level support. Mr. Olson pointed out that during his first year as Governor of Pennsylvania, Tom Ridge quickly recognized the dramatic implications of the year 2000 date field problem. Subsequently the Governor took quick action to ensure that Pennsylvania businesses and governments will be prepared before January 1, 2000.(8)

At the September session Harris Miller, president, Information Technology Association of America, presented an outline of how the year 2000 situation presents three problems for personal computer users in homes and businesses across the country:

(1) the BIO's chip of individual machines; (9)

(2) the operating system that generally comes bundled with new computers; and

(3) the commercial software purchased for those machines. Most equipment manufacturers in the past 18 months have modified their products. Operating system software is also an issue. Operating systems in personal computers in most cases can have their operating systems "fixed" through a simple procedure using the computer's mouse. Commercial software products may or may not be year 2000 compliant. An issue of great concern for personal computer users is the increasing interconnectedness with other systems. In order to ensure that computer systems are operational in the year 2000, most systems will need modification.

Mr. Miller testified further that personal computer users as well as mainframe information technology managers need to be aware of this issue and take appropriate corrective steps.(10)

In her testimony Sally Katzen, Administrator, Office of Information and Regulatory Affairs, Office of Management and Budget, provided an outline of the Clinton administration's current strategy for solving the problem:

(1) raise the awareness of the most senior managers in Federal agencies to the dimensions of the problem;

(2) promote the sharing of both management and technical expertise; and

(3) remove barriers that may slow down or impede technicians fixing systems.(11)

B. Oversight Activities of the Subcommittee

Alarmed by what the subcommittee had learned at its April 16 hearing, Subcommittee Chairman Stephen Horn and Ranking Minority Member Carolyn Maloney sent a joint congressional oversight letter. The letter was addressed to the heads of each executive department and 10 additional agencies. The letter, dated April 29, 1996, asked 13 detailed questions intended to ascertain the status of each agency's software conversion preparation for the year 2000.(12)

The agencies receiving the letter were selected by the subcommittee because each would be required under the Information Technology Management Reform Act to appoint chief information officers.(13)

The overall response the subcommittee received was discouraging. Only 9 of the 24 departments and agencies responded that they had a plan for addressing the problem. Five of them had not even designated an official within the organization to be responsible for the problem. Seventeen of the departments and agencies lacked any cost estimates for addressing the problem. Even those with partial cost estimates could only provide projections for a limited part of their agency.(14)

Four agencies surveyed did have superior records, compared with the others. The Social Security Administration began its year 2000 initiatives in 1989. Although it should be observed that their efforts are not yet near completion. The Agency for International Development wrote the subcommittee that a "system migration" to newer technology had addressed the problem. Both the Office of Personnel Management and the Small Business Administration also had more advanced year 2000 efforts.

However, none of these four agencies is a Cabinet department. Each organization has a more focused information technology mission than other agencies.(15)

Several Cabinet departments, with diverse subagencies and bureaus, reported to the subcommittee that they only had limited year 2000 projects underway. Efforts at the Departments of Energy and Transportation were so underdeveloped that both could not answer any of the 13 questions posed by the April 29 oversight letter. Many agencies with direct responsibilities for furnishing services to the public, such as the Departments of Labor, Veterans Affairs and the Federal Emergency Management Agency, had only minimal year 2000 initiatives underway.

Subcommittee Chairman Horn, Ranking Member Maloney and other members of the subcommittee released their conclusions based on the agency responses at a July 30, 1996 press conference. To underscore their conclusions, each of the 24 departments and agencies received letter grades based on the subcommittee's assessment of their relative performance. Four were given "A's" and four agencies were given "F's." Ten agencies were given "D's," none of which had any plan in place for addressing the problem, or available cost estimates. The decision to give each agency a grade was intended to emphasize the that individual departments and agencies have for their own performance.

[The information referred to follows:]

Insert offset folios 1-2 here.

002

Other major findings resulting from the April 29 oversight letter which were presented at the July 30, 1996 press conference with Representatives Horn, Maloney and other members of the subcommittee include:

- ✦ Major departments are in the initial planning stages of this effort, even though, agencies need to have their systems inventoried and fixed by 1998, in order to provide sufficient time to test and ensure complete accuracy. This means, in the next year and a half departments and agencies must complete their plans, inventory and fix millions of lines of code, while simultaneously meeting agency needs.
- ✦ Even those agencies considered leaders in this effort, such as the Social Security Administration and the Department of Defense are not close to completing the inventory and solution stages of the conversion process.
- ✦ According to the information received, only six agencies have cost estimates on the monetary resources needed to address the problem. These agencies include, the Department of Agriculture, the Department of Education, the Department of Health and Human Services, the Office of Personnel Management, the Small Business Administration, and the Department of State. In fact, the Department of Health and Human Resources, has cost estimates for only two divisions, amounting to $125 million and the Department of

Agriculture has cost estimates for only one division, amounting to $5.6 million. The total estimate for these six agencies and their departments is $298 million.(16)

- The Department of Defense has not yet completed its inventory of the computer software code which needs to be converted.
- The cost estimate to fix the 358 million estimated lines of code to be reviewed is between $1.02 and $8.52 per line. This means the cost to review and fix Department of Defense's systems could range somewhere between $358 million and $3 billion.(17)
- NASA, one of the most innovative, advanced and computer dependent agencies in the Federal Government, has not prepared a plan to solve the problem and does not anticipate having a plan completed until March 1997. With this schedule, the agency will have less than a year to inventory, and fix systems.

C. Committee Findings

The committee finds the following:

1. The year 2000 problem results from the unanticipated consequences of data processing decisions made decades ago. The two-digit year date field in many computer systems perform various functions, such as calculating the age of U.S. citizens, sorting information by date, or comparing multiple dates. When computer technology was developed 20 years ago disk storage was very expensive.(18) During this time, many computer programmers never considered an alternative format, because of the cost and the idea that these programs would not last 10 years let alone through the year 2000. Systems which have been in place for nearly 30 years have been enhanced through advanced technology development but continue to be programmed for the 20th century. During the development of

computer technology many experts within the Federal Government and the private sector believed that the rapidity with which technology advanced could always yield a "silver bullet" solution to any technical difficulty. Others believed that the software services industry was overstating the problem in order to sell their product solutions. It has been noted that while correcting the date field is technically simple, the process of inventorying, correcting, testing and integrating software and hardware among all interactive systems (both among and between industry and Government) is a very complex management task.

2. Senior management involvement is required to address the year 2000 problem. According to the various witnesses who appeared before the subcommittee, the key to success is support from senior level management to fix systems accordingly. Witnesses revealed the fact that many information technology experts have been aware of this issue, in some instances for a decade, but have been unable to take corrective action because the issue has been perceived as irrelevant to the success of agencies' missions. According to private sector witness, Michael Tiernan, it was only after senior level management realized the potential economic impact of this issue did they move quickly to develop a plan to resolve the problem.(19)

Within the Federal sector an interagency committee has been established to raise awareness of the daunting task facing Federal information technology managers. The "Interagency Committee on the Year 2000" has taken several actions including requiring vendor software listed in future procurement schedules to be year 2000 compliant.(20)

3. The year 2000 deadline cannot be extended; no schedule slips are possible. According to Kevin Schick,

research director, The Gartner Group, the crisis revolves around three considerations: time, cost and risk. Businesses, Federal agencies, and State and local governments need to understand that this is the only information technology project that will not allow for a schedule slip. Saturday, January 1, 2000 cannot be moved to another day or time. Federal, State and local governments may need to shift resources from other projects in order to work on year 2000 efforts.(21) In most cases, Federal agencies are running out of time.

4. The cost of addressing the year 2000 problem is expensive. Addressing the year 2000 computer problem will be very expensive. Estimates received by the subcommittee run as high as $600 billion for systems worldwide. The cost for the Federal Government alone, could reach $30 billion. These estimates are based upon the private and public sectors developing plans to inventory their current programs; analyze the percentage of code affected by dates; implement a "fix" to the problem, and provide for testing to ensure that the changes are correct.(22) All of these solutions need to be applied while successfully operating current information technology programs.

Only six agencies furnished any cost estimates on the monetary resources needed to solve the problem to the April 29, 1996 oversight letter. These agencies include, the Department of Agriculture, the Department of Education, the Department of Health and Human Services, the Office of Personnel Management, the Small Business Administration, and the Department of State. In fact the Department of Health and Human Services, has cost estimates for only two divisions, amounting to $125 million.(23) The Department of Agriculture has cost estimates for only one division, amounting to $5.6 million. The total estimate for these six agencies and the remaining 22 departments is $298 million.(24)

As of this date, there are no estimates for solving the problem within and among the various departments and agencies.

5. There is a high risk of system failure if the year 2000 computer problem is not corrected.

As stated by the Congressional Research Service, it may be too late to correct every system in the Nation before the clock strikes twelve on December 31, 1999.(25) If this is the case, then, businesses need to know what steps they must take in order to avoid disruptions in normal business operations. Federal, State and local governments, need to prioritize mission critical systems, immediately correcting those systems which have the greatest human impact.

Federal, State and local governments, must ensure that the American public is not at risk of losing any currently available government service. Additionally, agencies, such as the Department of Defense, the Federal Aviation Administration, and the National Aeronautics and Space Administration, need to ensure that January 1, 2000 will not be a day when computers go haywire and life as we know it is severely disrupted.

On June 7, 1996, the Congressional Research Service (CRS) provided both the House and Senate with a memorandum on the various issues complicating the year 2000 solution process. The CRS also identified the potential consequences resulting from a failure to address this problem at the Federal level. Some examples of the impact of system failures could include:

- ✦ Miscalculation by the Social Security Administration of the ages of citizens, causing payments to be sent to people who are not eligible for benefits while ending or not beginning payments to those who are eligible;

- ✦ Miscalculation by the Internal Revenue Service of the standard deduction on income tax returns for persons over age 65, causing incorrect records of revenues and payments due;
- ✦ Malfunctioning of certain Defense Department weapon systems;
- ✦ Erroneous flight schedules generated by the Federal Aviation Administration's air traffic controllers;
- ✦ State and local computer systems becoming corrupted with false records, causing errors in income and property tax records, payroll, retirement systems, motor vehicle registrations, utilities regulations, and a breakdown of some public transportation systems;
- ✦ Erroneous records by securities firms and insurance companies;
- ✦ False billing by telephone companies resulting in errors in consumers' bills or lapses in service.(26)

6. <u>There are potential liability issues if the year 2000 computer date conversion is not completed</u>. In the future, industry may face potential liability for failing to provide year 2000 compliant products or services. These same providers need to ensure that their databases are not corrupted by bad data from other sources. This issue may cause banks, securities firms and insurance companies to ascertain whether the companies they finance or insure are year 2000 compliant before making investment decisions. Additionally, governments and businesses will need to protect themselves from purchasing noncompliant software products and services through the use of commercial market warranties.

7. Interconnected computer systems pose international risks. As the leading user of computer technology the United States probably has more at risk, in terms of economic loss, if the year 2000 issue is not resolved properly. The economic impact on businesses both domestically and internationally could be dramatic, especially if our allies do not quickly take action to correct date dependent software. In fact, Federal agencies and the private sector need to emphasize the urgency of this problem worldwide.

III. Recommendations

The year 2000 is less than 40 months away. The problem, although not technically complex, is managerially challenging and will be very time consuming for private and public sector organizations. Additionally, the task may be more difficult for the public sector, where systems which have been in use for decades, may lack software documentation and therefore increase the time it takes from the inventory phase to solution. Further increasing the time to solve the problem could be a lack of qualified personnel willing, or able, to correct the problem.

According to estimates received by the subcommittee during the hearing process, the cost to fix Federal systems, is estimated to be at least $30 billion. After requesting budget information from 24 departments and agencies, Congress still does not have a complete picture of the cost of solving this problem. This lack of cost information may hinder Federal agency efforts to correct every system. In fact, as stated by the Congress Research Service memorandum dated April 12, 1996, "it may be too late to correct all of Nation's systems". The clock is ticking and most Federal agencies, have not inventoried their major systems in order to detect where the problem lies within and among each Federal department, field office and division. The date for completion of this project cannot slip.

The administration, particularly, the Office of Management and Budget must ensure that agencies convert two-digit date fields to recognize the year 2000 by ensuring the necessary and appropriate resources_including both human and capital_are available to senior agency managers. The Government has a responsibility to its constituents and we must not fail to ensure that Government services and public safety are available to all of our citizens.

Additional specific recommendations for the Federal Government by the committee include:

- ✦ Agencies must prioritize mission critical systems, and determine the resources needed to make these systems year 2000 compliant.
- ✦ The Office of Management and Budget should direct Federal agencies to begin implementation of agency year 2000 plans by January 1, 1997.
- ✦ The Office of Management and Budget should work with Federal agencies to ensure appropriate funding levels are allocated to solving this problem.

(1) Richard Nunno, Analyst in Information Technology, Science Policy Research Division, Year 2000 Computer Problem, Congressional Research Service, April 12, 1996, p. CRS-2.

(2) Rules of the House of Representatives, 104th Congress, X, 1(g)(6) and (12) and X, 2(b)(2).

(3) Rules of the House of Representatives, 104th Congress, X, 4(c)(2).

(4) The decision to record two-digit date fields as "66" rather than "1966" was a way to save very limited storage space on computers. Many believed at the time that there would be difficulty in the year 2000, but they assumed that any systems already in operation would be replaced by the year 2000. At this point no magic bullet has appeared to solve this problem.

(5) Opening statement of Representative Tom Davis before a hearing of the Subcommittee on Government Management, Information, and Technology, House Committee on Government Reform and Oversight, Is January 1, 2000 the Date for a Potential Computer Disaster? April 16, 1996.

(6) Statement of Representative Peter Blute before a hearing of the Subcommittee on Government Management, Information, and Technology, House Committee on Government Reform and Oversight, Is January 1, 2000 the Date for a Potential Computer Disaster? April 16, 1996.

(7) Oral testimony of Kevin Schick, research director, The Gartner Group, before a hearing of the Subcommittee on Government Management, Information, and Technology, Committee on Government Reform and Oversight, Is January 1, 2000 the Date for a Potential Computer Disaster? April 16, 1996.

(8) Statement of Larry Olson, Deputy Secretary for Information Technology, Commonwealth of Pennsylvania, before the Subcommittee on Government Management, Information, and Technology, Committee on Government Reform and Oversight, Subcommittee on Technology, Committee on Science, September 10, 1996.

(9) The BIO's chip instructs the basic input/output system of a computer.

(10) Oral statement of Harris Miller, president, Information Technology Association of America, before Subcommittee on Government Management, Information, and Technology, Committee on Government Reform and Oversight, Subcommittee on Technology, Committee on Science, Solving the Year 2000 Computer Problem, September 10, 1996.

(11) Statement of Sally Katzen, Administrator, Office of Information and Regulatory Affairs, Office of Management and Budget, before the Subcommittee on Government Management, Information, and Technology, Committee on Government Reform and Oversight, Subcommittee on Technology, Committee on Science, Solving the Year 2000 Computer Problem, September 10, 1996, p. 3.

(12) Letter from Representative Stephen Horn and Representative Carolyn Maloney to 24 departments and agencies, April 29, 1996 (letters on file with the subcommittee). It is attached as an appendix to the report.

(13) National Defense Authorization Act for fiscal year 1997; Division E; Public Law 104-106.

(14) Refer to appendix (on file with the subcommittee).

(15) Each of the four also has some comparability to the private sector financial services industry which also moved faster than other private industries in addressing the problem.

(16) Letter from Representative Stephen Horn and Representative Carolyn Maloney to the Honorable Donna Shalala, Department of Health and Human Resources, April 29, 1996 (on file with the subcommittee). Letter from Representative Stephen Horn and Representative Carolyn Maloney to the Honorable Dan Glickman, Secretary, Department of Agriculture, April 29, 1996 (on file with the subcommittee). Letter from Representative Stephen Horn and Representative Carolyn Maloney

to the Honorable Richard W. Riley, Secretary, Department of Education, April 29, 1996 (on file with the subcommittee). Letter from Representative Stephen Horn and Representative Carolyn Maloney to the Honorable James B. King, Director, Office of Personnel Management, April 29, 1996 (on file with the subcommittee). Letter from Representative Stephen Horn and Representative Carolyn Maloney to the Honorable Philip Lader, Administrator, Small Business Administration, April 29, 1996 (on file with the subcommittee). Letter from Representative Stephen Horn and Representative Carolyn Maloney to the

Honorable Christopher Warren, Secretary, Department of State, April 29, 1996, (on file with the subcommittee).

(17) Tom Backman, MITRE Corporation, MITRE Assessment on the Effects of Two-Digit Years for the Year 2000, January 10, 1996.

(18) Oral testimony of Kevin Schick, research director, The Gartner Group, before a hearing of the Subcommittee on Government Management, Information, and Technology, House Committee on Government Reform and Oversight, "Is January 1, 2000 the Date for Computer Disaster?" April 16, 1996, p. 8.

(19) Michael B. Tiernan, chairman, Year 2000 Subcommittee, Data Management Division of Wall Street, Securities Industry Association, testimony before the Subcommittee on Government Management, Information, and Technology, April 16, 1996, p. 79.

(20) Richard Nunno, Analyst in Information Technology, Science Policy Research Division, Year 2000 Computer Problem, Congressional Research Service, p. CRS-3.

(21) The State of Nebraska has imposed a new tax to pay for the cost of the year 2000 computer conversion.

(22) Kevin Schick, research director, The Gartner Group, testimony before the Subcommittee on Government Management, Information, and Technology, April 16, 1996, p. 16.

(23) Stephen Horn, chairman, Subcommittee on Government Management, Information, and Technology, Ranking Member Carolyn Maloney, "letter", April 29, 1996.

(24) Letter from Representative Stephen Horn and Representative Carolyn Maloney to the Honorable Donna Shalala, Department of Health and Human Resources, April 29, 1996 (on file with the subcommittee). Letter from Representative Stephen Horn and Representative Carolyn Maloney to the Honorable Dan Glickman, Secretary, Department of Agriculture, April 29, 1996 (on file with the subcommittee). Letter from Representative Stephen Horn and Representative Carolyn Maloney

to the Honorable Richard W. Riley, Secretary, Department of Education, April 29, 1996 (on file with the subcommittee). Letter from Representative Stephen Horn and Representative Carolyn Maloney to the Honorable James B. King, Director, Office of Personnel Management, April 29, 1996 (on file with the subcommittee). Letter from Representative Stephen Horn and Representative Carolyn Maloney to the Honorable Philip Lader, Administrator, Small Business Administration, April 29, 1996 (on file with the subcommittee). Letter from Representative Stephen Horn and Representative Carolyn Maloney to the Honorable Christopher Warren, Secretary, Department of State, April 29, 1996 (on file with the subcommittee).

(25) Richard Nunno, Analyst in Information Technology, Science Policy Research Division, Year 2000 Computer Problem, April 12, 1996, p. CRS-2.

(26) Richard Nunno, Analyst in Information Technology, Science Policy Research Division, Year 2000 Computer Problem, Congressional Research Service, June 7, 1996.

Agency Report Card

The House Government Reform and Oversight Committee's Subcommittee on Government Management, Information and Technology conducted a survey of US Government Departments. Here is the Government Department's Report Card:

AGENCY	GRADE	PLAN?	PROGRAM MANAGER	COST ESTIMATE?
AID	A	YES	YES	Y2K Compliant
OPM	A	YES	YES	YES – $1.6M
SBA	A	YES	YES	YES – $4.9M
SSA	A	YES	YES	YES
Education	A	YES	YES	YES ($60 M)
NRC	B	YES	YES	NO
State	B	YES	YES	YES $33–$66M
Defense	C	NO	YES	YES
NSF	C	YES	YES	NO
Treasury	C	YES	YES	NO
Agriculture	D	NO	YES	NO
Commerce	D	NO	YES	NO
EPA	D	NO	YES	NO
GSA	D	NO	YES	NO
HHS	D	NO	YES	NO
HUD	D	NO	YES	NO
Interior	D	NO	YES	NO
Justice	D	NO	YES	NO
NASA	D	NO	YES	NO
VA	D	NO	YES	NO
Energy	F	NO	NO	NO
FEMA	F	NO	NO	NO
Labor	F	NO	NO	NO
Transportation	F	NO	NO	NO

This table refers to the information received from the joint letter of Rep Steven Horn & Carolyn Maloney, sent April 29th, 1996. The replies were published Sept. 24th, 1996.

Testimony Of George Muñoz Assistant Secretary of the Treasury for Management/Chief Financial Officer House Subcommittee On Government Management, Information And Technology

April 16, 1996

Introduction

Representative Horn, distinguished members of the Committee, ladies and gentlemen. On behalf of the

Department of the Treasury and Secretary Rubin, I want to thank you for the opportunity to speak with you about the Year 2000 Date Transition, more commonly known now as the Y2K problem.

I want to commend Representative Horn and this Committee for taking the leadership to bring this important issue before Congress. As you have heard from the other witnesses in this hearing, it is essential that the Federal government begin defining the government solution for the century date change and, by drawing attention to it at this level, much needed resources can be focused on that process.

I would also like to applaud OMB for having taken the initiative to sponsor the Interagency Committee work that has recently begun. GSA and NIST are also to be commended for their part in developing recommended guidelines and standards.

Credit is also due to those agencies like Social Security and Department of Defense which have demonstrated foresight in initiating projects within their own departments. I also want to recognize the Financial Systems Committee of the Chief Financial Officers Council (CFO) for their leadership in this effort. In addition, I would like to thank the Treasury Office of Security and the Office of Information Systems as well as our bureau information technology officers for having identified this issue and coordinated our response.

I plan to present here not only the position of Treasury, but, as Executive Vice Chair of the Chief Financial

Officers Council, my comments will reflect information gathered from several state governments, Federal agencies, and the CFO Council's Financial Systems Committee.

My comments today will briefly address the **three main components** of the Year 2000 Date Transition:

- ✦ The reality and severity of the problem;
- ✦ The additional risks in the Federal environment and how we in Treasury are addressing the problem; and
- ✦ Finally, lessons learned, opportunities, and recommendations for successfully moving into the 21st Century.

Severity of the Problem

A description of the problem here may be repetitive of what my colleagues have presented, but I would like to define the issue from the financial perspective. Clearly, if a solution were delayed, we would be courting disaster and may be facing chaos. That would not happen.

When I use the term "problem," I am referring to the challenges that I and many other managers have to assure that key systems will process smoothly into the next century. It is a challenge which we will meet. I am confident that systems in the Treasury Department and other agencies will work on January 1, 2000. As others have said, the challenge comes from the inability of some computer systems to process dates after 1999 accurately.

It is not a problem that is limited to either the Federal government or other public sector information systems. It is widespread throughout the public and private sector information systems, systems that impact our lives daily. It involves deeply embedded manipulations that have the potential to affect almost all automated systems, from small, single user systems, to massive transaction systems.

In reviewing the missions of our agencies, the effect of Federal government computer processing on the American economy becomes abundantly clear. For example, in the Treasury Department, we have large, extensively complex systems:

- ✦ Treasury collects $1.4 trillion annually through IRS, Customs and ATF, representing over 97% of the total Federal revenues. Last year, 250 million returns were processed.
- ✦ The Treasury Financial Management Service (FMS) oversees a daily cash flow in excess of $10 billion and issues over 800 million payments totaling over $1 trillion each year for all executive agencies.
- ✦ The Customs Service collects over $20 billion in duties, taxes, and fees. They assist in the administration and enforcement of some 400 provisions of the law on behalf of more than 40 government agencies and process 456 million persons and 127 million conveyances a year.
- ✦ Public Debt auctions $2 trillion marketable Treasury securities annually. They issue and redeem 150 million savings bonds annually and they account for the $4.9 trillion Federal debt and over $300 billion in annual interest charges.

I have described these key activities to provide you with a sense of diverse areas of potential impact and the magnitude of work needed to address these seemingly simple date problems. It is important to stress that the business of the Federal government is intricately interwoven with the commerce and welfare of the rest of this country as well as other nations. Because of those critical relationships, it is essential that we in the Federal government address the Year 2000 problem aggressively.

Before I go any further, I think it is important to address a question which naturally emerges from a cursory examination of this problem: "Did this problem arise because of someone's negligence?" To this, we emphatically respond: NO!!! Not many years ago, computers were not measured in gigabytes and terabytes, but in kilobytes. As is often quoted these days, people today have computers in their homes that have more storage space and processing capacity than many mainframes of thirty years ago.

In those days, saving storage space in computer files was critical to the efficient operation of systems that used very expensive resources. As a result, software was developed to solve complex technical problems and serve intricate, critical business needs using only two digits for the year. Many of those systems are still in use, which is a testimony to their quality but also, to the complexity and cost of migrating these systems to newer technology. These systems are central to many of our most critical operational functions—they are at the heart of the Year 2000 problem.

The enormous scope of this conversion effort is only clear when the steps involved locally within an organization are multiplied across the world-wide enterprise of information systems. Resolving Year 2000 issues will require extensive examination of applications, data items, and systems. While the legacy systems are the most likely to include the two-digit year, we must be sure that all dependencies have been identified and addressed.

For some Year 2000 compliant systems, complex interfaces will need to be built to handle data to and from systems that may or may not be compliant yet. Typical of most organizations, within the portfolio of Treasury production systems, not all systems will be updated at one time, requiring complex configuration management as sections of code are made compliant.

Bridges will have to be built between systems as changes are introduced. Firewalls and other protections will need to be developed as part of contingency plans to ensure the success of critical system if interfaces fail. Comprehensive test environments will have to be built to ensure that applications can successfully process 21st century dates.

Finally, all of this must be accomplished while still operating these systems for critical production activities.

Government Environment

As we prepare to address this issue, it is important to recognize the realities of the environment in which these conversion activities will take place in the Federal government. Many Federal systems are larger and older, and perform unique tasks so they are less likely to be included in the Year 2000 upgrades provided by vendors. Simply put, our challenge is greater than that faced by the private sector.

In addition, there are some obstacles to resolution of the problem, which hinder, rather than support, the technical and project management efforts to move the Federal Sector forward toward full compliance. Those obstacles include the limitations of the acquisition cycles, dwindling pool of experienced personnel, application systems unique to the Federal sector, and a huge inventory of legacy software and hardware. Further, as opportunities to cut expenditures are sought, the budget environment may limit aggressive conversion activity in favor of continuing current operations.

Given the size of this effort for the Federal government, sufficient quantities of competent vendor support services are absolutely essential. There will be fierce competition for technical contracting services to assist public and private organizations world-wide with this conversion effort. The longer the Federal government agencies wait to purchase these services the higher the costs and the more likely all competent sources will already be fully committed. In this regard, the recently enacted Information Technology Management Reform Act of 1996 should help immensely to provide flexibility in acquiring the needed technology and systems.

Personnel issues are another category of Federal government difficulty. Work on this problem is occurring at the time of downsizing the Federal workforce. We must be careful as we downsize to maintain the critical expertise we will need to address this Year 2000 problem.

One of the most significant features of the government environment is the huge inventory of legacy software. Many times that software is characterized as being monstrously complex and run on outdated hardware. As can be seen from the attached charts, the Federal government has large numbers of older mainframe systems which may be suspect. For many of these legacy systems, the vendors who originally provided the software are either no longer in business or not upgrading these early versions of their products. Funds may be required to upgrade or replace that software, in order to ensure the continuing operation of systems.

Finally, the testing environment for implementing the solution may require duplicate resources for a limited period of time. There has never been a time when so much code was being examined, changed and tested at the same time. Not only will most of the software in each agency be changing, but simultaneously, most of the code in every other interfacing agency will also be changing. The rigorous testing environments required to implement such a complex scenario will require careful planning.

Budget cycles for purchasing much needed services, software, and hardware require extensive multi-year

projections and must be submitted months and years in advance. It may be difficult to finance a conversion effort of this magnitude within existing program funds.

Treasury Year 2000 Initiatives

As I stated earlier, Treasury's systems will not fail at the beginning of the next century. To ensure that, we have already begun necessary steps to address the Year 2000 issue. Every bureau within Treasury has made progress towards the Year 2000 solution and some have made significant progress within their information systems in resolving the Year 2000 problem.

- The Department has been an active participant in the OMB Interagency Year 2000 Committee since its beginning in December 1995.
- A Treasury-wide group has been established to highlight the problems, work the issues, and share lessons learned.
- Milestones have been given to bureau information technology executives which will provide a vehicle by which the Department can track progress.

The bureaus are at various levels of progress. Some bureaus have completed one or more of the following key steps in the Year 2000 conversion process:

- used four-digit year fields for many years;

- completed conversions for legacy applications;
- developed blueprints;
- inventoried systems;
- evaluated tools;
- or identified potential systems at risk.

The bureaus have been requested to include estimated Year 2000 costs in the FY 1998 budget submissions.

Our Chief Financial Officers are aware of the issue and are monitoring the compliance of fiscal systems across Treasury.

Lessons Learned

Turning now to what can be done, I would like to discuss the lessons that have been learned, the opportunities that we have for making improvements, and how Congress can proactively address the Year 2000 problem.

No silver bullet. There is no one solution for all situations because of the inherent complexities. Huge legacy systems are full of homegrown routines, adapted for specific agency requirements, many of which have dates. There is no way a quick fix or new product can address all of the embedded date usage. The only solution is addressing each technical problem internally and coordinating the project centrally.

Planning is paramount. The temptation to rush in and attack the technical problem is great, especially with the added pressure of the inflexible deadline. This would be a huge mistake. Planning is essential because approaching a project of this size must be done strategically and tactically. Thinking outside the box may give us the chance to evaluate opportunities to improve business processes and computer processing. Taking the additional time to plan is imperative and will prevent costly errors later, when there will be no time to recover.

Good project management is essential. The challenge of project management in an effort of this size is

unprecedented in the information systems environment. This is not strictly, or even primarily, a technical problem. Treasury's financial systems, especially those related to revenue collection and disbursement of funds, represent the crossroads of financial activity for the Federal government. Consequently while addressing the Year 2000 issue, Treasury must also ensure that the integrity of all existing financial systems is maintained during this conversion. We cannot off-load these processes while we make corrections to them. It is analogous to trying to repair a Boeing 747 while in flight. Managing all of the components simultaneously while continuing to execute the mission is absolutely imperative.

More effort than expected. Planning and testing, which are critical to success in this effort, are requiring

significantly more resources than expected. Neither the government nor industry has ever attacked a computer systems problem this massive or pervasive. The brittle nature of the homegrown systems, the monumental coordination with external agencies, the heterogeneous existing technical environment all contribute to the complexity, and therefore to the effort, of this project.

More costly than expected. As the effort was underestimated, so was the cost. Because of all the elements that must be brought to bear (planning, testing, project management, unexpected hardware and software upgrades) cost estimates continue to rise. And, as increasing numbers vie for the same limited number of service providers, rates may escalate as well. A year ago initial projections indicated that anticipated costs would be less than $.50 per line of code. Today, current industry metrics reflect that estimates have risen to $1 — 2 per line. Even this number primarily reflects conversion costs and may not include testing, hardware replacements, and systems software upgrades.

Testing is the key According to industry estimates, the actual conversion may represent only 10 -20% of the total effort. The critical component, testing, will actually consume most of the resources: 45 — 55% of the total effort. With so much of the code being modified, we must verify that, in the process, we do not break something that was not broken. Certifying those changes will be essential to continuing our normal processes. The remaining 25 — 35% is accounted for with required planning.

Standards facilitate process. A recommended standard for data exchange was developed by NIST and endorsed by the OMB Interagency Committee recently. Such standards will help to create much needed common ground for project coordination and data exchange between government agencies and the business community.

Good solutions — Bad solutions.

There are several ways to approach this project. Anyone who promises to quickly and cheaply fix the problem is offering a "silver bullet" and clearly is not doing us a favor. The Year 2000 problem emerges from the context of the technical and organizational environment in which it was created and in which it resides. And it will require the functional and technical stewardship of the individual government owners to correct it.

Allow agencies to perform their own solutions. The key to success is that the converters must know the systems. Each department and agency internally has the best perspective on what should be done to resolve the technical issues. In-house expertise is your best expertise.

Chain is only as strong as its weakest link. Government agencies and the business community continually exchange data, creating intricate interdependencies. Those interdependencies create potential weaknesses that are not related to the internal health of systems, but to those external groups upon which certain processes and business functions are dependent. Firewalls can be built to protect each agency's information assets, and that covers the possibility of unconverted data. But if their systems fail and data is not available, contingency plans are needed.

Opportunities — Silver Lining

Coming Out Ahead

If we address these problems correctly, some significant benefits can come out of the effort. We will not only ensure survival but also improve practices. Specifically, we will end up with a more complete, accurate and usable inventory of hardware and software assets; a comprehensive evaluation of our capabilities; relevant metrics and measures; streamlined project management practices; and the technical infrastructure to improve tracking, accounting and transitioning. This information is what was envisioned under the Government Performance and Results Act in terms of well-defined outcomes and performance measures, resulting in better service.

Leveraging Government Resources

An immediate benefit of multiple agencies working together is the opportunity to leverage tools, expertise, and best practices. Already, OMB s Interagency Committee has put a website in place to facilitate the exchange of best practices and project experience (http://www.it-policy.gsa.gov). Software routines that have been developed for the government have also been exchanged. The development of common approaches and standards will benefit the government by using common resources to build benchmarking frameworks and to encourage franchise funds for sharing products and deliverables.

Next Steps

Expand OMB Year 2000 Interagency Committee. OMB has demonstrated leadership in establishing the Year 2000 Interagency Committee to provide a forum for exchanging information and making Year 2000 recommendations. This Committee should be expanded to include all agencies and formally chartered. While each agency would be responsible for ensuring Year 2000 compliance for its information systems, the Committee could provide high-level direction to agencies for resolving the Year 2000 problem. Its responsibilities would include the development and communication of Year 2000 data exchange, contracting, and software procurement guidelines. Likewise, the Committee would facilitate the exchange of strategies, best practices and resources across the government.

As a first order of priority, each agency must assess its own systems for vulnerability to the Year 2000 problem, decide which of the systems to convert, prioritize its application inventory, and prepare a Year 2000 conversion project plan. As part of its prioritization, each agency must, with a very critical eye, identify which systems will be upgraded, what solutions will be employed, and which systems will be replaced. This battlefield triage is absolutely necessary to protecting the most vital systems from failure.

Support from Congress. Congress can assist the Federal community by understanding the enormity of this

challenge. I commend you, Representative Horn, and your Committee for having taken leadership in promoting Year 2000 awareness. An increased awareness of these issues will be critical when considering legislative requirements that will result in new tasks that affect information systems. In addition understanding these issues will be essential as budgets are being considered. In fact, financial resources are needed to address all the tasks discussed in the testimony heard today.

I would like to thank this Committee for the opportunity to speak to this issue which is so important to our financial and Federal community.

U.S. Senate, Washington, D.C.
July 31, 1966

The President,
The White House, Washington, D.C.

Dear Mr. President:

I hope this letter reaches you. I write to alert you to a problem which could have extreme negative economic consequences during your second term. The "Year 2000 Time Bomb." This has to do with the transition of computer programs from the 20th to the 21st century. The main computer languages from the '50s and '60s such as COBOL, Fortran, and Assembler were designed to minimize consumption of computer memory by employing date fields providing for only six digits. The date of this letter in "computerese," for example, is 96-07-31, The century designation "19" is assumed. The problem is that many computer programs will read January 1, 2000 as January 1, 1900. Computer programs will not recognize the 21st century without a massive rewriting of computer codes. I first learned of all this in February and requested a study by the Congressional Research Service. The study, just now completed, substantiates the worst fears of the doomsayers. (A copy of the CRS study is attached.)

The Year 2000 problem ("Y2K") is worldwide. Each line of computer code needs to be analyzed and either passed on or be rewritten. The banking system is particularly vulnerable. A money center bank may have 500 million lines of code to be revised at a cost of $1 per line. That's a $500 million problem. (I learn from Lanny Davis that his client, the Mars Company, estimates the cost of becoming Y2K date compliant at $100 million to $200 million. Mars is only a candy company.)

One would expect that a quick fix of the problem would have been found but it hasn't happened and the experts tell me it is not likely. There are three issues. First, the cost of reviewing and rewriting codes for Federal and state governments which will range in the billions of dollars over the next three years. Second, the question of whether there is time enough to get the job done and, if not, what sort of triage we may need. I am particularly concerned about the IRS and Social Security in this respect. Third, the question of what happens to the economy if the problem is not resolved by mid-1999? Are corporations and consumers not likely to withhold spending decisions and possibly even withdraw funds from banks if they fear the economy is facing chaos?

I have a recommendation. A Presidential aide should be appointed to take responsibility for assuring that all Federal agencies including the military be Y2K date compliant by January 1, 1999 and that all commercial and industrial firms do business with the Federal government also be compliant by that date. I am advised that the Pentagon is further ahead on the curve here than any of the Federal agencies. You may wish to turn to the military to take command of dealing with the problem. The computer has been a blessing; if we don't act quickly, however, it could become the curse of the age.

Respectfully,
Daniel Patrick Moynihan

February 14, 1996

Moynihan Requests Analysis of Y2K Problem

Re: Treasury Dept and Social Security Administration

Possibly no person in American public life has consistently demonstrated greater foresight over the last 40 years than New York's senior Senator Daniel Patrick Moynihan — witness (1) his early '60s speech warning the auto industry that safety would become a major issue of contention for the Big Three before anyone had ever even heard of Ralph Nader, (2) his seminal study analyzing the breakdown of the negro family and its widespread social implications, (3) his comment to John Westergaard in 1968 that bureaucrats were being measured by the acre in certain Washington agencies and that the public would react eventually by becoming anti-beltway, and (4) his 1979 article written for Newsweek where he predicted that the major historical event of the 1980s would be the collapse of the Soviet Union.

Now, once again, the Senator is onto something big — the "Year 2000 (Y2K) Problem" which has to do with the need to rewrite all mainframe computer code written over the last 40 years in Pascal, Fortran or Cobol to take account for the transition from the 20th to the 21st century. To reduce code, these computers were programmed to only recognize the last two digits designating a given year (i.e. 72, 84, etc.) with the first two digits assumed always to be "19". Problem is that come year 2000 the computers will assume it to be 1900. You'd think it would be simple to fix but in fact it is estimated to be a $300 billion to $600 billion problem worldwide. Moynihan worries about how the IRS and Social Security Administration will deal with this.

For Immediate Release
February 13, 1996
Contact Michele Kayal, 202-224-2668

NY Senator Daniel Patrick Moynihan Reflects Concern Over The "Year 2000 Problem"

Sen. Daniel Patrick Moynihan announced today that he has asked the Congressional Research Service to study and provide a report on the implications of the so-called "year 2000 problem." The year 2000 problem (also known as the "Y2K problem") refers to the computer reprogramming that experts say will be required in order for government and private-sector computer systems to adjust for the correct time and date in the year 2000 and thereafter.

Existing computer programs express years using only two digits, such as "96" for the year 1996. The first two digits of the year are "assumed" by current programming to be 19. As a result, at the turn of the century, computers will mistakenly interpret the two-digit indication of the year ("00") to be 1900 rather than 2000. According to analysts, this problem may cause widespread errors in computation of government benefits and taxes as well as in private sector record keeping and any other calculations in which reference to the date is made. The costs of reprogramming computers worldwide to correct the problem may be in the hundreds of billions of dollars, according to some industry estimates.

"The Department of the Treasury and the Social Security Administration have established working groups to address the year 2000 problem. As Ranking Minority Member on the Senate Finance Committee, I am concerned about how the problem will affect these agencies as well as other government and private computer systems,"

Senator Moynihan said. "I have accordingly asked the Congressional Research Service to report on the costs of the year 2000 problem and on the status of efforts to deal with it."

Senator Moynihan is the Ranking Minority Member of the Senate Committee on Finance, which has jurisdiction over the Department of the Treasury and the Social Security Administration.

104th Congress — 2nd Session
S.2131
In the Senate of the United States

September 25, 1996

Mr. MOYNIHAN introduced the following bill; which was read twice and referred to the Committee on Commerce, Science and Transportation.

A BILL TO ESTABLISH A BI PARTISAN NATIONAL COMMISSION ON THE YEAR 2000 COMPUTER PROBLEM

Section 1. Short Title.

(A) This title may be cited as the "Commission on the Year 2000 Computer Problem Act."

Section 2. Findings.

The Congress makes the following findings:

(A) Whereas the Congress of the United States recognizes the existence of a severe computer problem that may have extreme negative economic and national security consequences in the year 2000 and beyond.

(B) Whereas most computer problems (particularly in mainframes) in both the public and private sector express dates with only two digits and assume the first two digits are "19", and that therefore most programs read 00-01-01 as January 1, 1900; and that these programs will not recognize the year 2000 or the 21st century without a massive rewriting of codes.

(C) Whereas the Congressional Research Service (CRS) has completed a report on the implications of the "Year

2000 Computer Problem" and according to CRS, each line of computer code will need to be analyzed and either passed on or be rewritten and this worldwide problem could cost as much as $600 billion to repair. We recognize that no small share of the American burden will fall on the shoulders of the Federal government and on state and local governments.

(D) Whereas six issues need to be addressed:

(1) an analysis of the history and background concerning the reasons for the occurrence of the Year 2000 problem;
(2) the cost of reviewing and rewriting codes for both Federal and state governments over the next three years, including a legal analysis of responsibilities for such costs and possible equitable bases for sharing them;
(3) the time it will take to get the job done and, if not by 2000, what agencies are at risk of not being able to perform basic services;
(4) the development of balanced and sound contracts with the computer industry available for use by federal agencies, and if such outside contractual assistance is needed, to assist such agencies in contracting for and effectuating Year 2000 compliance for current computer programs and systems as well as to ensure Year 2000 compliance for all programs and systems acquired in the future.
(5) an analysis of what happens to the United States economy if the problem is not resolved by mid-1999;
(6) recommendations to the President and Congress concerning lessons to be learned and policies and actions to be taken in the future to minimize the Year 2000 public and private sector costs and risks.

(E) Whereas the Congress recognizes that an Executive Branch Interagency Committee has been established to raise awareness of this problem and facilitate efforts at solving it; but that in order to best minimize the impact and cost of this problem, and recognizing the extreme urgency of this problem, this bipartisan commission will be established to both address these issues and take responsibility for assuring that all Federal agencies be computer compliant by January 1, 1999.

Section 3. Establishment of Commission.

(A) There is established a commission to be known as the "National Commission on the Year 2000 Computer Problem" (hereinafter in this section referred to as the "Commission"). The Commission shall be composed of fifteen members appointed or designated by the President and selected as follows:

(1) Five members selected by the President from among officers or employees of the Executive Branch, private citizens of the United States, or both. Not more than three of the members selected by the President shall be members of the same political party;

(2) Five members selected by the President Pro Tempore of the Senate, in consultation with the Majority and Minority Leaders, from among officers or employers of the Senate, private citizens of the United States, or both. Not more than three of the members selected by the President Pro Tempore shall be members of the same political party;

(3) Five members selected by the Speaker of the House of Representatives, in consultation with the Majority and Minority Leaders, from among members of the House, private citizens of the United States, or both.

Not more than three of the members selected by the Speaker shall be members of the same political party.
(4) The President shall designate a Chairman from among the members of the Commission.

Section 4. Function of Commission.

(A) It shall be the function of the Commission to conduct a study on the historical, current and long term condition of computer programs as they relate to date fields and the year 2000;identify problems that threaten the proper functions of computers as the public and private sectors approach the 21st Century; analyze potential solutions to such problems that will address the brief time there remains to meet this problem, the substantial cost of reviewing and rewriting codes, and the shared responsibilities for such costs; and provide appropriate recommendations (including potential balanced and sound contracts with the computer industry available for use by federal agencies) to the Secretary of Defense (as this is a matter of National Security), the President and the Congress.

(B) The commission shall submit to Congress a final report containing such recommendations concerning the Year 2000 Computer problem; including proposing new procedures, rules, regulations, or legislation that is needed to ensure the proper transition of the computers of the Federal government and local and state governments from the year 1999 to the year 2000.

(C) The Commission shall make its report to the President by December 31, 1997.

Section 5. ADMINISTRATION.

(A) The heads of Executive Agencies shall, to the extent permitted by law, provide the Commission such information as is may require for the purpose of carrying out its functions.

(B) Members of the Commission shall serve without any additional compensation for their work on the Commission.

(C) Travel Expenses. While away from their homes or regular places of business in the performances of services for the Commission, members shall be allowed travel expenses, including per diem in lieu of substance, in the same manner as persons employed intermittently in the Government service are allowed expenses under section 5703(b) of title 5, United States Code.

(D) The Commission shall have a staff headed by an Executive Director. Any expenses of the Commission shall be paid from such funds as may be available to the Secretary of Defense.

Section 6. Termination.

(A) The Commission, and all the authorities of this title, shall terminate thirty days after submitting its report.

Wednesday December 18

SEC Asked To Speed Work To Avert Computer Chaos

Washington — Rep. John Dingell, a Michigan Democrat, called on securities regulators to speed up work to address a computer problem that could affect the securities industry and stock markets by 2000.

Dingell was referring to the so-called "millennium bug," in which some computer programs fail to recognize dates after 2000, or confuse 2000 with 1900. The problem stems from computer programmers who used only two digits to identify the year, instead of four.

Unless corrected, the problem will cause chaos in all kinds of computer systems, computer experts have said.

The problem is already well known and, at a House of Representatives hearing in September, a White House official said senior managers of federal agencies were being made aware of the situation and are taking steps to correct it.

Dingell, in a letter to Securities and Exchange Commission Chairman Arthur Levitt, said he wanted to know what the agency, which oversees the nation's equities markets and the mutual fund industry, is doing about the matter.

The lawmaker cited possible scenarios that could develop if the problem was not solved in time — brokerages' clearing and settling of stock trades would be jeopardized, trades may not be credited with the right investors, and liquidity could come into question if trades were not posted on time.

Dingell said he was aware of efforts by the SEC, the securities industry and exchanges to solve the problem, but he stressed that "more needs to be done immediately."

"Not addressing this problem promptly is not an option," he said.

Dingell asked the SEC to begin submitting annual progress reports on what it is doing to find solutions. He asked that the first of such reports be submitted on June 1.

An SEC spokesman said the agency is well aware of the problem and is working with other agencies to solve it.

Congressional Research Service Report Requested by Senator Daniel Patrick Moynihan

The Year 2000 Computer Challenge

Summary

Most computer systems in use today can only record dates in a two-digit format for the year. Under this system, computers will fail to operate properly when years after 1999 are used, because the year 2000 is indistinguishable from 1900. This problem could have a serious impact on a wide range of activities that use computers. Information systems must be inspected, and modified, if necessary, before January 1, 2000 to avoid major system malfunctions.

Many managers initially doubted the seriousness of this problem, assuming that an easy technical fix would be developed. Several independent research firms, however, have refuted this view, with the conclusion that inspecting all computer systems and converting date fields where necessary and then testing modified software will be a very time-consuming and costly task. Research firms predict that due to a lack of time and resources, the majority of US businesses and government agencies will likely not fix all of their computer systems before the start of the new millennium.

Most agencies and businesses have come to understand the difficulties involved, although some have not yet started implementing changes. Several companies have emerged offering services to work on year-2000 conversion, and software analysis product are commercially available to assist with finding and converting flawed software code. Even with the assistance of these products, however, most of the work will still have to be done by humans.

Federal agencies are generally aware of the year-2000 challenge and most are working to correct it. Agencies that manage vast databases, conduct massive monetary transactions, or interact extensively with other computer systems, face the greatest challenge. An interagency committee has been established to raise awareness of the year-2000 challenge and facilitate federal efforts at solving it. The interagency committee has initiated several actions, such as requiring vendor software listed in future federal procurement schedules to be year-2000 compliant and specifying four digit year fields for federal computers. The shortage of time to complete year-2000 computer changes may force agencies to prioritize their systems. Agencies may also need to shift resources from other projects to work on year-2000 efforts. State and local governments, as well as foreign organizations, will also have significant year-2000 conversion problems.

Congressional hearings have been held recently to investigate the year-2000 challenge, and a legislative provision was introduced directing the Defense Department to assess the risk to its systems resulting from it. Several options exist for congressional consideration. One option is to provide special funding to federal agencies for year-2000 conversion. While agencies are reluctant to request additional funds, some observers contend this may be necessary. Another option is to give agencies increased autonomy in reprogramming appropriated funds for year-2000 efforts. A third, less controversial alternative is to continue to raise public awareness through hearings and by overseeing federal efforts.

Contents

Description of the Problem/Challenge

Most computer systems in use today record dates in a format using a two digit number for the year; for example, 96 represents the year 1996. The two digit year field is very common among older systems, designed when memory storage was more expensive, but is also used in many systems built today. With this format, however, the year 2000 is indistinguishable from 1900. The year data field in computer programs performs various functions, such as calculating age, sorting information by date, or comparing multiple dates. Thus, when years beyond 1999 are entered under this format, computer systems will fail to operate properly. Given society's increasing reliance on computers, this problem could have a significant impact on a wider range of activities and interests worldwide, including commerce, government operations, military readiness, and the overall economy.

Computer systems of all sizes (mainframe, mini, and micro) as well as local area network and telecommunication systems must be assessed for this problem and converted to a four digit year field where necessary. Year data fields must be corrected in operating systems, compilers, applications, procedures, and databases. Unfortunately, it is often impossible to determine whether and how a computer system needs to be modified without reviewing all of its software code. While correcting the problem for standalone PCs may not be difficult, experts agree that all computer systems need to be inspected, corrected and tested before the start of the next millennium, January 1, 2000, to avoid mayor system malfunctions.

Should We Be Concerned?

Research conducted by several independent consulting firms concludes that the problem is formidable. The Gartner Group, an information technology research firm, estimates that it may cost $30 billion to correct the problem in government computers systems of the federal agencies and up to $600 billion worldwide. This is based on an estimated average cost of $1.10 per line of software code. Other independent research firms, including IDC Government (an information technology consulting firm) and the Mitre Corporation (a Federally Funded Research and Development Center), do not dispute this estimate. (See Note 1)

While correcting the year field is technically simple, the process of analyzing, correcting, testing, and integrating software and hardware among all computer systems that must interact is a very complex management task. In most cases, it is too expensive to re-write software code for the entire system. The overall task is made more difficult by the plethora of computer languages in existence today, the lack of source code and documentation for older software, and the shortage of programmers with skills in older languages. As a further complication, the year 2000 is a special leap year that only occurs every 400 years to keep the calendar accurate. Many software products will not account for the extra day needed in the year 2000.

Many business managers initially doubted the seriousness of this problem, assuming that an easy technical fix would be developed. Others suspect the software services industry was overstating the problem to sell their products ant services. For example, the Information Technology Association of America (ITAA), which represents the software and information services industry, has stated that for all US. computing systems, estimates for fixing the year field range between $50 and $75 billion. Some wonder whether ITAA could be exaggerating the problem to bolster the demand for consulting services of its member companies. Some question the objectivity of the cost estimates from other research firms, since these firms are providing services for year 2000 conversion. One critic suggests that because this is one of the few software problems that lay people can understand it is easy for software service providers to generate concern among managers and obtain additional resources for software maintenance. (See note 2)

After investigating the problem, however, many computer scientists, programmers, and more recently, their managers, appear to have assessed the magnitude of the problem, and the resources and time necessary to correct it, as formidable. Most agencies and businesses are convinced that this issue warrants executive-level attention. They point to specific problems that have already occurred and numerous others that will occur if it is not fixed. All vulnerable computer systems must be fixed by January 1, 2000 to avoid widespread erroneous automatic transactions that could be irreparable. Some programs that work with future dates may encounter problems before the next millennium. Others have already had problems. Some potential consequences of failing to convert systems using a two-digit year are listed below.

- The Social Security Administration would miscalculate the age of citizens, causing payments to be sent to people who are not eligible for benefits while those who should be eligible would not receive their payments.
- The Internal Revenue Service would miscalculate the standard deduction on its income tax returns for persons over age 65, causing incorrect records of revenues and payments due.
- Certain Defense Department weapons systems could fail to function properly if used during or after the turn of the century.
- The Federal Aviation Administration's air traffic controllers could generate erroneous flight schedules that may misguide aircraft or cause takeoff or landing conflicts.
- State and local computer systems could become corrupted with false records, causing errors in income and property tax records, payroll, retirement systems, motor vehicle registration, utilities regulation, and a breakdown of some public transportation systems.
- The banking industry's schedules for various loans and mortgages could be erroneously updated after the year 2000.

- Securities firms and insurance companies could produce erroneous records of stock transactions or insurance premiums.
- Telephone companies (both long distance and local) could record dates incorrectly, causing errors in consumer's bills or a lapse in service.
- Credit cards with expiration dates after the year 2000 could fail the credit check that is routinely performed when a purchase is made.
- Data on pharmaceutical drugs with expiration dates after the year 2000 would indicate that the medication is expired.
- Medical records could become corrupted leading to improper treatment of patients.
- Businesses of all types and sizes may make errors in their planning, budget, accounts receivable, purchasing, accounts payable, revenue, pension/loan forecasts, payroll, garnishments, material supplies and inventories.

Strategies for Correcting the Problem

Software analysis tools can be useful to assess the extent of the problem for specific cases. Software tools are commercially available to assist with the conversion of year fields to four digits. Various tools can identify locations in software code where date references occur, make the necessary changes, and test the upgraded system. Testing is particularly laborious because the modified software must be tested in conjunction with all possible combinations of other software programs it interacts with to ensure functioning has not changed. There may not be enough time, however, for in-house personnel at many agencies to purchase a software analysis tool, learn how to use it, and perform the software conversion and testing. According to one estimate, these tools can only reduce the human work-time by 20-30% at most. (See note 3) Furthermore, sharing analysis tools in most circumstances is prohibited under copyright laws.

Another consideration is whether to use contractor support, in-house personnel, or some mix of the two. Several companies have emerged offering services to work on year-2000 conversion. Many businesses and government agencies may be able to address the problem more efficiently and effectively by hiring experienced contractors. (See note 4). Unfortunately, many of the firms that specialize in year-2000 conversion are already under contract with the larger Private Sector corporations. If in-house staff have an in depth understanding of the software, the company may be better off working on the conversion internally. In many cases, a combination of in-house and contractor support will be used.

Several other technical issues must be considered. Many experts say that software should be analyzed, and modified if necessary, before the start of 1999, to leave ample time to test and debug the system while running in parallel with the existing system. This would leave only two and a half years to complete the conversion process. In some cases, the problem can be fixed without having to add two more digits to the year field. For example, in some cases where the date is printed rather than used for further calculations, the number 19 can be replaced by 20 in front of the two digit year for years after 1999. This would be easier than converting to a four digit year field, and would work until the year 2100, when new computer technology should be in use. Most computer functions that calculate an age or compares two different ages will likely require changing the year field to four digits.

Another major concern is that even if a company or government agency corrects the problem within its own system, it may need to interact with other computer systems. Other systems that are not year-2000 compliant could send file information into the corrected databases, corrupting those databases. Flawed data can easily enter from the private sector into government agencies' database, and from foreign countries into US computer system.

While the technology exists to address the problem, the two main constraints in the year-2000 challenge are funding and time. Because of the skepticism over the seriousness of the problem, computer programmers have had difficulty convincing their managers that resources should be put into this effort. The extra time to generate awareness at all levels in organizations has led to procrastination and delays in starting the work. Some of the blame can also be assessed to the programmers and software companies that did not use four digit year fields in their products. Correcting the year-2000 problem will prevent companies from making costly errors or going out of business but will not contribute to increased productivity or enable a business to provide any new service. In addition, for some organizations, analyzing, compiling, and testing the software will require more computer resources than are currently available without interrupting normal production. Companies may well experience substantial opportunity costs resulting from the need to use resources originally planned for other software projects.

Status of Federal Agency Efforts

The information resources management personnel at most federal agencies are aware of the problem and are beginning to take corrective action. The Social Security Administration (SSA) identified the problem in 1989 and is the furthest along among federal agencies. SSA plans to complete and test all software changes by December 31,

1998, and run the corrected software in production one full year before 2000.

The Department of Defense (DOD) has more recently become involved with the year-2000 challenge, with different DOD organizations at various phases of solving it. While DOD's finance community began to address the problem in 1991, for many DOD systems the work has not yet begun. A major problem for DOD is managing the efforts across all of the services and defense agencies to maximize efficiency and coordinate chances among system that interact across organizations. DOD has adopted a decentralized approach, letting each service and defense agency determine how to best solve its own year-2000 issues. The DOD coordinator is the Principal Director for Information Management under the Assistant Secretary for Command, Control, Communications, and Intelligence, in the Office of Secretary of Defense. This office, assisted by the Defense Information Systems Agency, serves to promote awareness, facilitate sharing of information, and avoid duplication within DOD (See note 6)

DOD has several unique concerns apart from other Federal agencies, For example hardware changes must be made in some weapon systems whose clocks store dates using two-digit codes. Computer chips that store dates in "firmware" may have to be replaced on missiles and other weapon components. Some of those chips,, however, may no longer be in production. In addition, DOD has many unusual computer languages for which software analysis tools are not commercially available. Given the limited time and resources, DOD is focusing on correcting its mission critical systems, and may use temporary fixes for other systems.

Many other federal departments and agencies face a major challenge in making their computer systems year-

2000 compliant to insure the safe and continuous operations of the federal government. The Department of Treasury oversees the massive databases of the Internal Revenue Service, Customs; and Bureau of Alcohol, Tobacco and Firearms. (See note 7) Other agencies with enormous task of correcting their computer systems include the Veteran's Administration, the Department of Transportation (which oversees the Federal Aviation Administration), the Department of Justice (overseeing the Federal Bureau of Investigation), and the Administrative Office of the US Courts.

Interagency Committee

Last year, the Office of Management and Budget (OMB) asked SSA to lead interagency discussions to raise awareness of the year-2000 challenge. As a result, SSA assembled an interagency ad hoc committee to facilitate the efforts of federal agencies. SSA has held several meetings with other federal agencies to help educate staff about the issue, and provide a forum to share cross-cutting ideas and strategies. Attendance at these meetings was initially small, but has increased to over 30 participating agencies. SSA emphasizes that the agencies that own the software are responsible for correcting it, and that the interagency committee can only facilitate their efforts.

The interagency committee has made some progress toward helping Federal agencies deal with the problem. With committee prompting, the General Services Administration (GSA) will require all vendor software listed in future GSA procurement schedules to be year-2000 compliant. The interagency committee is developing a precise definition of year-2000 compliance for GSA to use in future schedules. Due to contractual obligations with vendors, GSA is unable to place new requirements for year 2000 compliance on existing schedules. GSA will, however, collect information on products that are on existing schedule to determine which products are year-2000 compliant. Agencies can also use the definition of year-2000 compliance when they purchase software outside of GSA schedule.

In concert with efforts of the interagency committee, the National Institute of Standards and Technology (NIST) published a Federal Information Processing Standard on March 25, 1996, regarding Federal software purchases. The announcement (change no. 1 to FIPS 4-1) recommends that for purposes of electronic data interchange, federal agencies use four- digit year elements for data transmitted among US Government agencies. (See note 8) NIST chose not to require four-digit year elements for all interagency data transfer because it does not have authority to require federal agencies to comply. In addition, in many cases the four digit year field will not be necessary.

The interagency committee is involved with several other activities. On May 2, 1996, the committee cosponsored a conference bringing government and industry together to discuss year-2000 issues. The committee is currently developing a "best practice" report which will describe how agencies can best implement a solution. It will also include a comprehension conversion plan, setting milestones for Federal agency progress over the next few years. (See note 9) Through committee efforts, a site on the world wide web was developed to provide the latest information on year 2000 conversion activities. (See note 10) Private sector firms can also benefit from the information disseminated by the interagency committee.

Issues for Federal Agencies

Since there may not be enough time to complete year-2000 conversion for all information systems, federal agencies may have to prioritize their systems for repair. Several agencies are already admitting that there will likely be delays in other federal information technology projects due to the need to dedicate resources to year-2000 conversion. Non-critical computer systems may have to wait until after the start of year 2000. It is also possible that projects in areas other than information technology may have to be delayed or scaled back to divert funds to work on the year-2000 project. Funds may even have to be shifted from other agency accounts such, as research and development, procurement, operations, or maintenance. Individual agencies are confronting how they will prioritize their internal conversion projects. (See note 11)

The interagency committee recommends that Government agencies as well as private sector organizations conduct risk-benefit analyses before starting the conversion process. These analyses could help determine which systems absolutely must be fixed, and which could be terminated if their utility is not worth the effort needed to fix them. Unfortunately, the time taken to perform these analyses may delay the process of converting software. However, completing a risk analysis before starting the conversion is critical to help prioritize information technology systems. Even a system that is year-2000 compliant can be contaminated by incorrect data entering from eternal interactions.

Government agencies need to ensure that data entering their computer databases from other sources (such as state, county, municipal government, and the private sectors is accurate. To forestall contamination of federal databases, some suggest that OMB set a policy for how agencies monitor incoming data to insure its integrity. Many Federal agencies, however, would prefer to set their own rules for accepting eternal data.

Status of State Governments, Private Sector, and Foreign Government Efforts

Efforts needed to correct the problem in state and local government operations also are likely to be significant. The Gartner Group predicts that fewer than 25% of state and local government computer systems will be ready for the year 2000. The State of Nebraska estimates it will cost $28 million to pay for the conversion of its 12,000 computer programs and 12 million lines of code. Nebraska plans to divert part of its cigarette tax to provide $11.5 million toward conversion activities. Los Angeles county has made an initial estimate of $30 million for conversion costs, not including planning, testing, and unexpected hardware and software upgrades. (See note 12)

Major industry groups will need to make coordinated efforts to convert their software so that they can continue to interoperate as they do today. The securities industry, for example, must be able to perform stock transactions, access investor accounts, and record deposits and trades among business affiliates on a timely basis. For this to occur, all securities companies must agree on a standard year format for various types of data. Other industries that must coordinate their year 2000 efforts include banks, insurance companies, telecommunications providers, computer manufacturers, and airlines In addition to fixing their own systems, many computer companies are beginning to market their services in year-2000 conversion.

Foreign companies and governments appear to be further behind in addressing the year-2000 than their counterparts in the United States. In May, 1996, the Chief Executive of the British Government Central Computer and Telecommunications Agency met with representatives of US Federal agencies and congressional staff to gain insights into dealing with the challenge. The science and technology attaches at the embassies of Canada, Japan, Germany, and Australia were unable to provide an assessment of the efforts taking place in their countries. There has been little press and government published assessments, indicating a lesser awareness of the issue in these countries than in the United States. (See note 13)

Congressional Activity

On April 16, 1996, the House Government Oversight and Reform Committee, Subcommittee on Government Management, Information and Technology held a hearing to determine the extent of the problem, and how federal agencies are dealing with it. All witnesses stressed that federal government and other computer users must address this issue immediately. Following the hearing, the Subcommittee submitted a set of questions for major federal departments and agencies to determine their level of progress in addressing the issue. Information obtained from responses (due on June 7, 1996) will be analyzed by the General Accounting Office.

On May 14, 1996, the House Science Committee, Subcommittee on technology, held a hearing to review potential technical solutions to the year-2000 challenge, and to discuss a possible role for government in addressing the problem. Again, witnesses stressed the urgency needed to convert all software in a timely manner in both government and the private sector.

The FY1997 Senate Defense authorization bill (S. 1745) contained a provision directing DOD to assess the risk to its systems resulting from the year-2000 challenge, and to report to Congress on the resources necessary for conversion. The bill also require that all information technology purchased by DOD be able to operate in 2000 without modification. The bill was reported by the Senate

Armed Services Committee on May 3, 1996;. Other congressional committees are interested in the year-2000 issue and may hold hearings to pursue their particular interest in the issue.

Issues and Options for Congress

Is the Problem Serious Enough to Warrant Congressional Action?

Many in Congress would prefer to let industry solve technical issues of this sort, allowing market forces to work and avoiding cost subsidies and counterproductive regulation. Others are concerned that this problem is so pervasive that it could affect the entire nation, including Federal, state, and local government, businesses, and personal activities, with potentially harmful consequences to the overall economy. Some in Congress have expressed an interest in using legislation to help reduce the negative effects of what may become a crisis situation. Some are concerned that media sensationalism of the problem could effect consumer confidence in institutions, such as banks, and in public institutions that provide services to citizens. Effective management by Federal officials and communication by policy makers could mitigate those effects.

What Are the Options for Congressional Action?

More funding. One option is to provide specific funding for federal information resources management (IRM) offices to convert their agency software. Some in federal agencies have voiced concerns that in order to maximize additional funding, IRM managers might delay conversion effort. Congress could, however, use a funding mechanism that matches funds dedicated by agencies to work on year-2000 conversion. This could have the effect of — stimulating agencies to put more resources on the problem.

Finding new money, however, when Congress is focusing on reducing the Federal deficit will be a challenge. Some in federal agencies believe that funding could not realistically be provided until FY1998 appropriations, which will be too late for most agencies to begin work.

Reprogramming funds. The interagency committee advocates giving federal agencies greater autonomy in reprogramming funds to year-2000 efforts. Rules for reprogramming differ from agency to agency, and from year to year, however, depending on how each agency's appropriations legislation is written. Some appropriations subcommittees require approval before any funds are reprogrammed, while others allow various degrees of reprogramming among programs and accounts. Congress could create a special provision to allow agencies to reprogram for year-2000 efforts as part of a budget bill. If legislation to replace the process of reprogramming funds is passed this year, agencies could begin reprogramming in FY1997. Without general reprogramming authority for FY1997, agencies will have to wait another year to seek congressional approval, which may be too late to start year-2000 conversion.

At the April 16 hearing of the House Subcommittee on Government Management, Information and Technology, DOD expressed the need to be able to shift funds more quickly than the legislative process will allow in order to meet the year-2000 deadline. (See note 14) DOD has had problems obtaining timely approval for reprogramming funds for all of its programs. Currently, DOD can reprogram up to $10 million for procurement and up to $4 million for research and development in a given program without obtaining congressional approval. To reprogram funds in excess of these levels, DOD submits an omnibus reprogramming request each year containing dozens of requested funding changes. Only those items that receive the approval of all four defense budget oversight committees can be implemented.

DOD is now proposing legislation to allow it to double the amount of funds it can reprogram without congressional approval. DOD may also seek the authority to transfer funds between accounts (procurement to research and development, for instance) without congressional approval. (See note 15) While Congress may be reluctant to give DOD such a broad authority, a special limited provision might be considered for year 2000 efforts. Civilians agencies may want to gain similar authority for year-2000 efforts, although they have not requested it. Many agencies may not yet realize that they will need additional funds for year-2000 efforts.

Continued oversight. Others suggest that Congress take a different approach by continuing its oversight and scrutiny of federal efforts, and raising public awareness through hearings and written communication. While this may spur agencies into action, it would not help them to complete the work of software conversion. Congressional oversight can focus on how local agencies are prioritizing their computer systems projects, however money is being spent, and how potential delay could impact government operation. Further investigation into how state and local governments are preparing for year-2000 software conversion may be considered. The planned GAO study may provide information for Congress to take further action.

Standards issues. In the future, vendors might face potential liability for failure to provide year-2000 compliant products or services. Company managers may still need to be aware of whether their information suppliers are year-2000 compliant so that their databases are not corrupted by bad data. Businesses and government agencies may require software maintenance providers to accept contract provisions that require that computer systems continue to function properly after the year 2000. Banks, investment companies, and insurance companies may want to know whether companies they finance are year-2000 compliant before making some investment decisions.

These concerns raise questions about how consumer and government agencies can be sure that consultants and vendors are being honest about whether their products are year-2000 compliant. At the May 14 House Science Committee, Technology Subcommittee hearing, members raised questions as to whether the force of law is necessary to set standards for computer year fields. It was suggested that legislating a four digit year field standard for all electronic date interchange with the federal government would help bring the computer industry into compliance, and would at least raise awareness of the problem. Industry witnesses testified that if standards are necessary, they should be developed under the auspices of the American National Standards Institute (ANSI), a private sector, voluntary, consensus standards setting organization for the computer and electronics industry, rather than dictated by Congress. Other members warned that legislating standards was unnecessary and might not even contribute to raising public awareness. Notably, by the time an industry consensus standard is worked out, it might be too late.

International issues. Because the United States is more heavily dependent on computers than other nations, the year-2000 is probably a greater challenge here than anywhere else. The economic impacts of business failing to correct the problem, both domestically and internationally, could be dramatic. US businesses and government agencies will probably lead the rest of the world in fostering awareness and in assisting in software conversion. DOD is currently discussing with the NATO allies the need to ensure their year-2000 computer capability for future military engagements or other collaborative operations, and the general sharing of data. This area may require increased attention. The State Department may need to become involved in spreading awareness of this issue internationally through the diplomatic corps at US embassies in foreign countries. US. Federal agencies and businesses may need to emphasize the urgency of correcting the problem in making international agreements. Congressional attention to this issue helps to increase awareness other countries.

The future. This issue's sudden rise to public attention leads to the question of whether we can identify and prevent comparable technology problems before they reach these proportions. the computer industry has managed to deal with other problems reasonably well without federal intervention. Viruses, for example, became a widespread problem starting in the late 1980's. In response, anti-virus software was developed commercially and became widely used. Now, it is considered standard procedure for all data entering a computer to be checked first for viruses. Various security features are also now available and can be added to computing systems as threats are presented. Perhaps other unforeseen software upgrades will be necessary for widespread computer applications. As other computer-related issues continue to arise, Congress may again be faced with deciding what role the federal government should play in ensuring security and reliability in federal computer systems, and providing guidance and leadership into the digital age.

Notes:

1. It is assumed that the Mitre Corp. has no incentive to exaggerate, because its funding is limited by Congress and working on year-2000 projects would preclude it from working on other projects. Another independent source (Peter DeJager, private consultant) places the Gartner Group estimate at the low end of the range of possible costs.

2. Nickolas Zvegintsov, the Year 2000 as Racket and Ruse. American Programmer, Feb. 1966.

3. Bruce Hall, Research Director, Applications Management Division, Gartner Group, Federal Conference on Year 2000 Conversion, Dept. of Commerce, May 2, 1996.

4. Before hiring a contractor, some organizations have checked the validity of the contractor's assessment of the problem by running an independent software analyzer on their software code.

5. Testimony of D. Dean. Mesterharm, Deputy commissioner for Systems, social security Administration, before the House Subcommittee on Government Management, Information and Technology, April 16, 1996.

6. Testimony of Emmett Paige, Jr., Assistant Secretary of Defense (C3I) before the House subcommittee on Government Management, Information and Technology, April 6, 1996.

7. Last year Treasury collected $1.4 trillion and processed over 250 million returns. The treasury Financial Management Services oversees a daily cash flow in excess of $10 billion and issues 800 million payments totaling over $1 trillion each year for all executive agencies. The Customs Service collects over $20 billion annually in duties, taxes and fees. Public debt auctions $2 trillion marketable Treasury securities annually, issues and redeems 150 million savings bonds annually, and accounts for $4.9 trillion federal debt and over $300 billion in annual interest charges. All of these critical activities use computer support that must be inspected and corrected for year-2000 compliance.

8. Private industry currently uses a two-digit year standard for data interchange.

9. The best practices document offers a method for dividing year-2000 conversion activities into five phases: awareness, assessment, renovation, validation and implementation. The document should be available on the world wide web by mid July (information obtained from minutes of interagency committee meeting of May 8, 1966).

10. The address of the web page, managed by GSA, is http://www/it-policy/library/yr2000/y201tocl.htm. The web page is hyper-linked to DOD and other Federal agency year-2000 web pages. Numerous other World Wide Web pages are maintained by government and private sector organizations discussing activities and available resources on year-2000 conversion.
11. Information systems managers in the House, Senate and Library of Congress are working on the year-2000 for their systems, and expect to be compliant well before the end of the century.
12. The Clock is Ticking: Year 2000 does Not Compute, County News, National Assn. of Counties, April 29, 1996.
13. Personal telephone conversations with foreign attaches, March-April, 1996.
14. Testimony of Emmett Paige, Jr. before the House Subcommittee on Government Management, Information and Technology, April 16, 1996.
15. Pentagon to Propose Thresholds for Reprogramming, Inside the Pentagon, May 23, 1996.

Report of the U.S. Office of Management and Budget

February 6, 1997

The Year 2000 computer problem is a seemingly simple one: assuring that computers will recognize the correct year when the year 2000 arrives. If software programs are not prepared to handle the change of date on January 1, 2000, there is a risk to government information systems and the programs they support.

This report responds to 1997 appropriations language which directs OMB to submit to the House Committee on Appropriations, the House Committee on Government Reform and Oversight, and the House Science Committee a report which includes: a cost estimate to ensure software code date fields conversion by the year 2000; a planned strategy to ensure that all information technology, as defined by the Information Technology Management Reform Act of 1996, purchased by an agency will operate in 2000 without technical modifications; and, a time table for implementation of the planned strategy.

The report is to be submitted with the President's 1998 budget. (Committee Report accompanying Public Law 104-208.)

Background

People often use short hand to describe the year. When asked what year it is, we answer "97". When we fill in the date on paper forms we write 2/2/97. The same approach was used in designing many computer systems.

With the arrival of the year 2000, people will know that the year "00" stands for 2000. However, the hardware and software in many computer systems will not understand this new meaning. Unless they are fixed or replaced, they will fail at the turn of the century in one of three ways:

- ✦ they will reject legitimate entries, or
- ✦ they will compute erroneous results, or
- ✦ they will simply not run.

Many systems which compare dates to decide which is earlier will no longer work. Comparisons of dates permeate Federal computer systems — they are how inventories are maintained (e.g., last in, first out), how the order of filings is handled (e.g., first come, first served), and how eligibility is determined (e.g., an applicant must have filed before a certain date).

Systems which calculate length of time also may not compute accurately. Computations of length of time are common in Federal computer systems — they are how benefits are computed (e.g., based on length of time), how eligibility is determined (e.g., based on length of service), and how expiration dates are calculated (e.g., expires after three years).

There are other possible effects of the date change in computer software, depending on the assumptions made and programming technique used by the designer of the software. For example, information relevant to a year could be found by using the year to find the information in a table. For example, information about 1997 would be at the 97th location in the table. Such a technique would fail in the year "00" because there is no 0th location.

Impact

The potential impact on Federal programs if this problem is not corrected is substantial and, potentially very serious. Federal agencies are therefore taking steps to ensure a smooth transition, and fixing the problem is generating, a high level of interest and energy. The challenge for the next three years is to manage that interest and energy effectively and efficiently so that the systems upon which Americans all depend will operate smoothly through the year 2000 and beyond.

There are several unique characteristics of this problem that shape the Federal strategy for addressing it. First, it has an unmovable deadline. Unlike other computer development or maintenance activities, the deadline for fixing the year 2000 problem is not set administratively, but by the problem itself. Repairs must therefore be fully tested and implemented by December 31, 1999. This characteristic makes time the single most critical resource.

Second, unlike a normal system development or maintenance activity, many systems must be tackled concurrently. Comparisons and computations using dates permeate computer systems within the Federal government, throughout State and local governments, and in the private sector. There is thus a real potential for substantial strain on another key resource — expertise.

Third, complexity is increased by concurrent changes to multiply systems and elements within a system (e.g., the operating system). Because computer systems inter-operate and share data, the modified systems must be tested together. Furthermore, all of these changes must be made and tested while the current systems continue to operate.

Chief Information Officers

Federal management of information technology has dramatically changed in the past year as a result of the Clinger-Cohen Act of 1996 (formerly known as the Information Technology Management Reform Act of 1996)(40 U.S.C. 1401 et seq.). That Act established Chief Information Officers (CIO's) in each Federal agency with responsibility for maintaining a sound information technology architecture for the agency. In addition, Executive Order No. 13011 (July 16, 1996) established the Chief Information Officers Council, chaired by OMB, as the principal interagency forum to improve agency practices on the use of information technology. Year 2000 issues have been discussed at every CIO Council meeting to date. Agency CIO's acting within their agencies and through the CIO Council will provide the leadership and assure that the work is done to address the year 2000 computer problem.

In 1995, OMB formed an interagency working group on the year 2000, chaired by a representative of the Social Security Administration. That working group was recently adopted as an official working group of the CIO Council.

Planned Strategy

The Government's strategy is predicated on three considerations.

First, senior agency managers will take whatever action is necessary to address the problem once they are aware of its potential consequences. Those consequences would, after all, directly affect their ability to carry out the agency's essential functions.

Second, there can and will not be a single solution. Solving this problem requires technicians and engineers to write or revise software code and to replace hardware. A "silver bullet" is a logical impossibility. There is only a need for hard work, strategically directed, and plenty of it.

Third, given the limited amount of time, emphasis will be on mission critical systems. In many agencies such systems are large and complex, which means they will require the most time and be the most challenging to fix.

The Federal strategy relies on the newly established CIO's to direct that work and to follow industry's best practices. Those best practices include five phases:

- raising management awareness of the problem,
- assessing the scope of the problem by inventorying systems and deciding which ones to change, replace or discard,
- renovating the system to be changed,
- validating and testing the changed systems, and
- implementing the revised systems (including developing a contingency plan).

Detailed steps in each phase have been developed by the interagency working group on the year 2000 and are available for agencies on the GSA sponsored year 2000 home page at http://www.itpolicy.gsa.gov.

Schedule

OMB, in consultation with the CIO Council, has set government-wide milestones (shown below) for completion of the majority of the work in each phase of agency year 2000 activities. These phases, while sequential, overlap. For example, the awareness phase continues throughout the entire process.

Government-wide Year 2000 Milestones

Phase	Completion Measure	Completion Date
Awareness	Agency Strategy Approved by CIO	12/96
Assessment		
Inventory and Scope Completed		
System Plans & Schedules	Approved by CIO 3/97	6/97
Renovation		
Coding Completed		12/98
Validation		
Management Sign-off		1/99
		Implementation
Integrated Testing Completed		11/99

Attachment A to this report shows major agencies' current progress and plans for completing each phase. In many cases the plans consolidate milestones from individual components and systems within the agency. Agency CIO's are taking steps to accelerate their year 2000 activities to meet these goals.

Cost

OMB Memorandum No. 97-02, "Funding Information Systems Investments" (October 25, 1996), outlines the policy criteria to be used in making funding decisions for all investments in major information systems. One of these criteria is that the investment be consistent with the agency's year 2000 compliance plan. In addition, agencies are funding year 2000 work by redirecting resources from other planned activities (e.g., modernization), because it does not make sense to spend money on upgrades if the basic system will fail to operate. These policies are reflected in funding decisions for major information systems in the President's 1998 budget.

Agencies estimate that they will spend $2.3 billion between FY 1996 and FY 2000 on the year 2000 computer problem.

Attachment B includes agency-by-agency estimates of the cost to ensure that systems will work smoothly through the year 2000. The estimated cover the costs of identifying necessary changes, evaluating the cost effectiveness of making those changes (fix or scrap decisions), making changes, testing systems, and contingencies for failure recovery. The estimates do not include the costs of upgrades or replacements that would otherwise occur as part of the normal system life cycle. They also do not include the Federal share of the costs for state information systems that support Federal programs. The figures provided by agencies are preliminary estimates. Better estimates will become available after all agencies have completed the assessment phase.

Government-wide Action

Five government-wide actions compliment individual agency efforts.

1. OMB is raising the awareness of the most senior managers in Federal agencies to the magnitude of this problem;
2. The Chief Information Officers Council and the interagency working group on the year 2000 are promoting the sharing of management and technical expertise;
3. The government is acquiring only year 2000 compliant information technology, using standard contract language;
4. OMB and the CIO Council are removing barriers that could impede technicians fixing existing systems; and
5. OMB is monitoring agencies' progress to assure they are on schedule.

1. Raising Awareness

The President' Management Council, comprised of the chief operating officers of major departments and agencies has discussed the year 2000 problem on several occasions. OMB has been meeting individually with those chief operating officers to ensure they are appreciated the risk this problem poses and the difficulty of solving it.

Raising awareness is a continuing challenge. OMB will continue to assist the agencies in this area as new senior officials comes into the government during 1997. The recent inclusion by the General Accounting Office of year 2000 on its list of "high risk" areas will also assist in focusing attention to the immediacy of the problem.

2. Sharing Expertise

Some Federal agencies have considerable experience working on this problem. The Social Security Administration, for example, has been actively engaged since 1989. The interagency working group is taking advantage of such experience and promoting the sharing of expertise and solutions across agencies.

The interagency working group has also developed a list of products that are being used by Federal agencies, along with information about whether they will work through the year 2000. That list is available on the year 2000 World Wide Web page products, which is also available from the year 2000 Web page. This information is invaluable to managers as they evaluate the extent of the year 2000 problem in their system.

The President's budget includes resources to establish a dedicated year 2000 program office at GSA. Such an office will provide a core of expertise government-wide to assist agencies in formulating approaches and evaluating options to solve the problem in their systems.

3. Acquire Only Products that are Year 2000 Compliant

At the recommendation of the CIO Council and the interagency working group, agencies have stopped acquiring information technology that will not work in the year 2000. Regulatory language to effect this strategy was developed by the interagency working group on the year 2000 and the CIO Council, approved by the Federal Acquisition Regulation Councils, and the published in Federal Acquisition Circular 90-45 (December 1996).

That language defines year 2000 compliant to mean:

> *"information technology that accurately processes date/time data (including, but not limited to, calculating, comparing, and sequencing) from, into, and between the twentieth and twenty-first centuries and the years 1999 and 2000 and leap-year calculations. Furthermore, year 2000 compliant information*

> *technology, when used in combination with other information technology, shall accurately process date/time data if the other information technology properly exchanges date/time data with it."*

Finally, GSA is revising its Multiple Award Schedule contracts to assure that products on those schedules identify whether they are, or when they will be, year 2000 compliant. This will help agencies to acquire only year 2000 products from those schedules.

4. Removing Barriers

Solutions to the year 2000 problem in operational systems require technicians to undertake the time-consuming work of analyzing and fixing systems. There are, however, things that only can be done to speed this work. The interagency working group is helping to identify such measures, and the CIO Council is working expeditiously to implement them. One example is specifying a standard way to communicate dates among agencies. At the urging of the interagency working group, the National Institute of Standards and Technology (NIST) amended the Federal digital date standard to a 4-digit years and strongly encouraged agencies to follow it for data interchange among agencies.[1] In January 1997 the CIO Council adopted the NIST standard for all data exchanges among agencies. Based on common industry practice, the NIST standard will probably become a formally adopted standard through the normal standards-development process. The Council adopted it now because agencies can not afford to wait on a lengthy formal process. Technicians need answers today.

FIPS PUB 4-1. Representation for Calendar Date and Ordinal Date for Information Interchange, March 25, 1996

5. Monitoring Progress

OMB will require agencies to report their progress quarterly. The interagency working group and CIO Council are helping OMB develop that reporting requirement. This report will be used by OMB to monitor agency activity to assure that year 2000 activities remain on schedule. With the assistance of GSA, OMB will publish a summary of these reports within one month of their receipt.

Conclusion

The Federal government is making considerable progress in addressing the year 2000 problem in Federal computer systems. We are also well aware of the work that has yet to be done, and appreciate that there is a limited amount of time left to do it — less than 35 months. But the new CIO's are working hard to accelerate agency activities to address this challenge, and we are confident that the problem will be solved without disruption of Federal programs.

Attachment A
Agency Progress and Plans for Achieving Year 2000 Compliance

Agency	*Awareness*	*Assessment*	*Assessment*	*Renovation*	*Validation*	*Implementa tion*
Agriculture	11/96	4/97	6/97	9/98	9/99	10/99
Commerce	8/96	12/96	3/97	12/98	1/99	10/99
Defense	12/96	3/97	12/97	12/98	6/99	11/99
Air Force	6/96	3/97	5/97	1/98	7/98	12/99
Army	12/96	3/97	3/97	9/98	12/98	10/99
Navy	12/96	3/97	12/97	12/98	6/99	11/99
Education	12/96	2/97	6/97	9/98	9/98	3/99
Energy	6/96	1/97	1/97	1/99	1/99	12/99
HHS	11/96	1/97	6/97	12/98	1/99	11/99
HUD	11/96	4/97	6/97	12/98	7/99	11/99
Interior	12/96	4/97	7/97	12/98	1/99	11/99
Justice	3/96	9/96	9/96	12/99	12/99	12/99
Labor	12/96	3/97	6/97	12/98	6/99	12/99
State	6/96	12/96	6/97	9/98*	10/98*	8/99*
Transportation	12/96	8/97	12/97	12/98	1/99	11/99
Treasury	5/96	4/97	7/97	12/98	12/98	11/99
VA	1/97	1/98	2/98	11/98	2/99	12/99
AID	11/96	3/97	6/97	11/98	7/99	7/99
EPA	12/96	3/97	6/97	12/98	1/99	11/99
FEMA	12/96	3/97	6/97	12/98	1/99	11/99
GSA	11/96	3/97	6/97	12/98	1/99	10/99
NASA	1/97	2/97	3/97	6/99	7/99	12/99
NSF	9/96	1/97	6/97	6/98	12/98	12/99
NRC	6/96	6/97	9/97	3/99	4/99	11/99
OPM	12/96	3/97*	6/97*	12/98	11/99	12/99
SBA**	4/96	6/96	9/96	12/98	12/98	12/99
SSA	3/96	3/96	5/96	11/98	12/98	11/99

* – Applies to Mission-critical systems only

** – Replacing system through planned migration to client/server environment

Estimated Agency Year 2000 Obligations

(Dollars in Millions, by Fiscal Year)

Agency	1996	1997	1998	1999	2000	TOTAL
Agriculture	2.6	20.0	34.3	26.6	5.7	89.2
Commerce	2.3	16.2	33.	28.3	9.3	89.7
Defense						
Air Force	0.0	98.5	259.7	14.8	0.0	371.0
Army	0.0	87.0	87.0	44.0	0.0	218.0
Navy	3.0	24.0	26.0	22.0	15.0	90.0
D — Other	N/A	N/A	N/A	N/A	N/A	290.6
Education	0.0	0.2	3.0	4.0	0.0	7.2
Energy	1.8	21.2	44.7	43.5	16.9	128.1
HHS	27.7	42.9	14.5	5.6	0.0	90.7
HUD	0.7	11.0	35.0	15.0	6.2	67.9
Interior	0.2	2.6	4.5	2.2	1.8	11.3
Justice	0.3	2.5	8.9	10.3	0.2	22.1
Labor	1.7	5.3	4.6	2.2	1.5	15.2
State	0.5	47.6	56.4	29.1	1.6	135.2
Transportation	0.2	12.4	22.1	39.7	6.1	80.4
Treasury	1.3	55.0	102.0	119.1	41.0	318.5
VA	4.0	49.0	49.0	42.0	0.0	144.0
AID	0.0	0.2	1.0	0.0	0.0	1.2
EPA	0.8	3.3	6.8	5.6	2.3	18.
FEMA	3.8	4.4	3.0	3.2	1.2	15.6
GSA	0.2	0.5	0.6	0.2	0.0	1.6
NASA	0.0	6.6	14.4	10.6	1.1	32.6
NSF	0.0	0.2	0.3	0.1	0.0	0.6
NRC	N/A	2.6	2.9	2.9	0.9	9.3
OPM	1.7	0.3	0.9	0.6	0.2	3.7
SBA	2.7	2.3	1.9	0.0	0.0	6.9
SSA	2.2	15.4	9.5	6.0	0.0	33.1
TOTAL	57.7	529.1	826.4	477.5	110.9	2292.4

Notes:

1) These estimates cover "the costs of identifying necessary changes, evaluating the cost effectiveness of making those changes (fix or scrap decisions), making changes, testing systems, and contingencies for failure recovery". They do not include "obligations for upgrades or replacements that would otherwise occur as part of the normal system lifecycle (OMB Circular A-11, Section 43.2(c))

2) These are preliminary estimates only. More accurate estimates will become available after agencies complete the assessment phase. These

estimates do not include the Federal share of the costs for state information systems that support Federal programs. For example the Agriculture total does not include the potential 50 per cent in Federal matching funds to be provided to states by the Food and Consumer Service to correct year 2000 problems. Similarly, while Labor's FY 1998 President's Budget includes $200 million for the states to correct year 2000 problems in State unemployment insurance systems, that amount is not included here.
3) N/A means "not available".

Appendix II

Clippings from the Press

Newsweek Magazine
June 2, 1997

"The Day The World Crashes — Can We Fix The Year 2000 Computer Bug Before It's Too Late"
By Steven Levy and Katie Hafner

Will power plants shut down and your phone go out? Will your Social Security checks disappear into cyberspace? Will your bank account vanish?

Drink deep from your champagne glasses as the ball drops in times square to usher in the year 2000. Whether you imbibe or not, the hangover may begin immediately. The power may go out. Or the credit card you pull out to pay for dinner may no longer be valid. If you try an ATM to get cash, that may not work, either. Or the elevator that took you up to the party ballroom may be stuck on the ground floor. Or the parking garage you drove into earlier in the evening may charge you more than your yearly salary. Or your car might not start. Or the traffic lights might be on the blink. Or, when you get home, the phones may not work. The mail may show up, but your magazine subscriptions will have stopped, your government check may not arrive, your insurance policies may have expired.

Or you may be out of a job. When you show up for work after the holiday, the factory or office building might be locked up, with a handwritten sign taped to the wall: out of business due to computer error.

Could it really happen? Could the most anticipated New Year's Eve party in our lifetimes really usher in a digital nightmare when our wired-up-the-wazoo civilization grinds to a halt? Incredibly, according to computer experts, corporate information officers, congressional leaders and basically anyone who's given the matter a fair hearing, the answer is yes, yes, 2,000 times yes! Yes—unless we successfully complete the most ambitious and costly technology project in history, one where the payoff comes not in amassing riches or extending Web access, but securing raw survival.

What's the problem? It's called, variously, the Year 2000 Problem, Y2K or the Millennium Bug. It represents the ultimate indignity: the world laid low by two lousy digits. The trouble is rooted in a seemingly trivial space-saving programming trick—dropping the first two numbers of the date, abbreviating, say, the year 1951 to "51." This digital relic from the days when every byte of computer storage was precious was supposed to have been long gone by now, but the practice became standard. While any idiot familiar with the situation could figure out that the world's computers were on a collision course with the millennium, no one wanted to be the one to bring it up to management. And, really, which executive would welcome a message from nerddom that a few million bucks would be required to fix some obscure problem that wouldn't show up for several years?

So only now, as the centurial countdown begins, are we learning that the digit-dropping trick has changed from clever to catastrophic. Because virtually all the mainframe computers that keep the world humming are riddled with software that refuses to recognize that when 1999 runs out, the year 2000 follows. When that date arrives, the computers are going to get very confused. (PCs aren't as affected; sidebar.) So that seemingly innocuous trick now affects everything from ATMs to weapons systems. Virtually every government, state and municipality, as well as every large, midsize and small business in the world, is going to have to deal with this—in fact, if they haven't started already it's just about too late. Fixing the problem requires painstaking work. The bill for all this? Gartner Group estimates it could go as high as $600 billion. That amount could easily fund a year's worth of all U.S. educational costs, preschool through grad school. It's Bill Gates times 30!

That tab doesn't include the litigation that will inevitably follow the system failures. "You can make some very reasonable extrapolations about litigation that take you over $1 trillion, and those are very conservative estimates," says Dean Morehous, a San Francisco lawyer. (Conservative or not, this is more than three times the yearly cost of all civil litigation in the United States.)

Come on, you say. Two measly digits? Can't we just unleash some sort of roboprogram on all that computer code and clean it up? Well, no. Forget about a silver bullet. It seems that in most mainframe programs, the date appears more often than "M*A*S*H" reruns on television—about once every 50 lines of code. Typically, it's hard to find those particular lines, because the original programs, often written in the ancient COBOL computer language, are quirky and undocumented. After all that analysis, you have to figure out how to rewrite the lines to correctly process the date. Only then comes the most time-consuming step: testing the rewritten program. It's a torturous process, but an absolutely necessary one. Because if we don't swat the millennium Bug, we'll have troubles everywhere.

Electricity. When the Hawaiian Electric utility in Honolulu ran tests on its system to see if it would be affected by the Y2K Bug, "basically, it just stopped working," says systems analyst Wendell Ito. If the problem had gone unaddressed, not only would some customers have potentially lost power, but others could have got their juice at a higher frequency, in which case, "the clocks would go faster, and some things could blow up," explains Ito. (Hawaiian Electric revamped the software and now claims to be ready for the year 2000.) Another concern is nuclear power; the Nuclear Regulatory Commission says that the Bug might affect "security control, radiation monitoring... and accumulated burn-up programs [which involve calculations to estimate the hazard posed by radioactive fuel]."

Communications. "If no one dealt with the year 2000 Bug, the [phone] network would not operate properly," says Eric Sumner Jr., a Lucent chief technology officer. He's not talking about dial tones, but things like billing (watch out for 100-year charges). Certain commercial operations that run phone systems by computer could also go silent if the software isn't fixed.

Medicine. Besides the expected mess in billing systems, insurance claims and patient records, hospitals and doctors have to worry about embedded chips—microprocessors inside all sorts of devices that sometimes have date-sensitive controls. The year 2000 won't make pacemakers stop dead, but it could affect the data readouts it reports to physicians.

Weapons. NEWSWEEK has obtained an internal Pentagon study listing the Y2K impact on weapons and battlefield technologies. In their current state, "a year 2000 problem exists" in several key military technologies and they will require upgrading or adjustments. One intelligence system reverts to the year 1900, another reboots to 1969. The report confidently states that as far as nuclear devices like Trident missiles are concerned, "there are no major obstacles which will prevent them from being totally Year 2000 compliant by Jan. 1999."

Money. Banks and other financial institutions generally will go bonkers if they don't fix the year 2000 problem. The Senate Banking Committee is even worried that vertiginous computers might automatically erase the last 99 years' worth of bank records. Some Y2K consultants are advising consumers to make sure they don't enter the 1999 holiday without obtaining hard-copy evidence of their assets. According to Jack Webb of HONOR Technologies, Inc., ATMs won't work without fixes.

Food. In Britain computers at the Marks & Spencer company have already mistakenly ordered the destruction of tons of corned beef, believing they were more than 100 years old.

Air-Traffic Control. "We're still in the assessment stage, determining how big the problem is," says Dennis DeGaetano of the Federal Aviation Administration. One possible danger is computer lockup: while planes will keep moving at 12:01 a.m. on Jan. 1, 2000, the screens monitoring them, if not upgraded, might lock. Or the computers might know where the planes were, but mix them up with flights recorded at the same time on a previous day. ("You can bet we're going to fix it," says DeGaetano.)

Factories. Ford Motor Co. reports that if the Bug isn't fixed, its buildings could literally shut down—the factories have security systems linked to the year. "Obviously, if you don't fix it, your business will stop in the year 2000," says Ford's David Principato. Even if a manufacturing company aggressively solves its own problem, though, it might be flummoxed by a supplier who delivers widgets in the wrong century.

Just About Everything Else. Larry Martin, CEO of Data Dimensions, warns that if not adjusted, "on Jan. 1, 2000, a lot of elevators could be dropping to the bottom of buildings," heading to the basement for inspections they believe are overdue. Similarly, automobiles have as many as 100 chips; if they are calendar-challenged, experts say, forget about driving. Computerized sprinkler systems could initiate icy midwinter drenchings.

Like leaves rustling before a tornado, there have already been harbingers of a bureaucratic meltdown. At a state prison, a computer glitch misread the release date of prisoners and freed them prematurely. In Kansas, a 104-year-old woman was given a notice to enter kindergarten. Visa has had to recall some credit cards with expiration dates three years hence—the machines reading them thought they had expired in the McKinley administration.

The $600 billion question is whether we'll fix the Bug in time. The good news is that the computer industry is finally responding to the challenge. For months now, squadrons of digital Jeremiahs have been addressing tech conferences with tales of impending apocalypse. The most sought-after is Peter de Jager, a bearded Canadian who scares the pants off audiences on a near-daily basis. "If we shout from the rooftops, they accuse us of hype," he complains. "But if we whisper in an alley, no one will listen." Last week in Boston de Jager demonstrated the rooftop approach: "If you're not changing code by November of this year," he warned, "you will not get this thing done on time—it's that simple. We still don't get it."

But we're starting to. Most major corporations now have year 2000 task forces, with full-time workers funded by multimillion-dollar budgets, to fix a problem that their bosses finally understand. They're aided by an army of consultants and specialized companies. Some, like Data Dimensions, offer full Y2K service, providing tools, programmers and guidance. Others, like Peritus, sell special software to help find offending code and, sometimes, even convert it. (The final, most arduous stage, testing, still defies automation.) These firms are the new darlings of Wall Street. But buyer beware—consultants are coming out of the woodwork to exploit the desperation of late-coming companies. Someone might promise a phalanx of brilliant programmers to fix the Bug, but "for all you know, it could be 10 people in a garage doing it by hand," says Ted Swoyer, a Peritus exec. Still, the creation of a Y2K-fixing infrastructure is encouraging.

It's not uncommon to find gung-ho efforts like the one at Merrill Lynch: an 80-person Y2K division working in shifts, 24 hours a day, seven days a week. It'll cost the company $200 million, a sum that could hire Michael Eisner and fire Mike Ovitz. "Our return on investment is zero," says senior VP Howard Sorgen. "This will just enable us to stay in business."

So maybe we're not in for a full-scale disaster. Let us assume—oh God let it be true—that those in charge of life-sustaining applications and services will keep their promises to fix what needs fixing. The costs and liabilities of not doing so are too huge not to. (On the other hand, when did you last see a huge software project that met its deadline and worked perfectly? Just asking.) Still, there will almost certainly be severe dislocations because of the mind-boggling enormity of the problem.

Even the most diligent companies don't have total confidence they can fix everything. Consider BankBoston, the 15th largest commercial bank in the United States. Early in 1995, the company realized that "it was a problem that could bring an institution to its knees," says David Iacino, who heads the bank's Team 2000. To stop a meltdown, BankBoston has to probe 60 million lines of code. The harder BankBoston works at solving the problem—it now has 40 people working full time on it—the more complicated it seems. "Every day, when we see something new we haven't thought about, we get additional angst," says Iacino.

Of the 200 BankBoston applications that need revamping, only a handful have been completed so far. BankBoston is now separating the essential work from the noncritical, and if the Bug causes less dire problems, like the heavy vault doors swinging open on New Year's Eve, it'll just cope: "Vaults are physical things," says Iacino. "If push comes to shove, we can put a guard in front."

Now, if BankBoston, which started early and has been driving hard, is already thinking triage, what is going to happen to institutions that are still negotiating in the face of a nonnegotiable deadline? The Gartner Group is estimating that half of all businesses are going to fall short. "There's still a large number of folks out there who haven't started," says Matt Hotle, Gartner's research director.

As businesses finally come to terms with the inevitable, it's going to be panic time. In about a year, expect most of the commercial world to be totally obsessed with the Bug. "Pretty soon we have to just flat stop doing other work," says Leo Verheul of California's Department of Motor Vehicles. But no amount of money or resources will postpone the year 2000. It will arrive on time, even if all too many computers fail to recognize its presence.

"It's staggering to start doing mind games on what percentage of companies will go out of business," says Gartner's Hotle. "What is the impact to the economy of 1 percent going out of business?" Or maybe more: Y2K expert Capers Jones predicts that more than 5 percent of all businesses will go bust. This would throw hundreds of thousands of people into the unemployment lines—applying for checks that may or may not come, depending on whether the government has successfully solved its Y2K problem.

What is the U.S. government doing? Not enough."It's ironic that this administration that prides itself on being so high tech is not really facing up to the potential disaster that is down the road a little bit," says Sen. Fred Thompson. If Y2K indeed becomes a calamity, it may well be the vice president who suffers—imagine Al Gore's spending the entire election campaign explaining why he didn't foresee the crisis. (Gore declined to speak to NEWSWEEK on the Y2K problem.)

Here's the recipe for a federal breakdown: not enough time and not enough money. While the Office of Management and Budget claims the problem can be fixed for $2.3 billion, most experts think it will take $30 billion. Rep. Stephen Horn held hearings last year to see if the federal agencies were taking steps "to prevent a possible computer disaster," and was flabbergasted at the lack of preparedness. His committee assigned each department a letter grade. A few, notably Social Security, were given A's. (The SSA has been working on the problem for eight years and now has it 65 percent licked; at that rate it will almost make the deadline.) Those with no plan in place—NASA, the Veterans Administration—got D's. Special dishonor was given to places where inaction could be critical, yet complacency still ruled, like the departments of Labor, Energy and Transportation.

State governments are also up against the 2000 wall. California, for instance, finished its inventory last December and found that more than half of its 2,600 computer systems required fixes. Of those, 450 systems are considered "mission critical," says the state's chief information officer John Thomas Flynn. These include computers that control toll bridges, traffic lights, lottery payments, prisoner releases, welfare checks, tax collection and the handling of toxic chemicals.

As bad as it seems in the United States, the rest of the world is lagging far behind in fixing the problem. Britain has recently awakened to the crisis—a survey late last year showed that 90 percent of board directors knew of it—but the head of Britain's Taskforce 2000, Robin Guenier, worries that only a fraction really understand what's required. "I'm not saying we're doomed, but if we are not doing better in six months, I really will be worried," he says. He expects the cost to top $50 billion. On the Continent, things are much worse; most of the information-processing energy is devoted to the Euro-currency, and observers fear that when countries like Germany and France finally tackle 2000, it might be too late.

Russia seems complacent. Recently Mikhail Gorbachev met with Representative Horn in Washington, expressing concern about how far behind Russia is in dealing with the Bug; Gorbachev raised its possible impact on the country's nuclear safeguards.

The list can go on, and on and on. "It's like an iceberg," says Leon Kappelman, an academic and Y2K consultant. "I would certainly be uncomfortable if Wall Street were to close for a few days, but I can live with that. But what if the water system starts sending water out before it's safe? Or a chemical plant goes nuts? Anybody who tells you 'Oh, it's OK' without knowing that it's been tested is in denial."

It's tough out there on the front lines of Y2K. And in less than a thousand days, it might be tough everywhere. "There are two kinds of people," says Nigel Martin-Jones of Data Dimensions. "Those who aren't working on it and aren't worried, and those who are working on it and are terrified." Tick, tick, tick, tick, tick.

— With Gregory L. Vistica and Rich Thomas in Washington, Deborah Branscum and Bronwyn Fryer in California, Julie Edelson Halpert in Detroit, Jennifer Tanaka in New York and William Underhill in London.

Newsweek 6/2/97 Society/
The Millennium: The Day the World Shuts Down
Print Version: Pages 52-59
Internet Version: Via America Online
From Newsweek Magazine, June 2, 1997.

Computerworld
11/11/96

TELCOS LAG ON YEAR 2000, ANALYSTS WARN

Kim Girard and Robert L. Scheier

Telecommunications companies should be knee-deep into analyzing potential year 2000 problems by now if they hope to avoid billing problems, blocked telephone calls or even outages, experts say.

But carriers on the whole are lagging behind the financial industry, which is leading the year 2000 charge, said Bruce Hall, a research director at Gartner Group, Inc. in Stamford, Conn. "The [telecommunications] projects aren't on the scale that they need to be to get them out from under where you're at risk," Hall said.

"This is a problem of gigantic dimensions and with so many complexities that it's very hard to think something will not slip," said Bichlien Hoang, executive director of year 2000 network solutions at Bellcore, a telecommunications software, engineering and consulting firm in Morristown, N.J.

Carriers need to fix code in the custom software used for customer service, billing and financial information and in systems that support network switches and network management.

Many carriers are more focused for now on fixing internal software code. They believe the switching problem will be handled by suppliers, including Lucent Technologies, Inc., Nortel, Inc. and Siemens AG. But for now, there is no way to be sure equipment is year 2000-compliant, Hoang said.

Analysts said companies should set aside a buffer period before 1999 to work out any last-minute problems. They said testing could be as expensive and take as much time as identifying and fixing the problems.

Year 2000 project managers at the telecommunications companies contend they are moving quickly to fix the problems.

Tricky testing

Testing is complicated because carriers must introduce year-2000-compliant products from vendors while testing links with new telecommunications providers. In the deregulated environment, those providers include cellular and personal communications services vendors.

"The [carriers] have so many points of entry," said Mike Egan, a year 2000 analyst at Meta Group, Inc., a consultancy in Stamford, Conn. "That's one screamer of a test job."

Bob Bender, director of systems development at Sprint

Corp., said the company must determine how many of its 100 million lines of code are date-sensitive. "It's a very wide problem, but it's not a deep problem," Bender said. "Once you identify it, it's relatively easy to fix."

AT&T Corp., which has established a year 2000 program office, plans to test in cycles during the next two years and will begin fixing code next month.

"I think it's going to be a fair amount of work, a lot of project management," said George Brucia, year 2000 project manager at AT&T. "Right now, it's really not keeping me awake at night."

AT&T must peruse 500 million lines of code. Many times, only 5% to 10% of the code will have to be changed, but all code must be scanned to find the rogue dates.

Sprint is hiring an outside firm to do a full assessment but has six full-time and 20 part-time employees devoted to the problem. The company hopes to begin testing by 1998.

MCI Communications Corporation officials refused to discuss year 2000 plans. The company has hired Data Dimensions, Inc., a technology consulting services company, to do an initial assessment and tools survey.

Wall Street Journal
Marketplace, Page B1
12/9/1996

A Look at Allstate Shows Why Preparing for 2000 Is So Tough

By Lee Gomes
Staff Reporter of The Wall Street Journal

Sitting at his desk deep inside the sprawling mainframe computer operation of Allstate Corp., programmer Dan Deco stares at a mystery by the name of "K7" hovering in the middle of his computer screen. "Right there," Mr. Deco says, pointing at the spot. "That's what the Year 2000 problem is all about."

By now, almost everyone has heard that the arrival of the new millennium threatens to throw mainframe computers into chaos. K7 is a tiny snippet of the problem, a minuscule piece of computer code unique to Allstate that was plucked from deep within the company's mainframe-computer system. But eliminating it and other slivers of rogue software is now a full-time job for about 100 Allstate programmers like Mr. Deco, and that number will soon double.

In the end, protecting the nation's second-largest insurance company against Year 2000 glitches will cost at least $40 million. To adapt all of the world's mainframe computers, the total price tag could reach $600 billion by 2000, says the research firm Gartner Group.

How can a computer problem that seems so trivial be so hard — and expensive — to solve? The recent morning that Mr. Deco spent tracking down K7 provides part of the answer. "Here," says the tall, beefy programmer, settling in front of his computer screen, "is some of the hairiest code you are ever going to see."

The mainframe computer programs at Allstate work fine, but like virtually all others in the world, they are a rickety edifice of tens of millions of lines of code, some dating back to the 1960s. Many programs grind away daily, even though no one remembers any more precisely what they do or how they do it. The company has found some programs on its computers it didn't even know existed.

To save memory, mainframe programs were originally written to think only in 20th-century terms and to use just two digits to store dates. Hence, the "00" that follows "99" in three short years would, to Allstate's computers, be 1900. Such an error would create a rolling wave of data-processing malfunctions that could quickly overwhelm the mainframes, impairing the company's operations.

To fix the Year 2000 problem, programmers like Mr. Deco must deftly pull out and repair just the pieces of programs dealing with dates, while making sure everything else doesn't crash down around them. Allstate figures it must finish the job by late 1998, when it begins mailing renewal notices for one-year policies expiring in 2000.

But when it comes to the Year 2000, Allstate is ahead of many mainframe operators. While some companies still haven't faced up to the problem, Allstate has been planning its attack for nearly two years. At the company's Northbrook, Ill., headquarters, there's a Year 2000 logo, a newsletter, spirit-building meetings and even a motto: "Staying Informed + Planning Ahead = Year 2000 Readiness."

As they go about their work, Mr. Deco and the others at Allstate are exploring every corner of Allstate's mainframes. The part that is giving them the most trouble — in fact, the single biggest reason for the effort's huge scope — is a computer programming element known as "fields." Fields are routinely used in programs as a temporary stand-in for a piece of information, and they can represent anything: a name, address, balance due — or date. They act the same way that variables like "x" do in high-school algebra.

These days, there are strict rules about the names programmers can give fields. A field that represents today's date, for example, might get the name "TDATE." But in the past, someone might have called the same field "NOW." And long ago, programmers made up whimsical names for fields. Mr. Deco, who is 30 years old and has worked for Allstate for seven years, says he has come upon fields named after rock 'n' roll lyrics, flowers, programmers' sweethearts and members of the Beatles.

These fields are such a big problem because there are so many. Allstate's mainframes use 40,000 separate programs, totaling about 40 million lines of code. Each program can contain scores of different date fields. Because the names of these fields are so random, there is no way to know which fields are associated with dates except by searching through the entire mainframe library virtually by hand.

Nonetheless, all of the date fields must be tracked down and made "Year 2000 compliant" before the 1998 deadline. "It's like some huge, weird puzzle. You split it into pieces, and everyone gets their piece," says Mr. Deco.

On this morning, Mr. Deco is electronically thumbing through a mainframe scheduling program named ARCAN02 when he finds K7. He figures out right away that the field involves a date because he can see it has been swapped with another field already known to refer to a date.

But before he can fix K7, Mr. Deco needs to know which of Allstate's half-dozen different date formats was used by the programmer who created K7. To find that out, he must run ARCAN02, then stop the program precisely at the moment K7 appears in the machine's active memory.

Mr. Deco presses a button and the computer streaks through ARCAN02, but it fails to stop at K7. Mr. Deco furrows his brow and draws up closer to the screen. He runs the program again. No luck. He rubs his hands together and tries a third time, but still no K7.

Now, Mr. Deco is mumbling to himself. He has chanced upon an especially devilish snag, precisely the sort that keeps bumping up the price for the Year 2000 overhaul.

Computers take various paths as they work through a program, depending on the real-world data they are using. K7, it seems, sits on a rarely used byway of ARCAN02. This path, Mr. Deco says, might be used only once every billion or so times the program is executed — when, for example, the program encounters an Allstate policy holder from Honolulu who has been in an accident while using a friend's vehicle in Las Vegas.

With no notes from the programmer who first dreamed up K7, Mr. Deco has no idea what real-world circumstances will trigger the field inside ARCAN02. But if K7 isn't analyzed and repaired, the inevitable post-2000 day will arrive when the right mix of facts will awaken K7, perhaps crashing not only ARCAN02 but the mainframe too.

Mr. Deco breaks for lunch, announcing he is resorting to computer triage; K7 will join the list of especially troublesome fields to be tracked down during 1997, when Allstate's Year 2000 effort will shift into an even higher gear. "You cut your losses," Mr. Deco explains.

No one knows how many thousands of other sprites like K7 remain hidden inside mainframes at Allstate. For Mr. Deco, who first applied for his job at the urging of his mother, a former Allstate executive secretary, there is a lesson to be learned from this. "When I started here, I thought I would come in, write a thousand lines of code, and change the world," he says. "Now, I'm afraid to change even a single byte. Everything is just so complicated."

The Wall Street Journal, Dec. 9. 1996.

Computerworld
December 23, 1996

Year 2000 may ambush U.S. military
By Robert L. Scheier, Gary H. Anthes and Allan E. Alter

Hundreds of feet beneath the ocean's surface, a horrified commander watches as a torpedo he launched veers off course and races back toward his submarine.

While simulating a war in the Persian Gulf, mission planners see their screens go blank. If this had happened during an actual war, 2,700 air strikes would have been canceled or delayed.

Both of these software glitches, which actually happened, show how errors in calculating times or dates could cost lives and cripple America's ability to defend itself. They also provide a chilling preview of what could happen if the Pentagon doesn't fix critical software. Most of that software now records dates using only two digits, so it cant cope with the date change from 1999 to 2000.

But with only three years to go before the turn of the century, critics charge that President Clinton, Congress and top Pentagon leaders are failing to move aggressively enough to avoid serious problems.

"I think the president or the vice president should declare that this is a potential national emergency," said retired Air Force General Thomas McInerney, now president of Business Executives for National Security in Washington. "He could get the resources and attention that would prevent it from becoming a national emergency."

Just as damaging as weapons failures would be snafus in logistics and transportation systems, which are very date dependent. In a national emergency, such failures could be "catastrophic," Pentagon Chief Information Officer Emmett Paige Jr. told Congress earlier this year.

"Will they be able to find every single date problem? Of course not," said Robert Charette, who wrote code for submarine combat systems at the Naval Underwater Warfare Center. He is now chairman of the risk management advisory board of the Software Engineering Institute and president of Itabi Corp. in Fairfax, Va.

Instead, he said, defense officials "are going to cross their fingers and toes and run with it. I will not be surprised if something real bad happens."

To be fair, the Pentagon is ahead of many civilian IS organizations, other observers said. Its top leadership recognizes the problem as critical and is pushing the armed forces to inventory their software. Various committees are also working on much-needed common standards for year 2000 testing. Managers in some defense agencies said they have already found and fixed problems in their most critical systems.

Yet despite outside estimates of up to $14 billion, Department of Defense (DOD) officials have only rough estimates in the mid-hundreds of millions of dollars. More significantly, Congress hasn't appropriated funds for the work, aside from $5 million to assess conversion tools.

The DOD established a central program office to coordinate conversion work and give advice to the services. But that office has no budgetary authority and is leaving most of the repairs to development organizations that have a 20-year record of producing poorly tested and hard-to-maintain software.

For IS managers, the Pentagon's problems could serve as Exhibit No. 1 for a strong, centralized approach to mission-critical software maintenance projects. They also show how poor development practices can force an organization to take its eyes off strategic threats to clean up problems it caused itself.

In the past, DOD developers could use obscure languages, such as Jovial, for which there are few debugging or analysis tools. Because different developers wrote date calculations differently, "there is no standard that you can scan code for," Charette said.

Agencies also must take money for year 2000 work out of existing programs. Paige told Congress earlier this year that could mean delaying other systems and re-engineering efforts. In some cases, rival agencies will have to compromise on which projects to kill or delay to pay for date-change work.

Cynthia Rand, principal director of information management at the Pentagon CIO's office, insisted she is seeing excellent cooperation among the services.

Defense officials said they are working aggressively to improve their software skills. But "little has changed" in the DOD's management and oversight of software development during the past 10 years, said John Stephenson, assistant director in the General Accounting Office's Accounting and Information Management Division. Stephenson is now studying the DOD's handling of the year 2000 but won't release findings until May.

Given all this, can the DOD get all its year 2000 work done on time? "Probably not," said Bryce Ragland, an electronics engineer who heads a year 2000 team at the Air Force Software Technology Support Center at Hill Air Force Base in Utah. "There's a real risk that some wacko in another country ... might decide to launch an attack against the U.S. a few seconds after midnight just to see if our defenses can handle it."

Financial Times of London
May 2, 1997

Millennium bomb: Threat to global telecoms links

By Alan Cane

Major telecoms operators have warned that it could be impossible to telephone some countries after the turn of the century because of the so-called "millennium bomb".

While large operators in the US and the UK are investing heavily to ensure their systems are free of the bomb — the inability of some computer systems to distinguish between this century and the next — operators elsewhere are behind in their preparations.

British Telecommunications, which has set up a program to ensure its systems will function correctly, has written to its counterparts abroad to ascertain their preparedness. Mr. Paul Harborne, head of the BT program, said: "We believe some European operators are working on it but is anybody taking any action at all in the Far East?"

He is chiefly concerned that the world's operators should not only eliminate the bomb from their systems but have time to spare to test the way they work together.

AT&T, the largest US operator, for example, has established a project team under Mr. George Brucia, a vice-president, and aims to have the work completed by January 1 1999. The company said: "We see this more as a task to be carried through than a problem. But if it is not completed in time, it will be a serious problem."

Major telecoms manufacturers, including Lucent Technologies of the US, France's Alcatel, GPT of the UK and Sweden's Ericsson, are addressing the issue. The expected ready availability of equipment tested for compliance could therefore provide a solution for operators who do not take action quickly enough, according to some experts.

The International Telecommunication Union, the Geneva-based organization which co-ordinates the activities of national operators, will, for the first time, discuss what action to take in talks beginning on May 20.

While it has no power to force individual operators to take action, it could set standards against which their compliance could be tested.

The bomb results from the common software practice of storing the year in a date as two digits — 97, rather than 1997 — to save memory. After December 31 1999, affected computers may malfunction in unpredictable ways because of their inability to recognise a 21st century date.

Financial Times of London
May 21, 1997

Banking: Are you safe from the fallout?

By James Mackintosh

If the doom-mongers are to be believed, the new millennium will start with a bang: aircraft falling out of the sky, nuclear weapons out of control and a worldwide recession. These disasters would be the result of the "millennium bomb"— computers registering the beginning of the new century as the beginning of the one before.

This is because computer systems store the date as just two digits each for the day, the month and the year — so "00" can mean 1900 or 2000.

The most terrifying problems will be solved — at huge cost — long before December 31 1999. But will your finances be affected?

The first potential problem is that the banking system could collapse. But the Bank of England is confident that banks will be ready to cope.

Another possibility is that share prices in companies hit by the bomb may collapse — according to predictions from the US, this is likely to happen to 1 per cent of businesses. Most UK companies have not yet tackled the problem. Taskforce 2000, the government-appointed troubleshooter, says it would cost £31bn to bring all British businesses into line.

So far only one large fund manager, Scottish Widows, has announced that it is limiting its investments to year 2000-compliant businesses.

What about your financial records? One UK regulator admits that she would never invest in anything — from a pension to equities — without checking first that the company had corrected its computer systems.

Robin Guenier of Taskforce 2000 says: "Everyone should ask their pension fund [if it is] fixing its own systems and investing only in companies which are compliant." He adds that it would be "very prudent" for everybody to get a hard copy record of their bank account, pension and investments towards the end of 1999.

IBM is more reassuring, but has the same advice. "Don't panic — there is no need to keep banknotes under the mattress. But it is worth asking the companies that look after your money if they have done anything about it."

CrestCo, operator of the Crest automated settlement and share registration system used by the stock exchange, says it will not be affected. "Small investors should not have any worries that their shares will just disappear - there is no risk of that."

Your monthly pay packet may present a serious problem. The big banks will have modified their computers in time, but if your employer has not taken the millennium bomb seriously your January 2000 salary may never reach your account.

US News & World Report
February 2, 1997

The millennium bug looms — PCs will freak on Jan. 1, 2000. Is a fix in the making?

By John Simons

What's got the Department of Defense, the IRS, and the Social Security Administration gathering in Washington for a strategy session this week? Budget deliberations? Government downsizing? Nope. The federal agencies are teaming up to combat one of the most potentially crippling forces known to modern computing: the Year 2000 Problem.

In case your favorite info-tech professional hasn't cornered you to lament what's variously known as the Millennium Bug, the Year 2000 Problem, or simply "Y2K," a bit of background is in order. During the 1960s, computer memory was extremely limited and extraordinarily expensive. As a result, programmers were forced to economize when writing software, allocating only a two-digit number for each year's date. So, the year 1997, to a computer, is simply "97" (the "19" is assumed).

It doesn't take a computer-science degree to figure out the pitfall in this penny-pinching scheme: As midnight revelers celebrate the new millennium on Jan. 1, 2000, some 90 percent of the world's computer hardware and software will "think" it's the first day of 1900.

What sounds like a simple computer glitch has enormous business ramifications. Although the bulk of Y2K foul-ups will occur in 2000, consumers won't have to wait for the new millennium to witness the effects. Most corporations and government entities refuse to talk openly about Y2K's effect for fear of public embarrassment and mass hysteria. But Y2K-induced snafus are already becoming the stuff of folklore. According to the Gartner Group, a Stamford, Conn.-based technology consulting firm, a state correctional facility (Gartner won't reveal which one) recently released several prisoners by mistake. The inmates' sentences extended well into the next century, but the prison's computer calculations showed they were long overdue for release. Some diligent human caught the glitch, and the prisoners were rounded up without incident. Says Gartner analyst Bruce Hall: "Mix-ups like this will consume tens if not hundreds of work-years within the typical organization." All told, Gartner estimates that corporations will spend between $300 billion and $600 billion grappling with Y2K over the next three years.

That's the jackpot that 500 or so software and computer service companies, each claiming to have its own Y2K fix, are vying for. The Y2K-busting firms are designing programs that sift through every line of a corporation's code for a fee of about 50 cents per line. These programs locate the offending date codes—which are generally written in a now archaic language called COBOL—and rewrite them. It's not as simple as it sounds. The average company could have millions and millions of coded data lines. The keys to correcting the matter, therefore, are speed and accuracy.

Possible leader. For the moment, no clear leader has emerged in the Y2K market. That could change this week, as Fremont, Calif.-based MatriDigm unveils what it says is the speediest Y2K solution yet. MatriDigm has spent more than a decade developing its "Code Analyzer." In a trial run with its first and only client, the state of Nevada, MatriDigm's product ferreted through a dizzying million lines of code per hour, making corrections with about 99 percent accuracy, according to officials. By contrast, its closest competitor, Peritus Software Services, has a maintenance program that performs corrections at a speed of 2 million lines a day.

Not surprisingly, MatriDigm is one of the chief beneficiaries of the recent hype surrounding Y2K stocks. The company is partly owned by software maker Zitel. During 1996, Zitel, along with three other Y2K companies—Information Analysis, TSR, and ViaSoft—made the Dow Jones list of top 10 performers; each saw its share price leap an average of 977 percent.

As one might expect with a market that has a finite life span, the Y2K arena is maturing quickly. In recent months, a number of firms have begun to form alliances. MatriDigm has entered into an agreement with ViaSoft, and IBM is partnering with Peritus. "There's $600 billion on the table, more than enough for everyone," notes Peter de Jager, a year 2000 consultant.

Jager, who has become the Cassandra of corporate computing, worries that only a quarter of all U.S. firms have earmarked budgets for tackling their Y2K problem. "They still don't have the sense of urgency that this thing requires," he says. "Time is of the essence." Two years, 46 weeks, and counting, to be exact.

Business Week
August 12, 1996

Financial Institutions Panic in the Year Zero Zero
Can the financial world reprogram its computers in time?

By Leah Nathans Spiro in New York

It's 11:59 p.m. on Friday, Dec. 31, 1999. As the ball drops in Times Square, computers at some of the world's financial institutions shut down. With their lifeblood cut off, these banks, brokerages, and insurance companies, most of which operate in a limited way over the weekend, are forced to close their doors, at least temporarily. Other financial firms whose computers are still functional try to keep operating. But because linkages among financial institutions are so elaborate, even healthy companies begin to falter. By Monday morning, billions of dollars in transactions have been disrupted or aborted. A domino effect goes into play, and in the ensuing confusion the entire financial world teeters into chaos.

The pitch for a Hollywood blockbuster? No, it's the daytime nightmare of one of the most technologically advanced and well-managed firms on Wall Street, Morgan Stanley & Co. It is deeply worried that the computers that keep the financial world alive have not been properly programmed to make the transition to the next millennium.

"In Denial." Wall Street is just one of many industries facing the "Year 2000" problem, which has been getting some press lately. The inability of many computer programs to make accurate calculations after Dec. 31, 1999, will affect everything from the Internal Revenue Service to computer-operated elevators.

The world of finance, though, is especially vulnerable. "Because of the interconnectedness of worldwide financial institutions, the absolute worst case, albeit highly unlikely, is a global financial meltdown," says Kevin E. Parker, Morgan Stanley's head of information technology. Says William Bautz, senior vice-president for technology at the New York Stock Exchange: "Due to the unique nature of this business, everybody has to have the problem fixed, or they create problems for somebody else." If the specter of financial chaos isn't enough, plaintiffs' lawyers are already viewing securities firms as juicy targets for a year 2000 litigation bonanza. Investors could sue their brokerage firms over failed trades, unpaid interest, or bad investment decisions caused by incorrect date-based calculations. Law firms are looking into holding boards of directors liable, says Kevin Schick, research director at Gartner Group Inc.

Yet despite the risks, the securities industry has been slow to respond, in part because they are not anxious to spend the estimated $4 billion it will cost to become year 2000-compliant. "Here is an industry that prides itself on risk assessment and management," says Schick. "And yet, when faced with this potential crisis, they are in denial." The problem began some 30 years ago. Because of the limited memory space of early computers, programmers didn't want to squander four digits writing out, say, 1962. So they designed software to store dates using only a year's last two digits. The conventional wisdom was that programs would be replaced before 2000 rolled around. But many are still in use. So when 1999 turns to 2000, many computer programs will go from 99, or 1999, to 00—or 1900.

If left uncorrected, this will throw the financial world into convulsions like it has never seen, say Morgan Stanley's computer whizzes. That's because it threatens the underpinning of all financial transactions: the accurate recording of time. The markets are utterly dependent on dates. There are trade dates, maturity dates, settlement dates, record dates, ex-dividend dates, and payable dates, to name a few.

If these dates get screwed up, Wall Street firms' computers will no longer accurately calculate any number of things, says Michael B. Tiernan, a vice-president at CS First Boston. He is also chairman of the Securities Industry Assn.'s Year 2000 subcommittee, and testified at congressional hearings in April. Clearing and settlement of transactions could break down.

Stocks held electronically and checking accounts could be wiped out. Interest might not be properly credited to accounts. Customers might be denied access to their accounts. Deposits or trades might not be credited to an account, and customers' funds would not be available. "If year 2000 problems are not addressed, the consequences may be catastrophic, from a business and economic perspective," Tiernan testified. And there's a further complication: 2000 is a leap year, which means computers may not assume there is a Feb. 29.

Yet common reactions are: The computer geeks can fix it, or it can't really be as serious as all that. Schick estimates that only 20% of the industry is taking action. Very few securities firms have done audits of their computer programs, the first step toward getting a handle on their situation, he says.

In fact, fixing the problem is far more time-consuming than might be imagined. All of the older programs used by all of the financial firms must be revised manually. Morgan Stanley alone is spending tens of millions to change 3 million lines of code. "It's ugly. You have to inventory every single piece of code and then manually fix it," says Parker. Programming work must be done on the weekends, since most of the programs are in use during the week. There are only 179 weekends left until Dec. 31, 1999. "You can't do it on the weekend of the greatest party of the millennium," says Joshua S. Levine, a Morgan Stanley managing director whose office overlooks Times Square. "The sand is running out of the hourglass." Morgan Stanley plans to complete the job well before Jan. 1, 1999. Then the firm will spend 1999 evaluating the efforts of its thousands of counterparties in correcting their year 2000 problems and deciding who to stop doing business with. "We can't assume the risk of being caught in a domino effect," says Morgan Stanley Managing Director Eric M. Kamen.

Overblown? The white shoe firm is also trying to get other financial institutions and U.S. government regulators to focus on the problem. In June, Elaine LaRoche, a managing director at Morgan Stanley and president of the Public Securities Assn., had meetings with Treasury Secretary Robert E. Rubin and Securities & Exchange Commission Chairman Arthur Levitt Jr. to sound the alarm. Sources at the meeting with Rubin say he was surprised and sobered.

"It is viewed as a technology issue," says LaRoche. "But this is a settlement, counterparty, and systemic financial risk problem." She is referring to huge risks that could be created if millions of transactions between thousands of institutions could not be promptly completed.

Despite these alarms, many institutions are reluctant to make a big investment to solve the problem. "Here we're spending tens of millions of dollars, and it's not going toward anything productive or improving our competitive position," says Parker. Firms that spend the necessary money get to stay in business. And some of those are plotting to take advantage of their competitors' possible demise, says Schick. "We have players looking forward to the great market crash of zero zero," he says. He thinks as firms run out of time to fix their 2000 problems, they will discontinue certain lines of business or even fail.

Of course, not everyone is as apocalyptic as Schick and Morgan Stanley.

Renee Nalitt, one of Chase Manhattan's main year 2000 techies, says: "For the most part, we're already in pretty good shape." Securities & Exchange Commissioner Steven M.H. Wallman does not believe the year 2000 presents systemic financial risks and says the issues are being addressed responsibly.

George Munoz, a Treasury Dept. assistant secretary who heads a year 2000 Interagency Task Force, says Treasury will be ready by yearend 1998.

The NYSE and Securities Industry Automation Corp., its trade-processing arm, predicts the transition will be seamless. Why? In June, 1996, the industry went from processing trades in five days to three days, a potential back-office disaster that went without a hitch. "There is no chance of the industry not making the changes that are necessary in time," says Michael Reddy, who heads the securities industry year 2000 unit of EDS Corp. He could be right. But if he's not, the next century will start with an unwelcome financial bang.

Appendix III

"The Y2K Investor" Interviews

WBZS BUSINESS RADIO (730 AM)
HOSTS: TONY KEYES AND ED MULHALL

Guests: IRENE DEC AND JOHN VAZQUEZ OF PRUDENTIAL SECURITIES
WITH THOMAS OLESON OF IDC INC.
Date: FRIDAY, NOVEMBER 22, 1996

Y2KI: Now it is time for the Y2K Investor Show with our co-hosts, Tony Keyes and Ed Mulhall.

Y2KI: Thank you, Keith. And welcome everyone, this is the Y2K Investor where we discuss the year 2000 computer problem and its implications for the individual investor. We have got a great show lined up today so I'm sure you're going to want to stick around for the entire hour. During the first half of the hour we are hosting Irene Dec and Irene is Director of Prudential's Y2K program. And she is going to be talking about that with John Vasquez, who is a familiar name to all of you, I know, because John is frequently on WBZS. He is Vice President of Investments and a portfolio manager with Prudential in Bethesda, Maryland. By the way, just for future reference, you can reach John at (301) 961-0101 or on an 800 number, 368-2704.

In the second half of the show we're going to have Thomas Oleson on, Oleson on, and Thomas was — recently conducting a study for IDC on the year 2000 problem and they interviewed 500 top executives investigating where they were from a status standpoint on the year 2000 problem, how they perceived it, and general background. So I'm sure you're going to want hear that, that's going to be very interesting. So right now, I'd like to welcome Irene. Irene are you there?

IRENE DEC: Yes, thank you, Tony.

Y2KI: Thank you for coming on. You know, I'm certain that everyone out there who has been listening to this show regularly is quite interested in what you have to say because you in fact are the first end user that we've had an opportunity to interview. And the perspective that we've gotten to date have been through consultants and through vendors, and you can't help but wonder if some of that isn't jaded. So we're certainly interested in what you have to say.

IRENE DEC: Okay. Thanks, Tony. First, thanks for the opportunity to talk about a very critical subject, year 2K and the crisis that it will present to all business, as well as the opportunity to discuss with you what Prudential has done. At this point, you know, there is always a lot talk out there, Tony, and stating is this hype or is this a reality. And there is no question that this a reality. We talk about touching people and to what degree is this going to touch people or businesses and it's really going to touch all businesses and all people. You hear some really extreme numbers, some of the industries indicating things like globally this is a 300 to 600 billion dollar problem to fix. We're talking some big numbers there.

Y2KI: You actually have COBOL programming in your background I see.

IRENE DEC: Oh, yes, did that, that's how I got started in this world.

Y2KI: So you come from a very credible background as having been in the trenches and understand the complexities of COBOL, the idiosyncrasies of the COBOL programmer and some of the complex problems that that represents, I guess.

Y2KI: Yes, the problem is actually, Tony, what they really do for this is they present us not so much with a technology challenge, even though we really have to get those COBOL programmers in there to fix it and, you know, client server doesn't, you know, escape, you still need to address it there in your distributing environments and even in your intra and internet development. But what you really have is the IT world is really faced with a project management challenge. And as an industry we're not really the ones that have always been that successful in meeting target dates, we've kind of always dragged through our target dates. I mean, this is truly one case where business can't change that target date, I mean, we're committed to it. Some of the things that Prudential has done to lead with this is recognize that in a sense and saying we need to take a lead, we need to put a structure, an organization structure together that's going to allow us to track and monitor this. We're moving aggressively. Some of the things that companies are also faced with, Tony, is perhaps the fact that their company or business hasn't even recognized it and said, yes, this is a problem to our business and yes, we will fund this and we will make a commitment, we will put on our best staff to work on this. It's those companies that are really faced with risk.

Y2KI: Irene, this is Ed Mulhall. I wanted to follow-up on that and maybe you can give us a little background. When did Prudential first really identify the problem and what did it take in terms of getting the corporate support to move forward on this?

IRENE DEC: What really started was, Prudential has actually been aware of the problem for quite a few years. It wasn't really though until last summer, summer of 1995 that a commitment was made, stating it as a critical and a number one priority project at the Prudential. And I have to say, I mean, you know, at this point Prudential has been identified as a leader in running this year 2000 project and what really allowed us to become that leader was last summer our CEO, Art Ryan, our CIO, Bill Freall (phonetic sp.) basically put their foot down and said, this is critical to our business, we will do what we have to, to overcome it. And that's what key, and again in organizations that don't have that, that's where their risk is.

Y2KI: Can you give us a sense of your organization once you got that corporate commitment what next steps you took and what your organization looks like?

IRENE DEC: Sure. Basically Prudential is a company that has six — well, five major lines of business of which one is the Prudential Securities where John comes from. The others you probably know is the health care business, the life insurance, et cetera. With that what we did is from a corporate perspective, I directly report to the company CIO, so it was a project that was given high visibility. And what we put together was a company wide team, basically the think tanks throughout the company that are both think tanks, as well as have accountability to resolve the issue. Our CIO made a statement and a statement which is our plan for the company, we will be compliant, by compliant — excuse me, compliant, we mean certified with year 2000 applications by the end of 1997 for all our mission critical. And then looking for mid-1998 for what would be the less mission critical aps. It was that kind of statement that really drove us to the point where we were able in the year to make progress.

Y2KI: And keeping to that schedule you would be way ahead of what, say the general industry is projecting as the target date of December 1998, so that the whole year of '99 could be spent testing.

IRENE DEC: Yes. One of the ways we looked at it was is to make this — taking a leadership in this position and being proactive, it actually allows us to reduce the risk, the risk of a last minute crisis, therefore really providing the best service to our customer. It's really saying we're customer focused and say, we're going to make this seamless to our customers, we're not going to let them see this, they will not be impacted.

Y2KI: That's great.

IRENE DEC: The funding was put in place, the commitment was put in place and the priority was given.

Y2KI: You know, 300 to 600 billion dollars is o hard for anyone to really conceptualize, could you bring that to into the Prudential world and let us know what the cost or budget is for your project?

IRENE DEC: Sure. Basically what we did at first as we got started last summer, one of our first steps was really is this a hype or a reality, and if it's a reality to Prudential, how much is it going to cost us. So what we did in the first quarter of '96 is actually assess, we sliced through our aps to make a decision as to what it was going to cost us and how bad is our problem. Our original estimates were based on what are the industry estimates which are anywhere from a .90 cent per line of code to a 1.50. Prudential has a portfolio of 120 million lines of code as an entire company, so we took that, I mean you could do your basic math there, right, and take it through.

Y2KI: Yes.

IRENE DEC: So we were estimating somewhere around 150 million dollars to solve the problem. Since then what we've done is put some aggressive newsman to cost reduction. By moving aggressively what we've really been able to do is kind of capture it before the price escalates.

Y2KI: Great.

IRENE DEC: By centrally managing it. One of my as the company year 2000 program manager is to track the entire project throughout the company, build best practices, et cetera.

Y2KI: Great. You know, I've got to cut you off, I'm sorry. But we'll talk more about this when we come back after the break, because this is something we really want to focus on.

IRENE DEC: Sure.

Y2KI: Thanks, Irene. You're listening to the Y2K Investor Show on Business Radio 730. We'll be back in just a few minutes.

Y2KI: And we continue now with the Y2K Investor Show. Once again, here is Tony Keyes and Ed Mulhall.

Y2KI: Thank you, Keith. And welcome back everyone. We're talking with Irene Dec, who is Program Director for the Prudential's Y2K program. We're going to spend just a few more minutes here talking about the cost of the project, which is what we left the first half speaking about. But then I want to shift over to John Vasquez, because John has put a lot of work into researching some of the other aspects of the impact on the financial community, the securities community. So we'll shift over there and I would be very interested to have you participate in that Irene.

IRENE DEC: Sure.

Y2KI: In the second half of the show I want to remind folks or let those folks know that just tuned in we're going to have Thomas Oleson on and Thomas just conducted a survey for IDC of 500 top executives and where they are in the year 2000 problem, and I think that will be very interesting. So Irene when we left you were bracketing for us the problem as you had scoped it out last year that you thought it maybe it would be somewhere as high as 150 million, but with aggressive cost reduction efforts you've been able to bring that down.

IRENE DEC: Yes, at this point we're at 100 million dollars for our portfolio which really includes our mainframe, midrange and distributor environments. With that we are managing the entire project with two key philosophies. And one is manage risk, look for opportunities and processes that we can bring in to reduce cost, and number two is really cost reduction, you know, tied to the risk.

Y2KI: Right.

IRENE DEC: I mean, this is, I think the key message on this, Tony, is this is truly a business problem, it isn't a technology problem, it's a technology solution and you've really got a drive it so that you really keep your customers seamless. One of our lines of business, which is Prudential Security, their committed in their targets dates, they've moved aggressively already. A good part of their portfolio is in fix, by fix meaning they are working on the compliance and have completed, and again, they are targeted for end of '97 to have that portfolio completely clean and fixed for year 2000.

Y2KI: Well, that's a great segway over to John. One of the points that is often forgotten as people think about this, and certainly not implying that you have, but I want to make this clear to our listeners. That no one is an island and I'm sure one of your concerns, even as you talk about your customers, is that it's very important for Prudential to get there, but also for everyone that Prudential interacts with. And John, you've taken a look at some of the entities within the financial community and have some words, I think, on that aspect of it.

JOHN VASQUEZ: Yes, Tony, you know, it is my industry so naturally I was a little concerned about how we're going to do because, I think, that, you know, if a mass consciousness all occurred at once, say in mid-1998 or 1999, I was in the business of October of '87 and I know what it's like to go through a bit of a panic. So I made an effort to call the NASD, I spoke to their chief of their year 2000 problem there. And I'd like to let you know how actually interconnected Wall Street is. You know, when you place an order with me, say at Prudential Securities or any member firm, your order goes from the firm, then it goes to the exchange, whether it's the NASD or the New York Stock Exchange or the American Stock Exchange, wherever you buying a security, from there it goes to the National Securities Clearing Corporation for Securities Clearing, from there the trade goes to DTC, the Depository Trust Corporation who then turns back and confirms it to the exchange upon which the security was purchased, which then finally confirms it back to the member firm. So we're talking about a link here for just buying a simple stock that goes through one, two, three, four different intermediaries. And one of the things that I found once, for instance, if Prudential Securities is put together and is fully compliant with the year 2000 problem and the NASD is fully compliant with the year 200 problem and all these other organizations are compliant, these programs have to be tested again and we have to work together. So that's, of course, the inter-relationship between these programs, so that's another big thing that everybody has kind of has to test. Another thing that I found out when I spoke with the NASD is just the — one of the biggest problems I understand is the manpower problem. This is an interesting comment that I got from Jack Samarias, who is the VP of Information Technology and he is responsible for the year 2000 fix throughout the NASD. And I said, what kind of personnel are you really going need for this, and he mentioned to me that at the peak they thought they would need 100 people to be working on this and I said, well, what is your staff now, and they presently have 10 full- time and 10-15 part-time. Well, what we're finding is maybe COBOL is an interesting occupation to go into, how quickly can you get a COBOL, how quickly can you learn COBOL, it's probably a good place to be in business for the next few years.

Y2KI: You had an interesting anecdote, I know you told me on the phone, I want to be sure it comes up. You spoke with someone else, I think, with Prudential, Bill Anderson, and he told you anecdote about someone who was on his staff.

Y2KI: Yes. He mentioned to me that one of his programmers who is a $50,000 dollar employee was hired away by, I think, it was Computer Horizons or a major firm and offered $150,000 dollars to go to work on one of the big New York banks. And that's a kind of thing we're seeing here. So it is, as Irene said, it's a management problem, it's not a technology problem, it's a manpower problem. So those are some of the interesting things that I found out. Naturally, everybody is starting to get busy on this. Prudential is, obviously, ahead of the pack. The NASD and the New York Stock Exchange appear to still be in the assessment program and will probably be moving towards 1998, 1999 fixes. The other thing I found, too, was this estimate that somebody said of a dollar per line of code, everybody that I talked to told me how many lines of code they had and it really almost corresponded exactly to a dollar a line of code. And I think a report that I recently read from J. P. Morgan expects that figure to escalate many times that size as people try to get this thing done at the last minute.

Y2KI: Just a point of clarification. Irene, the number we talked about with you was 100 million dollars and 120 million lines of code. I assumed, hopefully correctly, that that encompassed all of the companies in the Prudential family, is that right?

IRENE DEC: Yes, that's the entire Prudential with all lines of business, health care, Prudential Securities, life.

Y2KI: I think you got a cheap, Irene, by being there earlier.

IRENE DEC: Yes. Yes. Well, that's actually one of the comments that our CIO and Art Ryan stated, the reason we moved aggressively is as time moves the cost fix will increase because of what John said, lack of resources. So by moving aggressively you're actually able to kind of manage that cost somewhere around that dollar per code type estimate.

Y2KI: Well, that's really the area we want to focus on in the second half is investigating that, kind of

probing into that. John, did you have some more that you wanted to offer.

Y2KI: Yes, but I think we're coming off here in a few seconds.

Y2KI: Yes. In the second half, I want to remind everyone, we're going to talk with Thomas Oleson who conducted a survey of 500 top executives for IDC. He is going to have a unique perspective and kind of contrary to some of the things that we might have been saying here. So it will be interesting to have Thomas on and see what he has to say. Irene, thank you for sticking around, I'd appreciate that. We'll see you back here in just a few minutes.

Y2KI: You're listening to the Y2K Investor Show and we'll continue in just a few minutes.

(BREAK)

Y2KI: And we continue now with the second half of the Y2K Investor Show with Tony Keyes and Ed Mulhall.

Y2KI: Thank you, Keith. Welcome back everyone and for those just joining us, we're talking about the year 2000 problem and its implications for the individual investor. Today we've got a pretty interesting folks with us. Irene Dec has been kind enough to stay with us for the second hour — half hour of the show. And Irene is Program Director for the Prudential's company wide year 2000 effort. Here in the studio with me is my co-host, Ed Mulhall, and John Vasquez who is probably a familiar name to most of you because John is on WBZS quite often.

You know, I've got a personal history with John, he and I have been working together, he has been my broker now for over a year and it was John, in fact, who turned me onto Zitel and that was a very pleasant experience. That little — little idea had a lot of zeroes behind it for me and I want to thank you personally, John.

Y2KI: My pleasure, Tony.

Y2KI: John can be reached at (301) 961-0101 or at (800) 368-2704. Right now I'd like to introduce Thomas Oleson. Thomas, are you there?

THOMAS OLESON: Yes, I am. Can you hear me clearly?

Y2KI: Just great.

THOMAS OLESON: Wonderful.

Y2KI: Mr. Oleson conducted recently a survey of 500 top executives and the analysis was to determine the status of their respective Y2K programs and their perception of the problem, its cost, and it really hit the industry, I think, as kind of, kind of a grenade, if you will. It set off a lot of controversy and has led to a lot of discussion and I really appreciate, Thomas, your coming on the show today to talk with us about that.

THOMAS OLESON: Well, I'm happy to do so. The IDC — the company that represent is International Data Corporation which is well known for doing studies of this type, statistical studies that are research based and this is just one of the ongoing series of research projects that follow very strict guidelines for quality of research.

Y2KI: And IDC also is the parent of a number of publications in the industry.

THOMAS OLESON: Well the IDG, our parent company is the parent and computer — any of the computer magazines that have the name world in them are our –

Y2KI: Network World, Computer World –

THOMAS OLESON: And also CIO magazine. Computer-World, PC World, et cetera.

Y2KI: Great. I just think that's an important note because this is a company makes its living in this industry and certainly is highly credible. Well, let me just sort of layout why the results of your survey were controversial. In your summary, it pretty much indicated, at least at looking at the data and one point of view that everything was under control, that the CIO, CEOs felt as though their company would certainly make it on time, the cost was manageable and, in fact, some cases minimized the threat to their business. That was a surprise, so maybe you want to comment on that, because maybe it was a surprise to you as well.

THOMAS OLESON: Well, it was. I have been following fairly closely the year 2000 for the past year and I expected that the results would come back with a lot of concern. And when they came back differently then that I sat back and thought about it — now my background is that of being an IS executive at a very large company, and so I've been there and done that in a number of roles within the IS organization. And I began to think back on how areas are run, such as Irene's at Prudential, I happened to have been at one of her competitors. But the nature of the process is one where things are under control and if they are not under control they get a great deal of management attention right from the top of the house down. The type of concern that these people showed, you know, we asked them about what would happen to their company if the year 2000 problem was not solved in a timely manner on the financial health company, its competitive position, the customers, and the company, and its business partners. And they showed a good deal of concern there, but most of the concern was shown by the CIOs on an overall. But when you look at the six vertical industries that we studied here, there were differences and banks and insurance companies and investment houses had a much higher concern for their customers then the manufacturing companies and utilities. And so you do get some differences. And I don't want to say that this is not a problem. As I say in my very opening paragraph, this problem is big, it's the biggest maintenance project to hit IS, but it is manageable and the industry as a whole has the problem under control. Now if you think about industry, you think about companies that are very profitable that know how to meet challenges and who adjust to the challenges. I think that this problem began back in about 1993 with the opening shot being Peter de Jaeger's piece in Computer World in September. And I found companies that started right then on it. There was an options clearing house out in Chicago that started the project immediately in the fall of 1993 and completed by the beginning of 1995.

Y2KI: Tom, let me ask — this is Ed Mulhall, let me ask you a couple of questions concerning the makeup of the survey. You suggest in here that you had a total of 500 participants and you had the breakdown between CEOs, CIOs, and CFOs. First question I have, were these folks self-selecting in that you asked a wide range of people and these are the people that responded, or did you go out and solicit these people individually?

THOMAS OLESON: Now this was a blind call, it was run by a research house that we use quite often. And what we did is supply them with a list of companies that had 1995 revenues of more than 100 million dollars. So that the first cut-off was if they did not have something like that then they — then they were cut-off. And then they had to be one of six industries, either investment, banks, insurance or the manufacturing, utilities, or communications industries. Those were particularly chosen because of their sensitivity to the year 2000. There are other industries — we did not go into Government and Government is a big problem and we recognize that.

Y2KI: Now did — I'm not clear yet, did they ask a whole bunch of people and everyone they asked responded, or was it this is the 500 that would responded. No. They did have some refusals. The number of refusals were fairly, fairly small. There were, I believe, eight CEOs who refused to participate because they had already solved the problem.

Y2KI: Okay.

THOMAS OLESON: And then there were about 11 that didn't — didn't for some other reason, there were some that had outsourced the problems or — and they just felt they were not in position to respond. But that was the CFO and CEO response. I have the actual, the client, because they didn't know about the problem well enough to talk about it, there six CEOs and two CFOs. There were a 100 in the survey — there were declines because the job was all done and this just didn't have anything to say, 11 CEOs and 8 CFO's and then because they had outsourced, one CEO said I don't have anything to say, we outsourced our whole IS operation and four CFOs said that.

Y2KI: Question of anonymity, were these folks assured that whatever they told you, told your surveyors

that they would not be associated with their companies.

THOMAS OLESON: That is correct. Their answers were put into a statistical mix. But we did at the end and ask them if they wanted an executive summary and I did fax down an executive summary to you folks. Each one of the participants was mailed one of those yesterday. So — I'm sorry, not each one of the participants, each one of the participants who identified themselves at the end and asked then received one. And there were, out of the 500, actually there were 503 total and 375 did ask for copies of the results.

Y2KI: Irene, I'd like you to comment on this question because my conjecture is that this sort of gets at the heart of the problem. When you look deeply into these number, and I think you even made this comment, Thomas.

THOMAS OLESON: Yes.

Y2KI: The closer you get to the problem, to the trenches, then the concern increases, the appreciation for the scope of the problem and its impact on the business increases. In fact, you can see it just at the CEO or at the — excuse me, the officer level between the CEO and the CIO. The CIO is consistently more concerned and less optimistic, if you will, if you just put that name on it then the CEO. And to my way of thinking this is the nature of the problem. And, Irene, I think you are uniquely positioned to comment on this.

IRENE DEC: Sure.

Y2KI: I'm concerned that the CEO has a bigger problem then he appreciates.

IRENE DEC: Okay. Let's start with a couple of the questions. One is that first it is a business impact and there is no question in some organizations or some companies today knowing that their development environments were including with a century code, et cetera, feel they really don't have a problem. But the next word that I think is real critical is risk. If companies don't implement processes to eliminate the risk and truly prove it's not a problem, they really at risk to be out of business. I mean, you know, you hear what the industry states, 15 to 20 percent of the companies that live today, exist today will not do business beyond the year 2000. And some of the thing that I think companies need to do as something that we've built in and that is a certification process. Even though we have compliant aps and we know, you know, their fine, you know, they have the century, we can live with that. What we're doing is requiring stringent testing that exists before the year 2000 and beyond year 2000, so the testing and certification process — because a lot of it is, even though you may have that in place where your data is so formed that it has century, it may not be populated.

Y2KI: You know, we're going to have to go off now for just a minute or two. We'll come back and I'd like to discuss this a little further, because it's a very interesting aspect of this subject. You're listening to the Y2K Investor on WBZS AM 730. Please join us in a few moments and we're going to continue this interesting discussion with Irene Dec and Thomas Oleson.

(BREAK)

Y2KI: And we continue now with the final segment of the Y2K Investor Show with Tony Keyes and Ed Mulhall.

Y2KI: Hello folks, welcome back. We've been having a lively discussion. I think it's even going to get more interesting here in the last segment of the show. We have today with us Thomas Oleson, who is an analyst with International Data Corporation. And Thomas conducted a survey of 500 top executives recently asking questions about the status of their year 2000 project to try to ascertain where U.S. business was with this problem and what their perception was. We also have on the line Irene Dec, who is Program Director from the Prudential's Y2K program, an enormous company. And Irene told us earlier in the program that they have actually spent or plan to spend about 100 million dollars to fix the problem for the Prudential suite of companies. What we were talking about right before the break was the issue of the complexity of the problem and the distance between the CEO and the worker bees and what, if in that distance is a disconnection and the potential that there is a greater problem then the CEO perceives, and therefore it may not be addressed as aggressively as it needs to be, the funds may not be allocated, et cetera. So we're going to have to referee this because Irene and Thomas can't actually here one another very well. So, Irene, if you wouldn't mind both the data that you have personally and what you understand from the industry about the risks of businesses that might not get there by the year 2000 and then we'll go to Thomas and find out what his data is showing.

IRENE DEC: Yes. From an industry perspective some of the, you know, research companies that have been taking a look at it from a business perspective, they have stated that approximately 15 to 20 percent of the companies may not be in business after year 2000. And it really kind of covers two areas, one is that they were not able to afford to fix the problem, or two, they really did not manage it from a risk perspective and validate it. Again, it's kind of the process where Prudential is validating it through an official certification process through very detailed steps of how you validate and test, you know, in the year before and the year after 2000. And companies that who really ended up calculating information on dates and end up with incorrect data that impacts their customers. The latest number two that you hear from an industry perspective, and again, these are industry numbers that you can gather up from some of the research firms are things like litigation potential could be up to a trillion. You know, and you hear that and read that stuff from, you know, the research firm. Actually, I don't know if Thomas can hear me, but I find the results real — I think they are real important, I think surveys on this have really proven some facts. And one, I think it's great to hear that 11 out of the 100 or 500 actually show is done, I think that's real good to see. I think the CEO stating that, it's good to see that the industry is moving on it and understands its seriousness. But I think we've got probably about 90 percent of the rest of what we need to look at as companies and say, you know, really where are they at. Sometimes what companies don't realize is that not until they real get — you know, roll up their sleeves and get down, you know, up to the mud, up to their needs, do they realize the impact. So that's why aggressive movement becomes more important.

Y2KI: Before we go over to you Thomas, I want to give you equal air time on this. I do want to state again, I said this before the break, but I want to help people understand it. The world wide financial economy is an organism. No entity or country operates independent of any other. And so this really is an international business problem, an international management problem. And solving the problem here on U.S. soil does not mean that we're all going to be okay. It has to be a cooperative effort internationally or we'll still be in trouble. In fact, John point out earlier, in a specific example of a single trade on the stock exchange, the number of different entities that has to move through. Well, on an international basis we have countless transactions that happen every day that go through multiple systems around the globe. So at some point, it hasn't happened yet, but at some point we all have to come to agreement on who is going to win here, is it going to be the NC standard or the ISO standard for year 2000 compliance, because the vary. The EU has its own standards that it is going to want to promote. So it's a very complex problem. But you had some specific data, I think, that came out of your survey, Thomas, that indicated that it probably wouldn't be as dire as perhaps some of the other data or surveys are showing.

THOMAS OLESON: That's right. We — we have an econometric model that we've worked on for a number of years here that has been very accurate in terms of estimating the demand side of spending in a number of areas. And we have put our data through this econometric model and what I'm about to say has not been published yet, so that you folks listening in are hearing it for the first time. We expect the U.S. spending on the year 2000 problem now to be in the 50 billion dollar range. Most of that will be in the area of software and services and the services company and the software companies in this are going to do exceedingly well. There is some hardware spending also. Now because we track world wide spending a lot, we know that the U.S. software spending is 44 percent of the world spending, 44.1 percent if you want to get really precise. And the U.S. services spending is about 46 percent of world wide spending. So extrapolating and that's dangerous to do because you shouldn't really extrapolate beyond the model that you're in, but I would — I would say that roughly world wide the spending for IS expenses, now this is not litigation expenses, but IS expenses would be in the say 109 to 114 billion dollar range. Now that's significantly less, but it is fact based on what people are budgeting and what they are spending in the six areas of industry that we have — that we have measured and then bringing it from those six industries to all industries –

Y2KI: Thomas.

THOMAS OLESON: I'm sorry, I'm going to have to interrupt you.

Y2KI: Okay.

THOMAS OLESON: But I'd like to invite you both back later on the show, another date because it's information that is really vital to our listeners. So I'd like to invite you now, I'll follow-up with you and we'll set that up. Folks, you have been listening to the Y2K Investor on WBZS AM 730. Thank you for joining us. We're here Monday's and Friday's, Monday's at 11:30 to 12:00 and Friday's from 11:00 to noon. Please join us.

Guest: CONGRESSMAN STEVEN HORN
Date: FRIDAY, JANUARY 10, 1997

Y2KI: Today we're joined by Congressman Steven Horn of the 38th District in California. And before I bring the Congressman on I'll do a short bio. And at that risk of someone reaching his age being called distinguished, I hope I don't offend him, but it is a very distinguished career. Undergraduate degree from Stamford, Masters degree from Harvard, and PHD from Stamford and has been an assistant to Senator Thomas Kurchell (phonetic sp.) and also a fellow at the Brookings Institute, and a Dean at American University, a member of the U.S. Commission on Civil Rights, and the President of California, University of California at Long Beach for, it looks to be almost 18 years. Was elected to the House in 1992 from the 38th District. Welcome,

Congressman Horn.

CONGRESSMAN HORN: Well, it's a pleasure to be on your show.

Y2KI: I really appreciate your coming on. And while all of that is very important, I think the key to your involvement in this show is the chairmanship of the Government sub-committee on Government Management, Information, and Technology. And your committee has been one of the first to recognize the year 2000 issue. Can you tell us when you first became personally aware of the problem?

CONGRESSMAN HORN: Early last year my staff had been pursuing some of the issues that were coming up in technology and that seem to be a major one that not many people had paid attention to. We had about 53 different hearings in the last Congress and so we scheduled this one for April of '96 and it was fascinating in terms of the impact. Many people that should have heard of it that would be affected by it had never heard of the problem, I'm talking now about Chief Executives and others who hadn't really been informed by their technical staff or what we now call the

Chief Information Officer in various Federal agencies. So we started pursuing it on a bi-partisan basis with a questionnaire to find out just where were the agencies in this. Some Cabinet Officers as I suggested never heard of it. Some were working on it and Social Security gets the top star, probably an A+ for working on the problem since 1989. And the problem as you know is that 30 years ago, 25 years ago computers just didn't have much storage capacity, so somebody had the bright idea, well, let's just put the last two digits of the year in and forget the 19 business. The problem comes when you hit the year 2000 and its 00, and the computer doesn't know what it's doing at that point. Now what does it matter, because there are hundreds of millions of dates that guide many activities of the Federal Government, be it a maintenance schedule, be it eligibility for social security, be it eligibility for various tax breaks based on age. And if the computer systems go haywire in the year 2000 because a 00 pops up and they don't have the four digit year, we have a lot of trouble. And Gardner Associates, a rather respected group testified before us, they thought it was a 600 billion, that's billion with "B", billion dollar problem world-wide and we're half the computing. In the United States, that's a 300 billion problem and they thought the Federal Government might have a 30 billion problem. So we started looking into it, framed some questions, about 13 different ones, boiled down to four categories and then we graded these various agencies as to where they were. We ended up with four A's, since I'm a former university professor, in fact, on leave as one. Three B's, oh, a handful of C's and everybody else was the D and the F. And so

Y2KI: No, curve was used then.

CONGRESSMAN HORN: We got their attention, no curve. I never — I graded on an absolute as a professor and I'm grading the Federal agencies on an absolute.

Y2KI: Good for you.

CONGRESSMAN HORN: And we got their attention. And I talked, in fact, to the Director of OMB yesterday, Mr.

Raines (phonetic sp.), who is a very able person and he came in about the fall, in September or so, and he came out of experience in the private sector and he could see it was a problem. So he and his staff followed up and did a further survey and I reviewed that last week. And it's got their attention. And now that some of the Chief Information Officers are in place, hopefully, they can get on the top of the problem. And when the President submits his budget in early February, there will be response in that budget to try and deal with that problem. Now is it adequate, we don't know, because that budget is confidential until it's submitted to the Congress and then it's open to everybody.

Y2KI: What — what role do you think Congress, the U.S. Government is going to have to play to make sure that the problem is solved before the year 2000?

CONGRESSMAN HORN: Well, I think one of the problems we have here is that 30 years ago when somebody had the idea of how to save this inventory space, if you will, in your database, I think the problem has been that they thought technology would come around to solve it by the year 2000. At this point, technology is not solving it, but you've got a simply laboriously review the code lines in your database, identify the date situation and develop and use new software and, of course, with the tremendous capacity, even personal computers have nowadays, get that converted to a four digit year. Now during the hearings we asked the Information Technology Association of America to sort of try at being a good housekeeping seal of approval. The General Services Administration which purchases for the Federal Government has said that all software will now have to be 2000 year compliant. In other words, the four digit year. But nobody has the magic wand yet, so it's a very laborious project and that's why Social Security which would affect the most people and you'd have the phones ringing off the hooks in Congressional District offices, where is my check, at which we do sometimes now anyhow, Social Security began on this in 1989. They hope to have the files cleaned up by 1998. The stock market, they've begun on it. A number of Governors, Governor Ridge in Pennsylvania, Governor Wilson in California have led the pack in getting their own state Government to that year 2000 compliant. Governor Wilson bought off one of the top people in Massachusetts, took him out there, made him a member of the cabinet, and so he has the voice for technology and the impact on Government in the state of California, which is the second largest Government in the United States, they can now talk to their fellow cabinet members and get their attention. In terms of the budget implications, and I mentioned this to Mr. Raines the other day, I have said from the beginning, don't come to us and expect a lot of money out of us. Face up to it right now, get yourself organized, appoint someone in charge of the project and start reprogramming money that you always have at the end of fiscal year. And so and I think the Director agrees with me on that and we'll just have to wait to see what the President's budget says as to the degree to which money must be put up in this coming fiscal year, which is fiscal year '98 that begins on October 1, 1997.

Y2KI: Well, Congressman let me interrupt you right there. We're going to have to go to the first break and I'd like to follow-up on that when we come back. You're listening to the Y2K Investor on WBZS. If you have calls for Congressman Horn, you can call us on (202) 289-7730, that's if you have a question. It's (202) 289-7730.

(BREAK)

Y2KI: And we continue with more of the Y2K Investor Show. Our guest this morning is Congressman Steven Horn. Once again here is our co-hosts, Tony Keyes and Ed Mulhall.

Y2KI: Thank you, Keith. Welcome back everyone. This is Tony Keyes and Ed Mulhall is here with me this morning. Congressman, just to follow-up on the topic that you were finishing with there in terms of budget dollar, one of the issues that we've been concerned about in analyzing the problem that even if you accepted enough money will be there and so let's just assume that whatever is needed will be available to the Government, our concern is that since globally everyone will be competing for a common resource within a very short window of time now at this late date that that, in fact, will be the difficulty, the long pull in the tent in terms of getting there on time. Did your committee look at that problem at all?

CONGRESSMAN HORN: Absolutely, this would have been in my next point. The resource allocation and scarcity is a major problem, and that's why we urged the Federal Government last year to start put together responsibility with an individual, develop the plan, make an assessment of the cost, and the human resources. And that's — you're exactly right. As everybody wakes up about this, people that have had some experience in looking at these lines of codes, dealing with the conversion are going to be very scarce and the price for their time and their expertise is going to be rising proportionately. So that is a major problem.

Y2KI: One way to potential relieve that would be to raise consciousness in the commercial environment well above where it is today. I think you've also heard in the testimony that came before your committee that the commercial sector was really no better off than the Government in terms of awareness and having attacked this problem at all. There has been some improvement over the last eight to twelve months, but the commercial sector is still far behind and there is still a lack of awareness and people taking the problem seriously. Any thought to the Government stepping up a campaign to just raise awareness, because if that were done and the commercial sector got on this problem immediately, there is the potential that they could get to a point where they would consume the resource they require serially ahead of the Government and then there might be room for everybody to get the thing done?

Y2KI: Well, the stock market and the financial market people are very well aware and have been working very hard on this.

And they have assured us that they are okay, they are going to be compliant. So you're probably right, the average personal computer and others that might be affected in a minor way they might not have gotten the word yet. Although I must say, for the computer high tech industry there has been a tremendous number of articles on this and I think we are getting the attention. Now my colleague in the Senate, Senator Monaghan wrote me a note a month or so ago that said, how about let's getting a commission to be on this and they could make a report within months with all that publicity. Well looking at it from the Federal Government's stand, I thought a commission would just be a duplication of effort, because what's needed is management leadership. And one of my gripes about the Office of Management and Budget has been regardless of Administration, is that the budget problems are so great that they drive out people's discussion of management, and how you organize, and how you solve some of these problems. And that structural problem of responsibility, time tables, use of resources in a prudent manner, that's what the management side has to do. And I think they have finally faced up to it in the Federal Government with a new director.

Y2KI: That's an excellent point. A lot of people equate this situation to things we've experienced in the past like the mobilization after Pearl Harbor and the czar that was empowered to build our capability to respond. And then the obvious difference between a committee as you say, and that kind of leadership, it's a wide gap, and the committee is often lacking in terms of their ability to really get anything done. So I'm encouraged to hear that OMB is stepping up to it.

Y2KI: Congressman, one of the complaints we often here from the commercial sector is the potential tax treatment that's been proposed that allow any expenses incurred correcting this problem will have to be treated just that way as expense and hit the bottom line in the year it's incurred, and they would like to see a more favorable tax treatment. Is there any discussion about doing that in your committee or a more appropriate committee?

CONGRESSMAN HORN: Well, we don't have jurisdiction on that, the committee on Ways and Means does and obviously any tax benefits they give means one of two things, that either they are detracting from closing the deficit gap, or number two they are in competition with about 150 other forms of reduced taxation that people would like to have. The two big ones, being the charitable donations, which everybody wants to protect on capital hill, and the home interest payment on the mortgage deduction, that I think everyone wants to save on capital hill. So this year you're going to have a very extensive discussion in Ways and Means of not only the theoretical proposals to change the tax laws, such as the Chairman, who is probably one of our finest legislators here and I admired him because he is the only Chairman of Ways and Mean, Chairman Archer that never took any political action committee money, nobody else can make that statement.

Y2KI: Congressman, we're running out of time. It went very quickly. A couple things, I want to first thank you for coming on and I want to invite you to come on again. And maybe in the last 30 seconds, could you tell us what we can expect out of your committee in the next couple of months?

CONGRESSMAN HORN: Well, in the next couple of months we will go — after we see the budget we'll go back and make sure that what they are saying in the budget is accurate and if the agencies have not responded, we will raise the heat level by having in all the key people in a hearing, and that's one way we try to get everybody's attention.

Y2KI: Well, thank you very much, Congressman Horn, it's been a great pleasure having you on board, hope to speak to you again soon. You're listening to the Y2K Investor on WBZS. We'll be back after the break.

(END)

Guest: STEVE WHITEMAN — President Viasoft Corp.
Date: MONDAY, NOVEMBER 18, 1996

Y2KI: We're very pleased this morning to have Steve Whiteman, the President and CEO of Viasoft online. Are you there Steve?

STEVE WHITEMAN: Yes, I am, Ed.

Y2KI: Very good. Thanks so much for joining us. One of the things I wanted to get to right away so that we give you adequate time to respond if you are so inclined, would be Friday's heard on the street column in the Wall Street Journal. Do you have any comment on that?

STEVE WHITEMAN: Well, I saw the article clearly on Friday morning about, about our stock and our stock has done very well this year, I think we are the number one stock, certainly on the NASDAQ for the year and probably the entire market in terms of growth. And I think it was just an article that questions, you know, can a company keep growing and can a stock keep performing as well as it has performed. And early in the day clearly we were down. We came back some towards the end of the day. But we believe, you know, the year 2000 market certainly is a good market for us, but it's not the only that we do. We had a good business before year 2000. We'll have a very good business, we believe, beyond year 2000. In fact last week, we announced an acquisition of a company from Germany, Arano Software Company (phonetic sp.) that clearly will help us position ourselves and get ready for technology, providing technology and services beyond year 2000, in addition to what we already do today. So I guess my own opinion was perhaps, the article was maybe a little bit unfair and didn't really dig and find out what was really going on here at Viasoft.

Y2KI: Yes. Well, Steve, let me ask you another question, then, because one of the issues that always comes up when we're talking about the year 2000 is this — this notion that a lot of the companies that are involved are sort of going to fall off the face of the earth when the problem is theoretically solved. And one of the things that keeps on coming up is what is your game plan in terms of leveraging any year 2000 out into the future.

STEVE WHITEMAN: Okay. Just a comment or two here in this area, certainly a very good questions and we do get asked it quite a bit, is before our first — let me just backup a little bit. Before the year 2000 issue ever came on the marketplace we were just growing as a company roughly in that 28 to 30 percent per year growth rate and we were starting to grow a little bit faster, and this is before the year 2000 ever came on the market. We went public before the year 2000 issue arose as an issue in the marketplace. So we clearly had a strong business, a strong financial model before the year 2000 hit. Now the year 2000 opportunities are natural for us. It fits in with our technology and the things we are capable of doing very nicely. But to us the year 2000 is really a great way to get a lot of new accounts going. And the last year and a half, well over our license revenue business has come from brand new accounts. So we're using the year 2000 quite — especially as a way to get a foundation going, to get established into a number of very, very large accounts, financial institutions, credit card companies, insurance companies, manufacturing companies, Government installations, whatever it is around the world. And from there we're working to help those organizations do other thing. The year 2000 gives us a great ability to get in and help these organizations understand the large applications that run their business much more effectively than they have done in the past. And from there we can help them do whatever they want to with those systems, whether it be migrating them to new architectures, like a client server environment, or implementing new packages, like an SAP or a bond application package, or Peoplesoft, whatever it happens to be, or to just improve the quality of the maintenance of those environments. So clearly we believe year 2000 is a great opportunity to get a lot of business the next couple of years, get into a lot of new accounts, but clearly we're positioning ourselves to do a lot more with those accounts once we've helped them solve their year 2000 issues.

Y2KI: Okay. Michael, you want to jump in here.

Y2KI: Hi, Steve, it's Michael Tantleff, Prudential Securities. How are you?

Y2KI: Michael, yes, doing real well.

Y2KI: Good. I want to focus on the year 2000, you know, Gardner Group has said it's going to be 400 to 600 billion and now I'm hearing a $1.57 a line and all this talk about, you know, the article in the paper pretty much said, while it's going to be a big issue, it's not going to be a really big issue. An IDC Conference this weekend I read a text of it that saying that most companies are now aware of the year 2000 and are taking, and they believe that they are going to be compliant. You know, the way I see it is that there is this whole bunch of money needs to be spent and people really haven't stepped up to the plate and spent it. They bought a little of the type of stuff that you do in terms of figuring out what they have, but —

STEVE WHITEMAN: Right.

Y2KI: But we haven't even begun to do this. What's the — what's your sense of the marketplace and the attitude of the clients, and as to the ultimate resolution of this?

STEVE WHITEMAN: There are clearly are a number of accounts that have been very aggressive over the last year, year and a half at trying to solve this problem. And, you know, I won't mention specific names but, you know, some of the big banks and credit card processors have, you know, really gone after it very hard to get in and understand what the problem is and really are down the road to making the changes that needed to be made to make sure that they are year 2000 compliant in plenty of time, you know, to meet the January 1, 2000, you know, deadline.

Y2KI: But the big money has not yet been spent or contracts let yet?

STEVE WHITEMAN: Right. But a lot — but the truth is a lot of companies have gotten as far as, I think, we would have predicted. And I know people, even the Congress, believe is somewhat disappointed that the market has taken off faster than it has because logic says that a typical Fortune 1000 should be in the middle of making the year 2000 changes today and many are not. Many — most of them are aware of the problem or aware that there is a potential problem within their organization, but many of them have not really gotten into understand how severe a problem they have. The people that are most afraid of this issue are the people that have looked at it the most within their organization. The more you look, the more you realize you've got some serious problems. And —

Y2KI: So what do you think it's going to take for a concerted effort on the part of companies to start spending the money. Coca-Cola said they took a 55 million dollar after tax charge buried in their earnings report, but they really probably haven't spent dollar one in fixing yet.

STEVE WHITEMAN: Well, you know, I can't speak specifically about Coke, though, you know, they are beginning to spend dollar one in the area, and we've seen a few companies take a big write off in anticipation of this year 2000 issue. But I think what it's going to take, quite frankly, people at the lower levels in the organization and mid-level management within the information technology organization, they are becoming aware of the issue and many of them are becoming fairly panicked. But as they try and drive it up the organization each layer gets a little bit buffered, a little bit more buffered from the seriousness of this problem. And it's going to take a lot of money in a large organizations, it's going to take 10, 20, 30 million in some of the large companies and even more to fix this problem. What it's going to take is for senior management, the CEOs, people in the Board room, the CFOs to really realize that they've got a serious problem, and quite frankly that they have a liability as senior executives to get this problem fixed. And I do think that some of the audit firms are starting to get into the picture here. We've talked to many of the audit firms, the big six firms, and a couple of them now are going to make their clients aware of this issue, they are going to make it a part of their management letter in discussions with these organizations, large organizations, that they really need to begin to address this year 2000 issue. So it's really not an audit issue for — this last years numbers or anything, but I think they are going to make it an issue as they tell this to the senior management's, to the Boards, to the CEOs and I think that's what it's going to take to really drive the amounts of money that are going to be required for companies to get real serious about this problem.

Y2KI: Steve, let me ask you a question, maybe help explain what to me is an apparent contradiction in Viasoft and several other company strategies, and that is that on the one hand you seem to have a very impressive list of teaming agreements and Var agreements (phonetic sp.) where you're teaming with some of the larger system integrators and body shops, the like, and on the other the explanation of your long term strategy that suggest you're going to want to partner and become essential to these large corporations.

STEVE WHITEMAN: Right.

Y2KI: How do you reconcile the two?

STEVE WHITEMAN: Right. Yes, I think what you're referring to is potential loss of control by turning over —

Y2KI: Right.

STEVE WHITEMAN: A lot of our activity to the — our solutions providers and we have embarked on very aggressive program to get consulting firms, system integrators, people like Anderson Consulting Team, CTA, a number of others working with us, you know, to provide services and actually help sell the solution into the marketplace. Well, a couple things there, one is on these teaming situations, almost every one of them we're directly involved. So we do have some level of involvement directly with the customer, either from a sales perspective and/or from a delivery perspective. We do have some people involved in the effort. Though we don't have enough bodies to do all the work, you know, but we'd like to have somebody there to help monitor this situation and provide subject matter expertise. So I think in one way that we're kind of helping ourselves and buffering ourselves from the solution providers and losing control is the fact that we are closely involved in virtually every situation out there with our solution providers, just not to the same level that they are involved. The second thing though, is that our solution providers for the most part see the year 2000 very much like we see the year 2000. It's a great opportunity for the next three to four years, but it really is to them a foundation for establishing a long term relationship, you know, with those organizations. So they clearly want to work with us on some of our other strategies, some of our transition strategies, helping move some of these applications to a client server architecture, integrating the intranets into the picture, or to implementing packages as a part of it. So I think that our long term strategy fits very nicely with our solution providers long term strategy in most cases. And I think we'll have long term relationships with these firms as we continue to evolve our strategy beyond the year 2000.

Y2KI: Yes, what's your current head count and how far, how large do you predict you'll growth let's say two or three years out?

STEVE WHITEMAN: Well, you know, we've not given a lot of financial projections in terms of how big we'll grow as a company. We're about a little over 300 people in the company right now and that has grown. And a lot of the growth has come in the development area or the services area within the company. Development clearly we're trying to develop more technologies for year 2000 and beyond. And clearly on the services side, we need additional people to help support our solution providers, as well as, you know, help do the engagements that we are leading as project leaders. So we will continue to grow the company and, you know, we've grown very nicely as a company. The last couple of quarters we were up 66 percent last quarter, 61 percent the quarter before. For this last fiscal year we were up over 40 percent, that's July 1 to June 30 fiscal year. So we've seen some good growth and I think the analysts are expecting that we'll continue to grow at similar paces, similar growth rates probably the next couple of years.

Y2KI: Okay. We're going to a break now. Anyone who has call for Steve, give us a call on (202) 289-7730. We'll be back after the news.

(BREAK)

Y2KI: We continue now with the Y2K Investor Show, your host this afternoon, Ed Mulhall discussing the year 2000 computer bug and related investment opportunities. And now here is your host, Ed Mulhall.

Y2KI: Thank you, Jim. We're speaking with Steve Whiteman, the President and CEO of Viasoft Corporation and Michael Tantleff of Prudential Securities in Santa Barbara. And now we're joined by Alan Simpson of Comlinks. Good morning, Alan.

Y2KI: Good morning, Ed.

Y2KI: How are things, any news to report?

Y2KI: Oh yes, it's that time of year again. In every looming crisis there are those who want to profit by claiming it's all of hoax, and this time of year seems to bring them out. It's not really as serious as the media claims, and they've all got reports to sell. It's very easy to prepare the questionnaire so that you get the answer you want to hear. Ask the political pollsters in Washington, they are masters at the game. The other method is just to ask naive questions and I hope last Thursday's report from IDC, which is the International Data Corporations comes from the naive question category. This report has just sent shockwaves of disbelief to the information technology community. They claim in their survey of 503 executives that there was no problem and the corporations are well on their way to fixing the date fields and the report goes onto criticize the media for generating hype on the year 2000. So it's been a week of they just don't get it. A good example is the Wall Street Journal (indiscernible) and I'm sure you've talked about this with Viasoft. It would take many years to convert all these computer programs and archives. It will not all end on January 2, 2000. Suddenly these consumer interviews, which most of them are, they are from the consumer computer industry believes that all it takes to fix any computer program is a 49.95 package from the local computer retailer. The sheer size of this problem, Ed, has not yet hit home.

Y2KI: Alan. What's your comments on the article on Friday out of London quoting a David Atkinson, an MP who is going to draft a law that will force British companies to correct the year 2000?

Y2KI: Okay. We're all — in fact this Thursday we fly over to London for two weeks, so we're going to be interviewing as many of these people as possible for this show as you well know. It's like Congress, anybody can put forward legislation. The chance of it getting on the bill are very, very slim. It's an election period and the UK election system isn't like the U.S. one. The Prime Minister can call it at any time within a five year period. He's ready to call it, we believe, in March, April of next year. So he'll announce it very shortly. The conservatives seem as though they are going to low, so keep in mind there is a lot of election airing going on. This is a high profile issue over there. Robin Guerney who is head of their task force has spent a lot of time and effort and being very successful. The electorate are fully aware of 2000. The next government will have to fix it. So there is a lot — we've got the answer, hey, we're going to make people fix it, you want software, keep that in mind.

Y2KI: Alan, do you have any questions for our guest Steve Whiteman.

Y2KI: I'm sure you've covered all the points with —

Y2KI: I'd like to ask another question, Ed.

Y2KI: Sure, go ahead, Michael.

Y2KI: Well, anyway, Steve, Viasoft clearly has the best tools in helping corporations evaluate and do impact studies on what they have. I'm sure you're looking at the next level of automation which is actually helping fix and change the problem itself.

STEVE WHITEMAN: Right.

Y2KI: What search engines have you looked at, the MatriDigm and Forcross (phonetic sp.) and other companies like that and would be considering adding to your portfolio of tools?

STEVE WHITEMAN: Right. Yes, we believe very strongly that there is three levels. There is really three things that need to be done and I think one you didn't really talk about today, I think is worth mentioning. The first thing certainly is doing the impact and we clearly have very strong technology to help people really understand the size and scope of the problem that they do have, or at least potential problem that they need to take a look at. The second phase though, which we believe is probably the most important phase is if you go into a large, you know, Fortune 1000 organization, they will have many millions of lines of code in their application portfolio and it's very complex, very complicated. Most shops don't really know what they have, that's part of the problem. And the biggest challenge and the biggest most — perhaps most important part of this year 2000 conversion is to put together a plan. How do you go about making the changes to the code, and how do you isolate code from other pieces of code so you have minimum impact on the production environment. And so the planning process is very important and that is clearly something that we do and have done for a good number of organizations now. The third phase clearly is in the making of the changes, the conversion itself, and then testing of the changes. And, you know, we clearly have tools here, we have already done this for a number of organizations. We have actually acquired some bridging technology which will help to support certain types of data, archive data. A lot of companies have tapes that they've saved of many years of data. Well nobody wants to go back and make changes to that code. We can support that code without any change. So we have some technology there and clearly we have technology on the testing side. But our strategy is to support multiple conversion strategies. As we've gotten into this year 2000 issue, it's very complex for a lot of organizations and there is not just one conversion strategy that's going to work for every application. So we have looked and we have talked to and we're doing work with a number of, you know, "change players", mass change players, automated change players in the marketplace. None of them are a silver bullet by any means, but they — but many of them do have value and they can speed up a lot of the change process. And that would be people like Paradus (phonetic sp.) out there or an Alydar (phonetic sp.), MatriDigm is new to the scene. They are in the beta test process, so it's hard to know exactly what they have, but they clearly are a potential player out there in this market as well. And clearly part of our strategy is to support these mass change players and help a company, a Fortune 1000 organization through the impact, through the plan, help them figure out which is the best way to make the changes, because they all do it a little differently and it may not be the same for every company in terms of the right way to do it. And then we'll bring it back and help that firm, the organization test the changes and put it back in a production environment. So we see some good looking technology out there from these players that plays in a role in the year 2000. And clearly part of our strategy is to partner with these players and that would be the MatriDigm's and the Alydar's and the Paradus, those are the three that come to mind right away.

Y2KI: Well, we've exhausted our time allotment again and want to thank Steve Whiteman, President and CEO of Viasoft Corporation. Also Michael Tantleff, Prudential Securities in Santa Barbara, at 1-800-368-9370. Alan, looking forward

to talking with you on Friday and have a great trip to the UK I want to thank everyone for listening, we'll be back on Friday. And this is the Y2K Investor on WBZS. Thank you.
(END)

Guest: STEVE MCMANUS — BankBoston, Communications Director, Year 2000 Program
Date: FRIDAY, JANUARY 31, 1997

Y2KI: This morning we have a very interesting guest from Bank Boston, Steven McManus. Steven is the Communications Manager for Bank Boston's Millennium Project Team 2000. In his role he is dedicated for promoting the understanding nature and scope and complexity of the banks millennium challenge. He's also responsible for internal and external awareness, as well as securing the cooperation of many business partners, both technical and non-technical to achieve the banks goal of interrupted customer service into and beyond the year 2000. Recently he also helped establish the Boston Millennium Association, a local users group that was formed to share best practices. Steven are you there?

Y2KI: Nope.

Y2KI: Excuse me. Steven will be joining us later in the program. But I'd like to kick this off by talking about a subject that came up this week in the Wall Street Journal. You probably saw and perhaps many publications. And then there was also an article leading off on the New York Times front page, I believe today. It has to do with the Internal Revenue Service. And the fact that the Commissioner was recently discharged by Rueben. The essence of the article had to do with the fact that the IRS faces enormous challenges in trying to get its computer systems updated just to do business. In very general terms today's article in the New York Times, in fact, let it be known that the IRS has spent four billion dollars in trying to update their systems and they still cannot do the very basic functions that are required. No where in this article, I don't mean to imply, but no where in this article did they mentioned the year 2000. I am simply bringing up the subject that if they can't spend four billion dollars and get their systems just to do the standard day-to-day processing that IRS needs to do, later on top of that the challenge of the year 2000, and it really does get scary. Some of the systems they are using are 12 years old and are being patched together, and they are leaping — limping along to process the day-to-day business.

Y2KI: Well, and another system equally complex and equally fragile, and another one that's been plagued by very, very serious problems is the Air Traffic Control System. And I can speak with a little authority on that subject in that the system that is currently in use is 20 years old, and is beyond antiquated and is incredibly fragile. As a matter of fact, the equipment is no longer manufactured. If something breaks they either cannibalized the system or they have it specially made. And so, and the code is very old and very, very fragile. And as you see every once in awhile it comes unglued. And again, as Tony pointed out, that's just keeping this thing limping along. Now you add into the mix this opening up of the code, this change and review of the code, and I'll tell you what, you scare any professional programmer half to death when you say that. Now I had a discussion yesterday with Capers Jones, and as many of you are aware, he provides some very, very interesting statistics across the board, and very well research, very hard to refute. And he has issued a fifth version of his — of his report. And two major changes in this new report is that, one is that he's raised the price worldwide to 1.6 trillion dollars to fix. And the reason he —

Y2KI: Now he includes legal costs in that one, does he not, in that calculation.

Y2KI: I believe he does.

Y2KI: I'm actually asking — okay.

Y2KI: I believe he does. I'm not a 100 percent certain of that, but I believe he does. What he's added that he hadn't added in his previous estimates are serious regression testing that he hadn't fully included, and more to this point, the standard or typical number of injected errors. That is, when you open up code, and you fix something, you inject a certain amount of errors, and that's typically somewhere in the 7 to 15 percent range. And what he did, he went back and took a look at the type of programs we're talking about, the type of code we're talking about here, and he upped his estimate from 7 to 10 percent. And when you're talking about the amount of code here that's on the table, that three percent increase jumps the price up by several hundred million dollars. So anyway, we've —

Y2KI: A hundred billion, I think.

Y2KI: Yes, I think.

Y2KI: Hard to say that, billion, you know, it's tough, it doesn't roll right off your tongue.

Y2KI: And now we've got the trillion word in there, so it starts getting really serious. Before we go to the break we have a couple of minutes, and I wanted to welcome our special guest, Steve McManus from the Bank of Boston. Are you there, Steve?

STEVE MCMANUS: Yes, good morning.

Y2KI: Good morning, thank you for joining us.

STEVE MCMANUS: You're welcome.

Y2KI: Steve, why don't you tell us about your role at the Bank of Boston, and maybe a little bit about the year 2000 project there.

STEVE MCMANUS: Sure. I'm the Communications Manager for Bank Boston's Millennium Project Team. So I'm a dedicated full-time employee. We have a centralized project team here to address our millennium challenge of about 40 people. So there is a management team of about eight folks with various responsibilities. And then we have setup a factory process that ideally we would like to take our applications through the whole process of analysis, coding, and testing, and then ensuring that they come out millennium certified.

Y2KI: Now you've been at this for a couple of years now and that's really kind of unique. When, in fact, did the Bank of Boston begin this project?

STEVE MCMANUS: In 1994, late 1994, Ed. We had someone knock on the door to talk to us about our millennium problem, and we thought that, yes, this is certainly well worth looking into, of course, because at the Bank we have so much data sensitive material. And what we did at that stage of the game was we just took a high level view, a 50,000 foot fly by to measure lines of code, because that was the original measure of how large the problem was going to be. And then we went and we surveyed manually our application owners and asked them questions like, what's your inventory look like, how many languages are you using, what's been written by Bank of Boston programmers, what do we use from vendors, and how long has this stuff been around. And we found a couple of things from that high level survey that we had in the neighborhood of 45 or 50 million lines of code, half of it came from vendors and at that stage of the game the quote figure per line of code to solve the problem was .50 cents to a dollar, and it didn't take us long to realize that we might have a large, you know, a large problem on our hands.

Y2KI: Well, Steve, we're going to go to a break here in a few seconds, stay with us. And if anyone has any questions you can give us a call on (202) 289-7730. And we'll be back after the break. You've been listening to the Y2K Investor on WBZS.

(BREAK)

Y2KI: Here from Bank of Boston's Millennium Project Team 2000. And Steve, one of the first things you did is you got a partner, and I believe it was Datadimensions. Can you tell us, you know, a little bit about that decision process and what they have done for you?

STEVE MCMANUS: Sure. It was about March of 1995 where we had kind of reviewed a couple of service providers and DDI being one of the original — one of the original millennium solution providers. We were satisfied with what their approach was going to be, and we invited them in as our subject matter expert to get a closer look and perform a more accurate portfolio sizing to find out if our high level results were on the mark. And so we were taking a closer look, and one of the things they helped us find was that we had roughly 20 million lines of code that were written by Bank of Boston programmers. And we had another 20 million lines of code that were vendor supplied. And one of the — one of the key figures that they came back to us with was that this is going to take more than 100 staff years for us to fix.

Y2KI: Wow. And now they've been sort of your teeny partner for over the last couple of years subject matter expert.

STEVE MCMANUS: That's right.

Y2KI: Another issue I wanted to talk to you about, we get this question a lot, is who broke the bad news to the Board of Directors and how did they take that?

STEVE MCMANUS: Well, the — the guy who was our CIO, Michael Lezinsky (phonetic sp.), he was — he bought into the fact that we needed to resolve this, and start resolving it as soon as possible. And he is our senior manager of the technology division of the bank. It was his — he saw it as his responsibility to go into the Board of Directors, present it to them in business terms, because the Board of Directors doesn't want to hear about lines of code or COBOL or C++ languages, they think in business terms. Okay. What does this means in business terms to Bank Boston. And so he was able to convince them that, yes, this is a business problem, it's not just a technology problem, and that's how we got our funding.

Y2KI: Another thing I wanted to ask you about is the overall project management of this project as it's grown. How have you approached that and what tools have you used for the project management?

STEVE MCMANUS: Well, following up on receiving our funding, that's the stage that we kicked off our project team and there was one guy on the team, the project's manager, Dave Iacino (phonetic sp.) who certainly, he was bitten by the bug earlier and was interested in trying to solve it, and he did a lot of research. One of the other companies that we talked to was the Gardner Group and they had recommendations out there about setting up this project team that involved people with roles such as mine, somebody else to just do the project administration, which can be very complex if you have a lot of applications, and you have a lot of suppliers. Somebody just needs to organize that or organize the budget, where is the money being spent and where is the time going. We have a full-time vendor manager, half of our code comes from vendors, so this guy spends all of his time identifying who they are, who is the contact, what release do we have from this vendor, is that release millennium compliant, if not, when is the millennium compliant release coming. Under him is someone that just spends all her time looking at contracts, and do we have any kind of warranties in these contracts. A process manager is on board and this person has developed what the factory process is going to be, and how we are going to look at our applications and update them. We need somebody to interface with the data center, this is our technical support person. If we need files from the data center to do testing, she's the one that gets us those. If we need more horsepower to do testing, she'll arrange for that. And we also had somebody write millennium compliant date standards. Now this is the standard that will stop the bleeding going forward, where programmers have received this communication where this is — the bank is going to four digit years going forward in as many cases as possible, because one thing that people are beginning to realize is that there is not one single solution to this, it's going to take a combination of factors to solve this problem. So we have put a standard out there, and if we can get folks to abide by that, that's great. If we need to make an exception to that, then we're willing to look at that, the key is to get the job done.

Y2KI: You know you — I think I understood that you — this is Tony Keyes by the way, Steve.

STEVE MCMANUS: Hi, Tony.

Y2KI: That you were expecting to wrap up your project, is it late this year?

STEVE MCMANUS: No, December '98.

Y2KI: Okay. December '98.

STEVE MCMANUS: Yes.

Y2KI: In the —

STEVE MCMANUS: (indiscernible) 99 days.

Y2KI: You have that written on your — the inside of your eyelids.

Y2KI: That rolled right off your lips.

Y2KI: Where are you in the span of the process, have you actually started converting code or are you still in the inventory analysis planning phase, if you will?

STEVE MCMANUS: We have started converting code and we actually have three applications that are what we call millennium certified, they are back in production. So they have been through this process, and they are prepared for the year 2000, to go from 1999 to 00. We have tested those, we know that they will work. We currently have about 17 of our applications in our factory undergoing the analysis and update phases. And one thing that we have done is we had to prioritize of — we have more that 150 applications that we need to take a look at. And we need to take our critical applications first. We have what's known as a disaster recovery plan at the bank where if, God forbid, there were a disaster, what systems do we need to bring back the quickest to get back into business.

Y2KI: Steven, you may here our theme music there. We've got to go off for a break. Please stay with us, folks. You're listening to WBZS AM 730, the Y2K Investor. Thank you.

(BREAK)

Y2KI: We will return to the Y2K Investor Show discussing the millennium bug computer problem and it will get bigger. We have Ed Mulhall and Tony Keyes, your hosts joining us this afternoon. Gentlemen.

Y2KI: Thank you, Leslie. I wanted to give you a couple of phone numbers and a couple of addresses here, as we usually do. If you'd like to contact us you can call us at (301)

924-6643 and leave us a message and we'll get back to you, of course. And you can visit our web site and that's www.y2kinvestor.com, that's all one phrase. And check out what we — what we have to say there. And certainly you can E-mail us, leave us a message there, there is a facility to do that. Also, as some of you may have noticed, you can also get stock quotes and the like up on the web server there. I also want to mention Alan Simpson's web site, that's www.comlinks.com, again, all one phrase C-O-M-L-I-N-K-S.com. And he has an excellent page, and again a lot of very useful links. And again, we want to encourage anyone to give us a call if they have things they'd like to tell us about their progress or lack thereof as they try to fix the problem, whether in Government or in the commercial sector. We do appreciate those phone calls, and we do follow-up on all of them. We're speaking today with Steve McManus, and he's with the Bank of Boston, he's the Communications Manager. And we spent the first half hour just trying to get a feel for his — where he is in his process and where it's going. But as we spoke yesterday, Steve, no one is an island, and there are significant concerns about the fact that banks are linked and very dependent upon their links, one to another, and to certain service agencies. Why don't you talk a little bit about your strategy in dealing with that.

STEVE MCMANUS: Okay, sure. We have service providers like the Federal Reserve or any ATM network that we exchange data with electronically, international funds transfers, wiring money, et cetera. And, again, it's — that falls under our vendor management program. And it's identifying who the contact there is and what the application is all about. I think the progress there has been a little bit slow, because I think the volume of work, say, on the Federal Reserve side is — is just huge and it appears to me that they are still trying to negotiate what their strategy is going to be to address the banks going forward, and I'm very anxious to hear what their plans are, because obviously it's a critical, it's a critical pieces to the puzzle.

Y2KI: Yes, you mentioned yesterday that you've formed a users group up in that area. Can you tell us a little bit about that?

STEVE MCMANUS: You bet. It's called the Boston Millennium Association and our inaugural meeting is March 5th, it's going to be hosted here at the Bank of Boston. And really what this is, this is a group of companies that are going to get together, all different size companies with representatives from their project teams to talk about what the status of their projects are and what are solutions, can we share ideas that will speed up this process, because in the end we want everybody to make it to the goal line, we want everybody to see, you know, a successful New Year in the year 2000.

Y2KI: Well that's the essence of this problem, isn't it, this is not a U.S. problem.

STEVE MCMANUS: No, it's not.

Y2KI: Not a parochial problem, it's a global problem.

STEVE MCMANUS: It is.

Y2KI: And so the kind of effort that you've launched there in your community is one that really needs to be launched and led in the international community. We've been saying here on the air that we're disappointed that the Clinton Administration has done something more aggressive to take some leadership there in getting at least the dialogue going.

STEVE MCMANUS: Right. And well it kind of, it just makes me think of our, our battle cry here at Bank Boston, plan do, plan do. Too many organizations spend too much time planning what they are going to do or say and I certainly feel that the Government is guilty of that, but we don't have a lot of time.

Y2KI: Yes.

STEVE MCMANUS: The deadline for this project is not going to move. So, again, I'm anxious for as much information I can get, and I'm willing to share information, you know, or experiences that the bank has had already.

Y2KI: Chilling really when you think about the Government's track record on some time critical projects. The one that, you know, hit the New York Times today, maybe you saw the story, I actually have not read it, but heard about it on my way in here. That they finally shared the fact that they have spent four billion dollars trying to update their processing systems and still are not able to do the most basic work with those machines.

STEVE MCMANUS: Whoa!

Y2KI: They are still back on the 12 year old mainframes and hobbling along with them. So it just doesn't instill a lot of confidence —

STEVE MCMANUS: Right.

Y2KI: That they are trying to figure this thing out, they are going to budget for fiscal '98, really worrisome.

TEVE MCMANUS: Yes, I couldn't agree with you more. And it's — and it's a — it is a global problem as you mentioned a second ago, but it's up to each either company or each government to make sure that the work is reduced to an accomplishable level. And that means committing resources, and a lot of people are having trouble doing that, and there is going to be more competition for resources as the deadline gets closer.

Y2KI: Speaking of that, have you had any difficulty obtaining resources in the Boston area, are they readily available or is it a little tight up there too?

STEVE MCMANUS: They appear readily available right now. We really haven't had turnover on our project team or in our factory. But, you know, again, I think that since we have established what the process is, I don't know, maybe people are comfortable with what's going on here with the bank. But I still think that's kind of an open issue.

Y2KI: Are they, have you taken the step of putting people under contract or is that just not felt necessary to you at this point?

STEVE MCMANUS: Well, we haven't locked them in under contract.

Y2KI: Yes.

STEVE MCMANUS: I mean, we've contracted with two different vendors, Datadimensions and Keen (phonetic sp.) to provide us with that manpower and I'm not close to the language of that contract, so I really couldn't speak to that. But I know that they are providing us resources there.

Y2KI: One thing you mentioned yesterday is one of the keys to or probably right behind getting your corporate management to sign on board was getting the legal department involved early. Has that proved useful?

STEVE MCMANUS: It sure has because, again, it just continues to speak to this problem as a business risk issue. Also with the legal department we have appointed a corporate co-sponsor. So these two people basically can help promulgate awareness of the problem through, what we call our risk councils. Now each business unit of the bank, be it credit or retail, has a risk council. And we have brought this — brought an awareness campaign to about half of these risk councils so far and what we want people to do is to have a millennium headset, to think millennium, how did this impact my line of business. And let's have a conversation about it, and let's make sure that the bank is doing right thing going forward.

Y2KI: Right. You know, one other element of the — dealing with the outside community that I wanted to mention because it's something that's come up on the strings on the internet that we follow, and this that Visa has actually told their clientele that they will impose fines, the number is astronomical, I don't know if it's true, 160,000 dollars if they are not compliant and can't process credit cards with an expiration date beyond the year 2000. I think the deadline is April of this year.

STEVE MCMANUS: Yes, right.

Y2KI: Can you tell us something about that just in general terms, that seems so far ahead of the year 2000, it tends to, I guess, corroborate some opinions that we've heard that, gee, it's not going to take until January 1, 2000 for problems to pop-up, they are actually happening now.

STEVE MCMANUS: Yes, the event horizon, you know, at what stage of the game do you, does your Visa credit card, at what stage of the game does that get issued with a 00 expiration date, and it's my understanding that they don't want member banks issuing cards with the 00 expiration date because they have had something of a millennium problem. And by issuing this mandate, if you will, that their service providers need to be millennium compliant by April, otherwise suffer the penalty of fine, it's one tactic to take, I guess, and it certainly has gotten a lot of people's attention. And so if it's a matter of some department store testing whether or not their card swipe machines can receive dates with a 00 expiration date, I'm sure those people will rally around that effort.

2KI: Several months ago we — we went with a story that was on the press wire about a scam with a group of people going around to retailers with a card swipe machine and advertising it or describing it as century date compliant. That somehow this card swipe machine would solve their century date and was selling it for a couple hundred dollars more than even a regular one. And, in fact, it was nothing more than a regular card swipe machine, and they had just manipulated the cards that they were using to indicate that it would not take a card with a date beyond the year 2000, and then showing one that was and running it through their machine and it would, of course, go through. It was the card that had been manipulated. You know, so I — we're going to, I think you're going to see a lot of those kinds of scams coming up.

STEVE MCMANUS: So that was a credit card silver bullet solution.

Y2KI: Yes, right.

Y2KI: At the — aimed at the folks who simply don't understand where the problem resides, and it certainly doesn't reside in the — in the card swipe machines. So, you know, I guess that's buyer beware but, you know, we'll —

Y2KI: That's one of the things, we keep trying to validate some of these things with folks in the real world like yourself. Irene Dec was on a couple months ago, she's with Prudential and runs their program. We've run through some of the same questions, but they do keep coming up and we want to hear from end users like yourself that are experiencing the problems and get valid opinions on some of this.

STEVE MCMANUS: Yes, and I think we need to get to some success stories, certainly, and that was one of my intentions of helping to form the Boston Millennium Association as a users group. Let's get together and let's share what the successes are or what the challenges are and kind of map that out. Certainly people do need to be aware that there isn't a silver bullet, and I'm sure you've discussed that before on your show, that there is not one solution, there certainly is not one solution for Bank Boston. There is going to be a combination of solutions that we need to implement and we need to find what the best ones are.

Y2KI: We've got about 30 seconds, but when we come back I'd kind of like to jump off from where you just started there and talk about how Bank Boston sees their progress on this and their leadership as perhaps a differentiator in the marketplace.

STEVE MCMANUS: Okay.

Y2KI: What you intend to do with that. Well, you're listening to WBZS AM 730, the Y2K Investor. Please stick with us, we'll be back in just a few moments.

(BREAK)

Y2KI: And we return to the Y2K Investor Show. Our final segment for today taking your questions too in the studio at (202) 289-7730. Your hosts for the program, Ed Mulhall and Tony Keyes.

Y2KI: Welcome back, folks. We're speaking with Steven McManus. Steven is the Communications Manager for Bank Boston's year 2000 project. When we left for the break Steven had mentioned the — we were talking about the users association that Steven is responsible for kicking off up in the Boston area. That actually led to a subject that I personally have, I don't know if I could say, promoting, but it's really an idea that I've had and since it's my show I get to ask this question and validate my rumor. And that is, you know, there is a lot of speculation as to what — what's going to be the event that causes the year 2000 to break upon the American scene and eliminate the polarity that exists today. You know, there are the folks who get it, understand it, have internalized it, believe it. And then on the other end of the spectrum you'll have someone like Terano (phonetic sp.) who wrote a piece in the Wall Street Journal where he thought we were all on the lunatic fringe and was poking fun at us. My thought is, it's probably going to be the forces of commerce that actually bring this about. And it will be companies like Bank Boston, Prudential, Westminister Bank, Allstate, those folks who have been out ahead on this and will complete their projects perhaps ahead of time and can speak proudly about them that will go out to the marketplace and use it as a differentiator to their customers.

STEVE MCMANUS: Sure. I tend to agree with that. I think the discussion needs to be an ongoing discussion to continually be out there. And if that brings us a competitive advantage that's great with me, because I've always felt that investing is a matter of what kind of sleep factor can you live with and how much risk are you willing to take. And if we can go to our customers, and when I mention customers, I'm saying that, you know, a 50 million dollars is just as important as 50 dollar ATM withdrawal. I mean each of these are our customers that depend on the bank to do business with us. And the sooner we can get to them and say, okay, we have knocked off that application, we've tested it, that's millennium compliant, the sooner the better in my eyes. And that is on our radar screen, that is part of our plans.

Y2KI: Well, you know it's been proven over and over again that the market moves on perception and anticipation. So if your clients or just the general public begin to get nervous about the post year 2000 environment, whether or not their electronic assets will be safe.

STEVE MCMANUS: Right.

Y2KI: Can they really account for what is theirs and is there any question about that, those are fears that could be highly volatile in the marketplace. So companies like yours getting out in front of it and saying, hey, this is what we're doing, we feel very confident it's all going to be okay. If you are a client of ours rest assured we've got this well in hand. If you're not, come take a look at Bank Boston.

STEVE MCMANUS: Yes. Yes. And so it takes place at all different levels, too. Again, this goes back to why I'm anxious to hear what some of the plans are coming out of Washington, D.C. for either a national council or an international council that gives people that kind of security. I mean, we can all sit around and wonder about what if the lights don't turn on, or what if the elevator doesn't work. You know, there are so many examples that, and that's what will get people's attention is that fear factor that, you know, I have a concern about having access to my money or whatever. And I just want to avoid that as much as possible.

Y2KI: One of the stories we've been tracking and are trying to nail down is a story about the FDIC and a proposed rule making that suggests that if a bank can't prove that it is century date compliant by a given date, and I won't use the date I've heard because we haven't verified that date. But in not too distant future, if a bank is not compliant, that the FDIC is considering ordering an automatic merge, merging of that bank with a "healthy" bank. I guess rather than ask your — maybe I will ask your reaction to that, but more — more to the point, what if someone came to you and said, oh, by the way, you're doing a heck of a job at Bank Boston, now I've got a bank X that isn't and you take it over. How far would you run?

STEVE MCMANUS: How far would I run? Oh, I don't know, I don't —

Y2KI: That's leading the witness, Ed.

Y2KI: Okay.

Y2KI: I object.

STEVE MCMANUS: Yes, I have seen enough bank integrations and things like that. I mean, in 1990 when there were some problems in the New England economy, it was not a good feeling, people were, you know, people were not thrilled at the prospect of banks changing names. And I still think there is some, you know, cultural aversion to that, because it speaks to the security factors. If, I don't know, I guess we'll cross that bridge if it ever comes.

Y2KI: Right. Right. Well, again, we want to thank you for coming on, Steve, and we'd like to ask you if you wouldn't mind to come back several times over the next several months and give us an update and let us know how you're doing, you know, as you progress along your path.

STEVE MCMANUS: I would be more than happy to, Ed and Tony, and I think that the kind of work that you guys are doing in raising this kind of awareness is very important to the success of the project as a whole.

Y2KI: Thank you, appreciate that. One other quick question because we're curious about this one, this is another angle that we've discussed and, you know, would like to take every opportunity to talk with an end user. And that is, are you on a calendar fiscal year or is your fiscal year (indiscernible).

STEVE MCMANUS: Calendar fiscal year, yes.

Y2KI: Calendar fiscal year. Is there any mention in your annual report about your year 2000 project, its costs, the future liability, et cetera, et cetera?

STEVE MCMANUS: There — I don't expect it to appear in our annual report, which will be published for year-end 1996. And who knows what happens over the next 11 months with this issue that maybe it does end up being in the '97 annual report.

Y2KI: So essentially the cost that are associated with year 2000 problem for the bank are just buried in the information systems budget?

STEVE MCMANUS: Currently, yes, yes.

Y2KI: Yes. Okay. Great. Well, about 60 second left, Ed.

Y2KI: Thank you, again, Steve.

STEVE MCMANUS: I will give, you know, some more good news was that this past December our Chief Executive Officer actually invited our CIO back to the Board of Directors Meeting for an update on what the millennium project team has accomplished since its inception. So that really gave us a good feeling about that senior management buy-in, that they have taken this problem very seriously.

Y2KI: Boy, we certainly hope that you are the, not the exception, the rule. We'd love to hear from a lot more bank and financial institutions on that front.

Y2KI: Well, we've managed to go through another hour on the subject. Hopefully, interestingly, we will be back Monday at 11:30. We look forward to having you join us then. You're listening to the Y2K Investor on WBZS. And we'll see you on Monday.

(END)

Guest: Kevin Schick
Date: 3/14/97

Ed: Good Morning Tony

Tony: Good Morning

Ed: We have an interesting guest today, we're looking forward to getting to him. Anything you want to go with initially, Tony?

Tony: Well, just some interesting moves in the market in the last two days. Zitel was up 7 1/2 yesterday, it off 1/4 at 37 1/4 on news of the contract award from the State of Nevada to MatriDigm, and as many of our listeners will recall, Zitel owns 35% of MatriDigm.

Ed: Right, and that was a beta site that everyone was sort of waiting to hear the results from. So that is good news for them.

Tony: There were mixed reviews, actually coming out, from rumors that they weren't happy ranging to rumors that they were ecstatic.

Ed: Right. I think the truth probably lies somewhere in the middle and it really does coincide with what we've been hearing in terms of the software works but it's not nearly as easy and friendly to use as people might imagine, so I think that's where the rumors were coming from, that it was doing the job but it was a lot harder to use then anyone expected.

Tony: Ya, and BRCP, which is another company that I follow, and in fact, I own some of BRCP as well as Zitel, they own 7% of MatriDigm, but they didn't have the kind of move that Zitel did. Zitel I think is much more associated by the investor community with MatriDigm.

Ed: O.K. Let's get right to our guest, Kevin Schick. His name has been taken in vain probably more than just about anyone else's having to do with the year 2000 issue. Kevin is currently the Vice President of Strategic Initiatives for Viasoft and I think where he became best known was as research director with the Gartner Group for year 2000 issues. His background is in the applications development field. He has about 21 years experience and his bona fides are he has a Bachelor of Science degree from Central Washington University and a Graduate Degree from University of Southern California. We want to welcome you Kevin. How are you doing?

Kevin: Very good. Thank you for the opportunity to join you fellows this morning.

Ed: Well, we've been looking forward to it and we want to thank your very lovely administrative assistant, Linda Conell, though I know her name is Longo. But Linda Conell for helping us arrange this.

Kevin: Thank you.

Ed: pass that on to her for us.

Kevin: I certainly will.

Ed: O.K. I guess the first question, and I think the people who listen to this show regularly are interested in this or are terribly tired of it, but I ask everyone of our guests initially the same first question. And that is, when did you first become aware of the year 2000 problem?

Kevin: Well, my initial awareness of the year 2000 problem came in about 1979-1980 when I was involved in, I was part of a technical team for the ground support systems on the space shuttle. We obviously had to look at this as a very large project and, in fact, many IT people over the last 20-30 years have looked at the use of 2 digit versus 4 digit dates and had to make that call that says what's the cost, what's the benefit, and you know we always, over 20 years we all came to the same conclusion, right? The program won't still be used, you know, when the problem arises.

Ed: Right.

Kevin: And now we're all ...

Ed: Yeah, that has to go into the hall of fame of famous last words.

Kevin: Well, you know, it's an amazing industry , isn't it, that 20-30 years ago we all created this scenario thinking it wouldn't be here, now it is here, and we get to be the ones to fix it.

Ed: Hopefully.

Kevin: Hopefully

Ed: Right.

Tony: You know, if Peter DeJager was the voice of this problem in the wilderness some time ago, you certainly have been the voice that has raised the investor's consciousness around the problem, and the opportunity actually that surrounds it with the companies that are in business to fix it. your numbers of the $300 to $600 billion world-wide for the cost to fix the problem certainly are the most oft quoted numbers. Any change in that perspective since those were first published, which I guess was probably about 18 months ago now, huh?

Kevin: Well, I think the change that you will see in those numbers is that they were under estimated. The year 2000 has gone from being an event within the IT industry to becoming a market and actually a process by which all companies are going to have to go through to get into the 21st century. The reason why I think the numbers are under estimated is as we start to see more and more environments be included, the Unix world, the mid platform world, the desktop as you start to see the ramifications outside of IT, themostats, VCR players, things that we can all laugh about and make good stories about but will have a dramatic input or impact on our day to day lives, that's going to raise the total cost of year 2000 and let us not lose sight of the litigation issues that will come out of the year 2000, be it perceived or real scenarios. I think you're going to find that litigation costs will probably exceed the correction costs for year 2000. And so, when you think of 300 to 600 billion dollars, I believe now you can probably start moving correction costs over a trillion dollars, and the feedback I've gotten from the market on litigation, that's going to be over a trillion dollars, so those of us who come from IT countries, North America being on of the dominant players there, we're about to see an enormous amount of capital get sucked up into what ultimately will be an infrastructure correction versus a promotion to get to new technology. There's got to be a balance there and that's going to be a big issue.

Tony: You know, probably of anyone to watch in terms of making a move, you certainly were someone that was in the spotlight, and the choice that you made to go to Viasoft obviously was an endorsement. Rumors were flying, I guess prior to your making that move, of where you would end up. Somehow I guess it got to the street that you were considering making a move. What led you to Viasoft? What differentiates them for you and why did you throw your fortunes behind theirs?

Kevin: A good question, and the reason to come to Viasoft, interestingly enough, is that within the Viasoft technology and the Viasoft management team there's a vision and a direction to move beyond year 2000. The capabilities are here today to deliver. O.K. and that's a good thing. But, for someone like myself, who tends to look what's the next opportunity and how do you use today's scenario to get you there, Viasoft was a good fit. They've got the Roshet Repository capability that we will start to build component management around which is clearly going to be a 21st century and beyond strategy.

Ed: Kevin, let me interrupt you there, we've got to go to the break, we'll let you finish that thought when we come back.

Commercial break

Ed: Thank you, welcome back. We want to get right back to talking with Kevin. John Vasquez from Prudential Securities has agreed to do double duty and is standing by and has a couple of questions also for Kevin. Kevin you were, Tony asked the question I think it's a very good one. You could of had your pick of the litter, why Viasoft?

Kevin: well, as I was saying, they've got a vision and that was critical tome. Where do we go after year 2000 and in fact, how do you take advantage of the year 2000 to get where you wanna be? And, where we wanna be can be a lot of different scenarios. The one that I was most excited about was gathering all this inventory and all this information about our systems and then making use of that in tomorrow's world of creating components and bringing, you know, assembling components instead of doing code development. So the folks at Viasoft, I've known them for years, I have a high degree of respect for the management team here, they've got an excellent client base. So it was, it was a, and by the way you're right, I had a very broad pick of the litter and really wanted to go to a winner and wanted to be part of the solution and what happens after year 2000.

Tony: You know, it's kind of interesting , one of the companies that I think most people were assuming you were going to go to, or the rumors were flying, was Zitel because you were such a strong proponent of MatriDigm's solution. Um, and so I think folks were sort of surprised at Viasoft, at your choice of Viasoft. But that may also be somewhat of a misunderstanding about what Viasoft does and seeing Viasoft perhaps as a competitor of MatriDigm may not be the correct way to view it? Is that a fair statement?

Kevin: Oh, I think it's very fair. Where Viasoft and Zitel, they have a tremendous amount of synergy, and when I say Zitel, we should probably recognize that we're talking about MatriDigm. Zitel's the stock offering, I suppose. But there's a tremendous amount of synergy between what Viasoft does and what the MatriDigm factory and other factories in the marketplace need in take way of enablement and support. You know that the issues around factories isn't speed, it's more their predictability of the results. And if you don't have high quality input, and reliable and predictable input, into a factory then the factory will choke. And, think about that when you're building an automobile right, if you don't send steel and high grade steel into an automobile factory you can end up with a very low grade result, and not one the people are gonna want to buy. Viasoft, when I looked at the opportunities out there, Viasoft offered something that was throughout the process, whereas the factories tended to be a particular aspect, and, you know again, I want to come back to, I wanted to look at something that took my career and my own personal vision and the vision that I see that's taking place in the marketplace, the post 2000 vision, and I wanted to be in an organization that believed in that and was working towards that and be a part of that. So I have a high degree of respect for the people at MatriDigm and the factory world out there, they've actually changed the way we all look at development today and the way we look at our infrastructure and my opportunity was to go to someplace that wanted to exploit that, if that's fair, and then bring that into the day to day aspect, not just the year 2000 aspect.

Tony: You know, I think that's an issue that many of our listeners deal with. We certainly get calls on this subject. We get E-mail also as well. When anyone outside this industry just sort of intuitively looks at the problem it's easy to come to the conclusion that this is a market that falls off a cliff on Jan 2, 2000. And, so our counsel is that, ya know, that's not the case. In fact, we are in dire straits right now and are not going to finish the work by Jan 1st as it is. But, the smart companies, the companies who have been in business for some time, like Viasoft, CACI, American Management Systems, some of the companies we talk about on the show, are actually using this opportunity to solidify their relationships, get into new relationships that they don't currently have and build on those for a long term relationship, extending well beyond the year 2000.

Kevin: Absolutely, and in fact we've announced our new initiative, the C dot Era Initiative, where the C stands for cooperative. Within that initiative, we're looking at extending our own boundaries beyond the traditional maintenance and redevelopment world that we've really been an active part of, and I would dare say, a leader. And in doing so, looking at component management, repository based development, what does it mean to take an infrastructure, your existing application assets, and re-using them, instead of always just trying to continue to build onto the pile. So it's been very exciting and you know , you can either just fix the year 2000 and consider it an expense, or you could use the year 2000 as your catalyst for change and view it as an opportunity and take it more as an R&D investment strategy. So, it's more of an attitude, and it's more of a business understanding how to take advantage of challenge versus succumbing to just saying fix it and I'll expense it and then I'll fire everybody for creating this problem for me.

Ed: Kevin, we have about a minute left to go before we go to the break, quick question, another often quoted statistic is 30 percent of all systems non-compliant by the year 2000. you still think that's accurate?

Kevin: I absolutely do. And I want to emphasize that's 30 percent of all systems that will have an impact on your business and your customer. Companies had better wake up.

Tony: Yeah, it's disturbing. I attended the hearings that were held on the 21st of February where seven of the Federal Government CIO's testified and really sent a chill down my spine to hear where those folks thought they were based on where we truly believe they are.

Ed: Tony, let's get into that after the next half hour, we're coming up on the break.

Commercial break

Ed: Thank you Keith. Welcome back. We're speaking with Kevin Schick. Kevin, we're a, our primary market here is Washington, DC and we try to follow the government's progress in terms of solving the Y2K problem. And there's a rather wide discrepancy between your estimates while you were with the Gartner Group of approximately 30 billion dollars for the Federal Government's tab and Miss Katzen, who is the Clinton administration's spokesperson and lead person for the year 2000. She says it's somewhere on the order of 2.3 billion dollars. How would you explain the difference?

Kevin: Well, I guess I'd explain it first that it's about 27.7 billion dollars.

(Laughter)

Ed: You're quick.

Kevin: Yeah, I'm writing it all down here. **(Laughter)** And, that's a pretty big number. First, I think we have to all appreciate that we're both trying to come up with what is better described as guesstimates, and you know, maybe mine is too high and maybe her's is too low. The original estimate that was put out on the Federal Government, through myself when I was at the Gartner Group was actually 15-30 billion dollars. Giving some sort of a range of trying to understand what's the real depth of the problem and how much imbedded systems would be included in that estimate. And then, what would be some of the alternatives as far as solutions in that regard. Now, that said, I think we also have to temper in that what's politically correct to say and you know, I don't know that you can say what they say versus what is reality, but it's difficult within any organization, be it the federal or out in the private sector, to come up with an estimate on year 2000. It's just not politically correct to come back to somebody and say I've got a 30 billion dollar problem, and by the way, we've known about it for a long time. So, you know, this is a tough one and I, I have a high degree of respect for the Federal individuals and we all know they wanna do a good job. The challenge is going to be are they gonna have the opportunity to do a good job.

Tony: You know I was speaking to Steven McManus yesterday and he's the director of the communications effort for Bank of Boston's year 2000 program. One area that he's particularly nervous about is the Federal Reserve. They have been disquieting in that they haven't really said anything about what they're doing. Viasoft though is, at least has been, it's been reported that you folks are working with them. Any insight into the Federal Reserve from your point of view?

Kevin: Well, you know, clearly in their position you want to be very careful what you say, right? I mean, we're talking to just on this radio show a financial community that when you look at the comment made about the stock prices and then try to attach some rhyme and reason to how does a stock go so high or why is it at so low, you know there's a lot of emotion associated when you include money. So the Federal Reserve is rightfully been very quiet. The Federal Reserve is active on a year 2000 initiative. We're involved there and working with them and looking for further opportunities. The challenge that the Federal reserve has is going to be more around the supply chain, right? It, it, the Federal Reserve themselves could make their systems year2000 compliant. All companies need to think about what I'm about to say by the way. You can make your own self compliant and yet your partner upstream from you or downstream from you may also be compliant but do it differently. That means you're both year 2000 compliant, you solved it differently, you didn't communicate that difference and the first time you try to communicate with each other, you're gonna have a catastrophe. So the Federal Reserve's challenge is also going to all of the members of the Federal Reserve network and trying to resolve and reconcile what is everyone doing? And how will we take these disparate solutions and make sure that we still have an integrated and cooperative environment that we have today. So you wanna be careful about becoming year 2000 compliant and yet loosing the cooperative nature you have with your business partners. That's the biggest challenge faced by the Federal Reserve and they have a high degree of exposure because they're talking about money.

Tony: That's a great seque into another subject area. One that we talk about on this program and that I cover extensively in my book that will be coming out in the next 30-60 days, entitled The Investor's Survival Guide To The Coming Computer Crisis. And that's the dark side of this problem. The impact that the cost of repairing the problem will have on corporate profits. The psychology of the investor community when they really internalize what this problem means and the threat that it poses to their assets. And when you take the problem that you just articulated and you extend it globally and you even say gee, in the U.S. we've cooperated, we've brought our systems into compliance, in fact we've done it so that they're compatible, we have to now deal with the international community. And where are they vis a vis our progress? Some folks think that the U.S. is quite a ways ahead of the balance of the World. Another huge threat would be that the European community, Asia-Pacific doesn't get there in time. Or gets there in an incompatible fashion. Any thoughts on that?

Kevin: I honestly look forward to your book because it is a classic scenario here. You know the books out there, the death of competition, things of this nature. We really do have to step back and understand that the entire business ecosystem, and that based on a global level, and then you start to pull it back in and you see your national level and you see your local level and you see your internal level. This year 2000 issue is really based on infrastructure. And infrastructure spans the corporate climate. So, organizations that just solve the year 2000 are only going to get an expense. Organizations that understand their partnerships, their business ecosystems and not only start to include the ecosystem in the solution but also start to understand the firewall requirement so that they minimize and localize what 30 percent of their systems will not be compliant. Ideally, if the 30 percent that we talked about as not being compliant is those systems that do not have dramatic impact on the business, that's a good thing. You can't get to all of it, let's make sure we get to the right pieces and let's make sure, just as we're doing in our C dot Era initiative, that you've got your partners involved and your full business system, the supply chain involved. This is the whole point of me leaving Gartner Group by the way, was that sitting at Gartner Group I was able to research and talk to people about this. But I didn't, because of the nature of the business at Gartner Group, have the opportunity to actually get out there and be an active part of the solution and create a new initiative that drives people to work together to get the vendors to work together and create these technology frameworks that not only solve the problem, but look at the supply chain and the issues that faces and then also look at getting leveraged values so you have something post 2000.

Ed: Kevin, Viasoft's a world-wide concern so that gives you maybe a broader perspective than a lot of other companies. Briefly, where do you rank the various world segments in terms of Y2K compliance? Europe, the Far East and the like?

Kevin: You know, that's an excellent question because the difficulty of looking at the year 2000 globally is a lot of it has to do with cultural perspective. We in North America and particularly here in the Excited States of America (chuckles and laughter) tend to be more prone to, you know, let's go do something and let's figure out what we should have done later. And you go to Europe and they are much more pragmatic and they study and they plan and then they act and Asia, it is a much more, well, you don't say you have a problem. You have to be very careful about insulting someone, going to an organization and saying your programmers have created an error. So when you look at the status of the year 2000 it's very closed door in Asia, very difficult to get a feel for the status of the year 2000. However, when you look at their press, and you start to realize that in the press they're very concerned, you have to feel that because of their culture they're gonna have a great deal of difficulty in the business ecosystem, the supply chain because you now can't go to a partner and say I've got a problem. That's culturally difficult. In Europe, where you have many. many nations, let's appreciate that the Europeans can not even agree to a currency or to the fact that they are going to share a currency based system. So they've got some challenges there because their ecosystem is very integrated. And it's from country to country which heightens the sensitivity. So, in North America we have much greater activity and we have, we are probably going to be, at an individual company level, far more compliant then any other region in the World.

Tony: We probably have to go to a break here Ed in just a few seconds, but that really does lead to one other thought and that is will U.S. corporations be able, some of them be able to capitalize on this, have the vision to enhance and extend their market share.

Ed: Tony, you're right. We have to go to a break. Let's leave that to when we come back.

Commercial break

Ed: Thank you Keith. Tony why don't you go ahead and continue with your question to Kevin.

Tony: Gee, I was so busy here, punching up some of the issues in this arena on my Bloomberg terminal so I lost my train of thought.

Ed: That's O.K. Well let me go with mine. You had mentioned earlier Kevin that litigation costs could actually equal the remediation costs. Vito Peraino, who I know you know, is getting ready to speak before Connie Morella's committee here in the next week or so having to do with maybe some new legal initiatives to maybe manage or sort of mitigate those litigation costs. What's your thoughts on things like sort of declaring a legal holiday on culpability and things like that?

Kevin: Well, it was interesting, Congressman Horn who chairs the sub-committee on the year 2000 issue made a comment that, you know, have we in fact created the year 2000 tort act, right and see what happens here. I would be very cautious around some of the issues with litigation. If you declared a holiday, you know what, we're all going to dump every issue we have as a year 2000 issue. And, so then everything becomes year 2000 because that's the holiday, right? If you don't declare a holiday then we put an enormous amount of capital at risk here in the U.S. where we have more liberal litigation opportunities. You know, you go overseas and you talk about the litigation issues and they scratch their head. They're looking at you and they say, oh no, no that's an American issue. And unfortunately it probably is more Americanized than anywhere else which puts our capital at greater risk and it means that the focus is taken off the real issue of becoming compliant, dealing with the supply chains and seizing the opportunity to take advantage of year 2000. So, it's very concerning and this is a tricky one. This is not going to be an easy answer. You know, as you look at the year 2000, it is just about dates. Let's get real about it, right. It's just dates. Once you look at the business issues and the legal issues, the supply chain, where are the opportunities, how do I get into the 21st century, what do I do with my other development opportunities, object oriented client server, Internet. It gets very complex and there's not gonna be a simple answer.

Ed: Kevin, one of the things that's kind of a touchy question having to do with litigation, and we might as well make it specific, it has to do with Viasoft, but it applies to any company doing remediation. How much responsibility and accountability does a company like Viasoft or any of the remediation companies assume in terms of entering into a contract to fix some client's year 2000 problem? Should it not work, or work exactly the way the company expects, how much responsibility does a company like Viasoft have?

Kevin: Uh, I mean, and that's an excellent point. You know it comes up in our contracts and everybody you know, ideally if I was a client and not a vendor, I'd want my vendor to take 100 percent responsibility. Which is kind of a cool thing, right? But the truth of the matter is, when you look at companies like Viasoft, we are a technology company. More of the liability will be focused on service providers who in the past have ran projects that may have implemented non compliant systems or who are running projects today. One of the things out of Viasoft's technology that we talk to people about is you need to understand is just it's not able to be found by technology. So in our world, we have to protect ourselves from that kind of exposure. And really have to look at our clients and our partners of sharing that. And what I'd say to the business world is then, make sure that when you look at your solution and you look at your partners greater than one, when I say partners the vendors that you bring in, look to understand what it means to have shared liability and shared risk and let's make it worth everybody's while. But, this is a thorny one. And it's one that in many contracts you'll see that there are explicit limitations as to the liability that a vendor will take on. I like to refer to it by the way, when you come through factories, that what you give a factory probably has bugs in it. Non year 2000 bugs. When you get it back, that software will still be fully bug-enabled.*(laughter)* That means what didn't work before doesn't work now. But unfortunately, it's probably the first time you really paid attention and certainly you see all these things that were always there, but now they're very visible. This is where it get very thorny. Did you introduce problems, did you really solve the year 2000. Did you get everything. It's a tough one guys.

John: I have a question for Kevin

Ed: Go ahead John.

John: Kevin, hi it's John Vasquez, Prudential Securities. Naturally, my interest is in helping people decide how to invest and pick up opportunities in this whole scenario. My question to you goes back to the MatriDigm solution, which you've aligned yourself with. We've heard a lot of very powerful stories coming out of MatriDigm and I just wanted a comment from you on how good is it. Is it the best that's available today and what can it do and what can't it do?

Kevin: Well, and that's a very fair question, we have a relationship with MatriDigm where we will provide the front end which helps create better input so that the factory operates at a more optimal level and then we'll create back ends that you can take what comes out of the factory into a more effective testing environment, so we believe that the MatriDigm technology is going to be very effective. You know I'm always cautious that when you bring in new technology, no matter how impressive it is in the lab, which MatriDigm, by my own research and by comments that I've made in the past, is some of the best that I've seen. The truth of the fact is that once you get out there in the real world we've got some really strange shit up out there. This is tough for a factory to handle. Factories really need predictable input. I think what MatriDigm will do, is with their relationship with Viasoft, create a better factory process that includes an analysis and packaging phase that feeds more efficient into the factory so you get more effective results out of the factory, and then feed that into testing, so you know, we're happy for the folks at MatriDigm. They're a brilliant bunch of people there and we're very excited about our relationship with them and where Viasoft fits into that picture and then takes that picture again beyond 2000.

Ed: Well Kevin, we've managed to run through an hour. We want to thank you very much for adjusting your schedule and again, thank Miss Conell for us for helping us and we have Cathy Adams from the Social Security Administration as our guest on Monday and we'll see you then.

(END)

Guest: PETER DE JAEGER
Date: MONDAY, NOVEMBER 11, 1996

Y2KI: And time now for the Millennium Bug with your host Ed Mulhall discussing the year 2000 computer bug and how you can make it profitable for yourself here at Business Radio. Ed today will be joined by Peter de Jaeger of the Tenagra Corporation (phonetic sp.) and Alan Simpson from Comlinks Corporation. A little later on we'll also here from Michael Tantleff of Prudential Securities in Santa Barbara, California. And now here is your host of the Millennium Bug, Ed Mulhall.

Y2KI: Good morning everyone. Thank you, Jim. This is a very special program for us. We're very, very pleased that we're going to be able to bring you Peter de Jaeger. Alan Simpson is also going to join us in the first half and then we'll be joined by Michael Tantleff. The reason we're so excited is that Peter has been and is the guru of the year 2000 problem. He's been at it probably longer than anyone and he has a very reasonable voice, has traveled widely, spoken widely on the subject. And he's widely recognized as one of the premiere thinkers on this problem. He has spoken before Congress and as I said, he has written extensively. He is always turned to when someone needs an authoritative voice. So we're very pleased to have him with us. Peter are you there?

PETER DE JAEGER: Good morning. How are you?

Y2KI: Alan, are you there?

Y2KI: I'm here, yes.

Y2KI: Oh very good, very good, technology working so far anyway. Peter I would like you to begin by giving us a little bit about your background and how you came to this problem.

PETER DE JAEGER: Well, I went to university hoping to be a math teacher and got my degree. And then when I got my degree they decided they don't math teachers anymore in Ontario. So I got out of that. My background is mathematics and computer science. And — as a problem solver I saw this problem looming back in about 1979, as did a lot of other people. In 1991, people — no one was really talking about this, everybody was sort of keeping quiet and it needed to be talked about, otherwise we would be in the situation we're in today. So I decided to make this a bit of a crusade, a personal crusade to have an impact and that's what I'm been doing for about five years.

Y2KI: Well, I — I often say that there is two ways I can clear a room is start telling some jokes or start talking about the year 2000 problem and I will clear a room out. Until recently did you experience that kind of a problem in terms of getting people to take this seriously?

PETER DE JAEGER: Absolutely. When I first started to talk about this a lot of people laughed and said, you know, you're being silly, one you're being a doom sayer and you're crying wolf and you're chicken little, and all those good things. But as it turns out a lot of people are working on it now, today, and they are finding out that they really wished they had more time.

Y2KI: Right. That's one thing for sure we don't have anymore of is time, that immutable date. Alan, you want to jump in here.

Y2KI: Okay. Peter, hello, Alan Simpson.

PETER DE JAEGER: Greetings.

Y2KI: Peter, I just read you're about in the silver bullet article, an excellent article on your web site and I can relate to this as we get daily calls from publicists ourselves claiming that client's have the answer to the automatic solution.

PETER DE JAEGER: Of course.

Y2KI: How seriously do you think the credibility issue is with these claims?

PETER DE JAEGER: Well, anybody who claims that they have a silver bullet is, to put it bluntly, lying. And if you actually sent down with them and talk about it they will be the first to admit that the silver bullet thing is just for the PR and just for the hype. The reality is that nobody has a solution that does everything. And I've been criticized by some by saying, they say to me, Peter, of course we don't have everything, but can't we still call it a silver bullet because that will get people to buy. And I have a real hard — real problem with lying just to sell products. So I am — I'm out there trying to tell people that there is no silver bullet and these are the reasons why and we came up with 18 reasons without thinking too hard.

Y2KI: Okay. You just returned from Scandinavia, Britain, and Ireland out there spreading the message. How do you find the awareness in these markets compared to here in the U.S. and Canada?

PETER DE JAEGER: Well, the awareness in the U.S. is greater than the awareness in Canada. The U.S. and Canada is greater than that in the U.K., which is greater than that in Europe, and there is no real indication at all on any front that anything is being done in the Far East. So part of the issue is still awareness. I mean, it is November 1996 and I find it very, very difficult to believe that here, you know, we're still talking about this as if some people don't believe it's a real issue. It's very, very strange.

Y2KI: A few days ago BBC television had an excellent 30 minute money program which was aired nationally which featured yourself and Robin Guerney (phonetic sp.) from Britain. Now do you think the mainstream in the U.K., I'm just — your answer there, more conscious of the issues as opposed to the networks here. I mean, last — on Saturday night NBC New York had a very short editorial piece on the year 2000 as though they just found it.

PETER DE JAEGER: Robin Guerney and the year 2000 task force which is partly funded by the government over there has done more to create awareness on this issue in the last three months that all the rest of us combined have been able to pull off in the last five years. They have catapulted the

U.K. from being 18 months behind the awareness curve to being at least three or four months in front of the U.S. Now that's not to say that action has followed those ads and the awareness thing. But certainly everybody in England is aware that there is something called the year 2000 problem and it affects their computer and they have to be working on it.

Y2KI: I'm interviewing Robin in London next week with other government and industry leaders together European perspective on year 2000. So we'll be hearing their comments in their interviews. Now Peter you've been slugging away at this message for the past five years. Many time the lone voice and as history has proven the accurate voice, looking back what lessons have you learned?

PETER DE JAEGER: Well, the media don't get on this, management doesn't get on this until there is a real crisis, until they can actually see something fail. And in a real sense there is nothing that has happened in this that really surprises me. From time-to-time I get a little bit frustrated that things aren't moving faster. But the reality is that this quite frankly is an unbelievable story. The fact that we left off two missing digits and because of that we have major problems. It should not really surprise us. It shouldn't surprise us that people find it unbelievable. I mean, they trusted the computer people to do what was right and we didn't. And it takes a while for that to sink in. You know, in the year 10000 we'll have exactly the same problem. Thank the Lord I won't be heard to speak about it.

Y2KI: I looking at the postings on your mailing list and for the listeners people — Peter has got an excellent mailing list which is about 4,000 professionals subscribe to or are starting to subscribe to — now do you worry about the platen of different solutions that are being put forward. Shouldn't we be striving for a common international standard instead of all these different opinions at this late stage.

PETER DE JAEGER: It would be nice if we could have a common date standard world wide. But we've never demonstrated ourselves to be very, very good at creating anything that's common. We have different plugs, we have different T.V. systems, et cetera, et cetera. Let's not worry right now about creating a common standard. Let's take any solution that anybody can come up with and use it. The reality is, is that we don't have enough solutions to address all the different types of problems that the year 2000 poses for us. And the more solutions we can come up with the better.

Y2KI: Now you use to be a programmer, what do you think about the prospects of these legions of all the programmers that people are talking about coming out of retirement to fix these millions of lines of forgotten code?

PETER DE JAEGER: Not only should they come back out of retirement, but they should bring back the documentation they took with them.

Y2KI: How serious a problem do you think it is to actually located and fix this source code, is it — is it a big problem, or has been lost like you just said?

PETER DE JAEGER: Oh, there are companies who have lost more than 40 percent of their source code and that's the stuff that makes up the programs originally and without that you have to sort of go back to square one. There have been organizations who have lost a tremendous amount. Most organizations have lost about five percent of their source code. So it is a problem. What they do in those situations, usually it's smaller modules, ones that weren't that active. Sometimes they are very, very well defined, so you can rewrite them. It's a stumbling block, but it's not a major obstacle.

Y2KI: Okay. What about the export of the software for (indiscernible) in a reverse engineering and foreign third world countries. You know, I have seen the number of Indian and Philippine companies that are springing up to do this, what issue do you see here, giving away all this stuff overseas.

PETER DE JAEGER: Well, in the beginning offshore development was not really what you would call politically correct, because it wasn't correct to send your work away when there was lots of people here who could do it. But because of the year 2000 problem and the recognized shortage of people it's become more legitimate. It's okay now to send your stuff offshore. One of the fears I have with offshore development, it's got nothing to do with the practice, instead it's got to with the mess. That you can send your code to someone else and have them fix it without you being involved in the process. My strongest recommendation is if you are sending your code away send one of your managers as well at the same time so that they can be on the sight to keep a real eye on what's going on over there and help with situations that come up or questions that need to be asked.

Y2KI: Before I'm back to it, how is the book coming along. It's about time that your book was suppose to come out. Is it near or —

PETER DE JAEGER: Well, the sad part about this is that — I mean, a lot of people are asking where the book is, where the book is. In reality, is that we are still busy, you know, speaking and getting out in front of people that finding time to do the book has been tough. The good news is, is with John Wiley and Sons, they came after us and the book is with them. There is no title as yet. It is due to come out in December or January and the first run will be 50,000 copies. So they do expect us to be, you know, a best seller or at least on everybody's — all the programmers bookshelves.

Y2KI: Excellent. Now the final thing before I head back to Ed. Last Friday I spoke on this program about the military implications of year 2000 and how the Air Force and the U.K. military were getting on board. How do you see this affecting the military and national security, and how are we going to get the politicians in Washington to wake-up?

PETER DE JAEGER: Well, the politicians are beginning to wake-up, but politicians wake-up very, very slowly. It takes them a while to get the message, then it takes them a while to act. They put a bill forward together in the U.S. Government that there would be a committee formed who would have the mandate of finding out about this thing and looking at solutions and finding out what the impact to the economy would be and that they would report back at the end of 1997. We don't have time for committee reports that take that long. We have run out of time and we need to work very, very quickly. If the Government were really interested in doing this, they would put the committee together and say you will report back at the end of January. But a Government can't work that fast. Plus the fact that we've just gone through a major election which slowed everything down. And now, though, the people who are in power, this will happen on their watch. This will happen during their term. And it will go down on history as to how they handle the year 2000 problem.

Y2KI: Well, thank you, Alan, appreciate it. We're going to have to go to a break here in about 30 seconds. And when we come back we'll be joined by Michael Tantleff and we'll continue our discussions with Peter de Jaeger. Please stay tuned.

(BREAK)

Y2KI: And we continue now with the Millennium Bug. Your host this afternoon, Ed Mulhall, discussing the year 2000 computer bug and how it could be profitable for you. Joined today by Peter de Jaeger and Michael Tantleff of Prudential Securities in Santa Barbara, California also joining us for this final segment. And now here is your host of the Millennium Bug, Ed Mulhall.

Y2KI: Thank you, Jim. Welcome back. Peter, are you still there?

PETER DE JAEGER: Yes, I am.

Y2KI: Good. I'm going to bring Michael Tantleff on now and he has some questions perhaps more, more directed to specific companies and how they are faring, if you will. Michael?

Y2KI: Yes, hi, Peter, how are you?

PETER DE JAEGER: Greetings, Michael, very well, thanks.

Y2KI: Good. I've been a faithful members of the list for about 18 months.

PETER DE JAEGER: 5,000 E-mail messages later.

Y2KI: Yes, I've seen it grow tremendously. The thing that I am really amazed at is that companies still haven't let out a tremendous amount of contracts. There have been a lot of impact studies done, but companies are still not moving up to the plate and I'm wondering, you know, what do you think it's going to take before people get the message. I'm down here in the trenches and people just don't really get it yet.

PETER DE JAEGER: This is one of those situations where you feel like asking the kids question, what parts of this don't you understand.

Y2KI: Other than my kids, what part of no don't you understand.

PETER DE JAEGER: Exactly. When 00 enters your code the code stops. When the code stops the systems that you depend upon stop and when they stop you are out of business. What it's going to take, unfortunately, is a significant exposure of some organization that admits to that a problem was created by the year 2000 problem. And it needs to get high publicity. It needs to create a significant financial failure before company start moving. And unfortunately, that will come to close to the year 2000 to be of help to many, many people. This is like going to your doctor and they say, don't smoke, don't, smoke, don't smoke. And then you finally go to your doctor and they say you have cancer in both lungs. And you say if I stop smoking now will that help. And we're going to wake-up as the train goes over the break in the tracks, unfortunately.

Y2KI: So you don't see any way of getting out of this with a major, you know, blow up?

PETER DE JAEGER: I see most of the company who are working on it today will come out of this slightly bruised but capable of performing business. So the companies who are active today and maybe tomorrow and possibly next week might be okay. But if you leave it too much longer than that, I mean if you don't really have a plan in place by January of 1997, you really are playing a nasty game of Russian roulette.

Y2KI: It's called millennium survivable is what a client told me.

PETER DE JAEGER: Well it is, I mean it is a case of survival. And what these companies will be doing is they will be playing Russian roulette, the gun is firmly planted to the side of their head, all the chambers are loaded and they will be hoping for a misfire. And I don't want to do that with my business, thank you.

Y2KI: No, I say not. One of the problems that I see is as you see the growth in your vendor list on the year 2000 page, it's becoming increasingly confusing as to which way to go. What I'm hoping will emerge is some sort of virtual, to use a bad word, silver bullet, such that the best tools of the various vendors will be made apparent. Because right now it's a tremendous alphabet soup as to who works with what and when and how much and who can really do the job.

PETER DE JAEGER: There is no doubt about it, as more player come into the field it's going to be very, very tough to identify who has, you know, a better answer then someone else. This is like any situation, though, with computers. You have to start now, you can't wait for something to get better down the line or for the prices to drop. Most of the vendors, I would say a large majority of the vendors are fair and honest vendors. In other words, they have real solutions that are applicable to your situation. It doesn't really take that long to settle in on a couple of vendors who know what they are doing. Go to one or two conferences and take a look at the vendors there and ask the most important question. Give me four or five references of people who have used your tool. Now even a vendor who is just starting up will have used Beta —

Y2KI: Beta (indiscernible).

PETER DE JAEGER: Who will have used the tool at no cost. So even the most, you know, junior of the companies coming into this will have people they can refer you to. And if they don't have people, if they don't, don't go with them.

Y2KI: Peter, let me change the point of view just slightly. What would you suggest to an investor, someone who is heavily invested or is thinking about investing in a corporation, what question should they ask that company in term — hopefully, to illicit an answer that will make some sense in terms of whether or not this company is actually taking care of the problem and they remain a viable investment?

PETER DE JAEGER: There's really three things for any company right now who is getting into this and the first one is get some information on their tool and listen very carefully for what is not said. In other words, if a tool vendors says or a process vendor says that we can solve everything, run, do not walk to the nearest exit, they cannot. If they are very, very frank with what they can and cannot do and there are some out there who will tell you right up front, we cannot do this, when they start telling you what they cannot do pay attention. Because what you're dealing with is an honest broker and that's important. The next thing is how many people do you have on staff and how fast have you grown. Do you have the resources to handle the contracts that you might get. And then thirdly, ask them to see a two and half year business plan. In other words, show me what you expect your growth to be and how you're going to handle even those guesses. I mean, you're guess a certain amount growth, how will you handle that.

Y2KI: Okay. What about a company not involved in the solution they are just trying to do business, Coca-Cola, what questions should you ask them?

PETER DE JAEGER: Same thing.

Y2KI: Really,

PETER DE JAEGER: You want to see your plan. I mean, if you're trying to invest in a company now you had better be doing due diligence on year 2000. If you buy a company today sight unseen, if you're emerging with a company, then one of the most important questions you ask right up front there is how have you handled your year 2000 problem. Because everybody has the year 2000 problem. That is the first given right now is that you do have the problem, how have you attempted to solve it. If a company, an insurance company, for example, does not have a year 2000 project plan in place that they can show you within 20 minutes of you asking then chances are it doesn't exist.

Y2KI: Hey, Peter, have you seen the data dimensions R2K (phonetic sp.) is offering?

PETER DE JAEGER: I do not speak about vendors. As much as DDI is my corporate sponsor and who pays me to be a lot of places, I must stay clear of talking about vendors, otherwise I lose my credibility in an instant. Then I become someone who just pushes a particular vendor or product. So forgive me, but I'm going to back out of that question.

Y2KI: Okay. Well I was — at any rate, I was very excited to see that they had a soup to nuts offering on how to embrace — they were two independent and how to embrace your problem. I thought that was a real step forward in getting the ball rolling because everybody is talking about this, that, and the other thing, but no one has sewn it altogether. And I'm looking for processes and methodologies and I think that's very important now.

PETER DE JAEGER: It's very, very crucial to this. I made a prediction a couple of months ago —

Y2KI: I have them all on my wall.

PETER DE JAEGER: Yes, that January, February, March there will be sheer utter panic in business as we finally realize that this thing is real. And then after that, there will emerge from all of the noise one or several very, very similar methodologies and it's based upon those methodologies that will calm down the market and get people to work.

Y2KI: Peter, let's assume that a company actually does or has made the investment, is well along the way, and is going to solve its problem prior to the year 2000, what about defensive strategy for its trading partners, its customers who don't?

PETER DE JAEGER: They must absolutely do two things. They must look to their supply chain and do something that we've always talked about, supply chain management. In other words, are your critical suppliers year 2000 compatible. What are they doing? Do you choose to help them or do you take a dog in a manger approach and say no, no, you know, we solved our problem, you solve your own problem. Do you help your business partners get this thing solved and you look both up and down the supply chain. And the other thing too, is that this is not an IS problem, it's never been an IS problem, as in information services, it has always been a business management problem. And one of the things that your business management must look to is how do they from the business management perspective start taking proactive action. One of those ways would be to loosen up a great deal on just in time inventory philosophy.

Y2KI: Right.

PETER DE JAEGER: In other words, in 1999 start buying up warehouse space.

Y2KI: Peter, we're going to have to go. This went so fast. We'd love to have you back again.

PETER DE JAEGER: Be happy to.

(END)

Guests: JEFF JINNETT
Date: FRIDAY, DECEMBER 6, 1996

Y2KI: Now for the Y2K Investor Show. Here now is our host, Ed Mulhall.

Y2KI: Good morning. Thank you, Keith. It's been a very busy week in the year 2000 business. Starting out Wednesday we were at the Wall Street Wednesday Reception and it was a real pleasure to get to speak there and to meet many of you. I enjoyed that very much. It's nice to know that there are some folks out there listening and are interested. Also, yesterday I spent the day at the education foundation of Data Processing Management Association conference here in Washington and it was also very, very good, some excellent speakers and I hope to have several of them on the weeks to follow. Now to begin our show today we are joined by John Vasquez, Vice President of Investments at Prudential Securities here in Bethesda. Are you with us John?

Y2KI: Hi, Ed. How are you today?

Y2KI: Good talking to you. And very special guest this morning for the first half hour is Jeff Jinnett. Jeff is of counsel to the law firm of Labuff, Lamb, Green and McCray (phonetic sp.) up in New York City. And Jeff has been writing and very outspoken about the legal implications of the year 2000 situation. So he's been kind enough to agree to come on and talk some about this and some of his work and take any of your questions at (202) 289-7730. Good morning, Jeff.

JEFF JINNETT: Good morning, how are you doing?

Y2KI: I'm very fine, thank you for joining us.

JEFF JINNETT: My pleasure.

Y2KI: Let's jump right into it, Jeff. What — can you give us a quick summary of what you think the legal implications of the year 2000 situation are?

JEFF JINNETT: Sure. Do you want to deal with the private sector?

Y2KI: Yes, let's start with that.

JEFF JINNETT: All right. Private sector — some of the more interesting legal issues deal with public companies. Many of the public companies, as the Wall Street Journal has reported, as reported are a little leery of describing the status of the year 2000 corrective programs, they are nervous that if they overstate the case they — and then they fail to become compliant, then they end up having the words thrown back at them when they get sued, like plaintiffs attorneys a few years from now.

Y2KI: Right.

JEFF JINNETT: I think one of the things that public companies should focus in on is that if they, if they say that they fully intend to become a 100 percent compliant and then come January 1, 2000, they have system breakdowns and they have not become fully compliant and their stock prices drop a few points, you may have plaintiffs attorneys coming back and pouring over their annual reports on Form 10K and their quarterly reports on Form 10Q, to see if they fully disclosed the extent of the year 2000 problems and then argue that they haven't, and then institute securities suits against the public companies.

Y2KI: Well, we had Irene Dec from Prudential on here a couple of weeks ago, and she said that the Prudential companies were going to spend a minimum of 100 million dollars to fix this problem and actually had budget authority up to about 150 million. My question to you is does that sort of set a precedent for what, let's just say in the insurance industry, the level of effort and the degree of investment that other insurance companies are going to have to make to be seen as having taken a real stab at solving the problem.

JEFF JINNETT: Well, actually, I don't think from a legal point of view that really protects a company to just say we've got a 100 million dollar budget for this, it is a significant number certainly. What I recommend to clients is that they adopt a year 2000 plan, they develop one based on their technical needs, have top management involved, not just the chief information officer, have the CEO and the General Counsel involved and then take the extra step of presenting it to the Board of Directors. Have the Board formally consider the year 2000 plan, have an outside year 2000 expert review the plan, give comments to it, incorporate those comments, and then have the Board formally adopt a plan. That way if they have made a mistake, they missed something, and they do have a shutdown on January 1, 2000 or thereabouts, the Board of Directors if they get sued can say, look, we were involved, we made our best business judgment that this was the plan to adopt, we devoted 100 million to it or whatever it was, and so, you know, we were certainly not grossly negligent and we don't even think we were negligent. Under State law there is what is called the business judgment rule, which protects directors from mistakes and judgment as long as they have fully considered a problem and made a best decision in the best interest of the company, and act as a ordinarily prudent person would act in their place. If the Board makes no decision whatsoever, never has a meeting on it, and knows nothing of what's going on, they may not get the protection of that business judgment rule. So the one thing I'm recommending to public company is elevate this to a higher level, don't just have this be a decision made by the Chief Information Officer, and involve top management, and involve the Board.

Y2KI: Yeah, do you think directors and officers insurance is going to cover these folks should there be a problem down the road?

JEFF JINNETT: Well, there has been no cases yet. But when you look at directors and officers liability insurance, the types of things that are excluded in terms of liability or things like sexual harassment suits, actions where the directors acted criminally for their interests. The types of things that could happen or go wrong with the year 2000 plan don't seem to be excluded by the typical D&O policy. So my best guest is that if a company were to have a breakdown or shutdown due to year 2000, they would probably still be covered by their D&O insurance. But the limits on those might be 5 million dollars or a little bit more, and the damages sought in a year 2000 suit could be considerably higher.

Y2KI: Right.

JEFF JINNETT: So your D&O might not fully protect you if you end up with a serious year 2000 problem.

Y2KI: Right.

JEFF JINNETT: And on insurance is another interesting issue which is, it could be that your business interruption insurance may not cover you. Business interruption insurance normally is under a property and casualty policy, it usually protects against fortuitous events, things that happen by chance. The year 2000 problem has been known about for 20 to 30 years, it's certainly not happening by chance and the correction of it is fully within the control of the insured.

Y2KI: Right.

JEFF JINNETT: So in all likelihood an insurance company looking at their business interruption policy might take the position that it's really not covered.

Y2KI: We've got a minute to go before the first break, Jeff. Would — briefly, do you think the requirement 10Q and 10K requirement for stating the size of the problem that is now coming up next year would also require them to state there — the Board's response and their plan to solve the problem?

JEFF JINNETT: It probably does. When you look at the management's discussion and analysis section of an annual report —

Y2KI: Right.

JEFF JINNETT: The SCC has various releases that they've issued describing when you have to describe a particular problem. And if a company feels that it's reasonably possible that they might have a material year 2000 problem then they probably should strongly consider discussing that in their management's discussion and analysis section. Companies might decide at this point that they don't feel that it's — they have enough information to be able to disclose that. But within the next year or two, certainly, there will be many companies that will look at it and say, you know, there is a possibility we might not catch everything, we ought to make a disclosure about it.

Y2KI: Right. Well, we're going to the break now. If you have any calls for Jeff at — give us a call at (202) 289-7730. And when we come back John Vasquez will have some questions for Jeff. You're listening to the Y2K Investor on WBZS.

(BREAK)

Y2KI: We continue with more of the Y2K Investor Show on Business Radio 730. Here once again is our host, Ed Mulhall.

Y2KI: Thank you, Keith. We're here with Jeff Jinnett, lawyer — of counsel to the law firm of Labuff, Lamb, Green, and McCray in New York, and a leading writer on the issue of legal liability and legal problem dealing with the year 2K. John, you had some questions for Jeff, go ahead.

Y2KI: Yes. Hi, Jeff, how are you?

JEFF JINNETT: Hey, John, how are you doing?

Y2KI: Good, nice to meet you. There is an interesting question. It seems to me as far as legalities are concerned, money issues certainly bring up a lot of lawsuits in the world and Prudential has publicly stated it's going to be at last 100 million dollars to fix this problem. Well, let's assume that we and everybody else in Wall Street and everywhere very, very important gets fixed and we've all spent a couple of billion dollars doing this. Well, Jeff, couldn't we look around and say, who is responsible for this problem, why do we have to spend this money, you know, I mean, we bought this software and these systems in good faith, why do we have to pay this money, shouldn't we get some of it back?

JEFF JINNETT: Sure. I mean, it raises a very interesting issue. You know people refer to this problem as the Millennium Bug, as if it were a virus, I don't think technically it truly is a virus, but it certainly is a bug or a defect. It had an innocent origin, programmers were trying to save memory during processing, so they used six digits for the date rather than eight. But they are definitely some liability issues as to who should pay for the corrective work. You may, for example, as a company, have licensed some software on a long term license, say a 20 year license and have taken out a maintenance agreement to run the same 20 year period, running past the year 2000. And the vendor would say I'm going to agree to maintain this software to meet specifications for that 20 year period. You might have an argument to that vendor that the vendor should correct the year 2000 problem, because otherwise it won't meet spec.

Y2KI: That's really interesting.

JEFF JINNETT: Same as with an outsourcing agreement. You may have a company in a outsourcing agreement saying I will do all your data processing for a 20 year period, past the year 2000, and I'll fix any bugs or defects in your system. You might be able to argue to that outsourcing vendor, well, look, this may not be a virus technically, but it is a bug, you should fix it at your cost as part of the outsourcing agreement. Now the vendors are going to say, this is crazy, even though we didn't think to expressly disclaim the year 2000 bug, the cost is in the millions of dollars and it's more than we are getting onto the main contract. We couldn't possibly have meant to take on that liability. And what will happen is the vendors lawyers, and the client lawyers will have very heated negotiations and discussions back and forth and maybe there will be some settlement in between.

Y2KI: Well, would you consider that would be, if some major case were settled that way, could that be used as a sort of benchmark case for everybody to settle their cases with.

JEFF JINNETT: Definitely. Definitely it will be very interesting to see what happens with the first case if it ever went into litigation. One problem is many companies are just going out and pay for corrective work and not even thinking of making a claim against their vendors. If they don't make that claim and they fix it on their own they are going to have waived their claim in all likelihood and they won't be able to go over to the vendor later and say, reimburse me. You need to make the claim up front.

Y2KI: Ah, okay. So why couldn't you go back and sue them later and say, hey, we had to spend this on our own?

JEFF JINNETT: Oh, because the vendor will say, had you come to me I would have used in-house labor and it would have been free to me. I'm not going to pay your cost to go hire expensive outside vendors to do it, I would have done it at my own cost.

Y2KI: But that's a kind of catch-22, because, as we all know, legal battles can be protracted (indiscernible).

JEFF JINNETT: Well, if you make a claim and the vendor says it's not going to be responsible for this, but you've made the claim in writing, and then the vendor refuses, you're free then to mitigate your damages, go out and fix it yourself, but preserve your right to go back later for reimbursement.

Y2KI: Ah hah, okay. Very interesting. So you couldn't — but it is a kind of catch-22, if it takes a long time to institute some lawsuit.

JEFF JINNETT: Well, in some instances they may be class action lawsuits. Major vendors use the same contracts uniformly with all their clients, so you have the same contract terms as everybody else. You could band together in a class action suit, conceivably hire one law firm and reduce your cost that way.

Y2KI: Have you seen anything along these lines beginning to happen?

JEFF JINNETT: Nothing. There have been a lot of talk, a lot of rumors, a pocket full of stories, but as far as I know there is no reported decision on any issue like this.

Y2KI: Yes. Jeff, I've heard it said that one man's bug, is another man's features, and that, the companies may argue that count — go back and count up all the cycles and all the storage, of course, that you saved by not having to input and store those two digits and we did it as a feature as opposed to a bug.

JEFF JINNETT: It would hard for a vendor to argue that, like say, for example 1998. If a vendor licenses new software in 1998 that's going to shutdown in two years —

Y2KI: Right.

JEFF JINNETT: It's going to be hard for the vendor to argue that they year 2000 bug was an accepted risk. Software, it usually has an intended life of more than two years.

Y2KI: Right.

JEFF JINNETT: So right now vendors are looking to change their contracts, their license agreements for future software to expressly disclaim year 2000 compliancy unless it is going to be compliant. Because they recognize that the closer you get to the year 2000 the more likely that the Court would deem it an assumed ability for software to handle the date change.

Y2KI: Jeff, I know you've also been following on the Government side, the Senate Bill 2131, and you've had some comments on the initial — to make the bill better when it gets resubmitted here in the next session.

JEFF JINNETT: Right.

Y2KI: What do you think has to be done with that?

JEFF JINNETT: Well, Senate Bill 2131 is a bill that Senator Monaghan introduced in the Senate. There is no counterpart House Bill at the moment. But Monaghan recommended that there be a bi-partisan year 2000 commission created of 15 members to help the Federal Government and the State Governments coordinate the year 2000 efforts to reduce duplication of effort, reduce cost and basically streamline their corrective efforts. I think it's a great idea. There were a few problems with the Bill though, which is that Senator Monaghan recommended that it only exist for one year, issue one report at the end of '97 and then disband. I really think the year 2000 commission is so important and so valuable that it ought to last through the year 2000 and issue multiple reports. And it's first report should be early enough to take into account the next budget, so the funding can be given to the Federal agencies in time.

Y2KI: What do you think State and local Government's liability is on this issue?

JEFF JINNETT: Well each State has or not each state, but many States have torque claims acts, where if a citizen is injured due to an act of a Government official they can sue. In certain limited cases the States have sovereign immunity they can waive in certain cases. Usually the waiver is if it's a ministerial act of an official that breaches a special duty owed to a citizen.

Y2KI: Right.

JEFF JINNETT: Not to the public at large.

Y2KI: I see.

JEFF JINNETT: So, let's say for example, there is a computer glitch and a prisoner is paroled out of prison early and he killed somebody.

Y2KI: Yes.

JEFF JINNETT: Typically that's viewed as a duty of the public at large, so the tort claim act doesn't cover it. If, however, you're issuing checks to somebody specifically, like welfare checks, veteran checks, and the computer fails to process those in time, there it's a more open question as to possibly the state might be liable for the damages that ensue. Or for example, they are operating traffic lights and the microchips in the traffic lights don't work and there is a car crash and the State knew years in advance that that was going to happen.

Y2KI: Jeff, Jeff, we're going to have to cut you off. I do appreciate your joining us, we'd like to have you come on back. We're going to the break now on WBZS.

(END)

Guest: BRIAN KEANE
Date: Friday, April 11, 1997

Y2KI: Good morning, everyone. I'd like to introduce our special guest for this morning, it's Brian Keane, and he is Senior Vice President with Keen — let me see if I can get that right now — it's Keane Associates, and —

BRIAN KEANE: — Incorporated.

Y2KI: All right. And welcome, Brian.

BRIAN KEANE: Good morning.

Y2KI: Well, let me tell you right off the top, I was looking over your — the financials and it sort of caught me by surprise that Keane just about a half a billion dollar company, and while I've heard about Keane — known about Keane for many years, I didn't realize how it's rapidly grown from 1968, I believe. Why don't you give us a brief history of Keane and how it's evolved over the years.

BRIAN KEANE: Well, we were started in 1965 up in the Boston area by my Dad, John Keane, and at that time he had been IBM prior to that, and the 360 architecture had just been announced, of course those of you computer hardware processing power and the great gap was between the processing and the business need of company, and he went out on his own and started a company to develop software — the business application software, to bridge that gap. So since our founding to today our primary business is developing and managing software assets. We're a large corporation. Currently we are — you're correct — our run rate right now is about $560 million. We've got about 40 branch offices throughout the United States and Canada, and our primary business areas are out-sourcing — application out-sourcing, large scale application development and that includes whether it's client servers as well as Internet, help-desk out-sourcing, and of course, Year 2000 compliance.

Y2KI: And how would you break down the mix between say government and commercial and also maybe between is there any one sector where you focus more than others?

BRIAN KEANE: In terms of our break-out between commercial and federal business, approximately less than 10% of Keane's business is from the federal and state government. But that difference continues to grow and actually it's doing quite well. But our legacy as a company has been in the commercial side of things. In terms of our break-out of industry sectors, we can look at that in a few different ways, if we're looking within the Year 2000 industry segment alone, the highest percentage is with financial services institutions — banks, insurance companies, etc. If we look at the company as a whole, probably manufacturing maybe the largest industry segment. How many folks do you have aboard. We have at the close of the third — the first quarter, I think we had about 7,002 and employees. Give or take one or two.

Y2KI: Give or take one or two.

BRIAN KEANE: We just gave our earnings report yesterday, so we had all the statistics as of the end of the quarter, so the number sticks in my mind.

Y2KI: We had, I guess, twice now the Bank of Boston on our show. Steve McManna(sp) and your one of their key partners in terms of addressing the Year 2000 problem. Could you maybe talk a little about what your role is for Bank of Boston

BRIAN KEANE: The Bank of Boston — what we're — and that was one of earlier projects and we are working along side the Bank of Boston. They have some pretty aggressive plans to bring their systems into compliance. I think that they've been very progressive in that respect and we are involved in what we would call the implementation phase or Phase III, converting the code and moving it into tests. I don't recall at this point exactly how large our staff is there, but we have a fairly large contingent over at the Bank.

Y2KI: And earlier you mentioned that less than 10% of your business currently comes from federal or state government, and that you in fact were focusing on increasing that. Have you done that through any partnerships? Do you have established partnerships with say traditional government system integrators that will help you into that market?

BRIAN KEANE: Well, as you know, many of the government contracts are bid out through partnerships and through primes and subcontractors, and we have a number of those relationships, have had a number of those relationships for years, so we were leveraging those and we're working with in some cases a lot of the big boys the EDS and the CSC and others, but we're also working with a number of the AideAide(sp) firms. I think there's probably a couple of dozen firms that we're working with at any given time. Within the Year 2000 arena, interestingly we are just seeing momentum start to significantly pick up with Year 2000. We're doing work for a handful of agencies right now and I think with LNB(sp) February 6th meeting, hopefully that paves the way for that work to increase significantly in the months ahead.

Y2KI: Any personal opinions on where the government stands, you know, there's quite a bit of controversy that we've talked often about on this show about the disparity between OMBs estimates for the cost, CIOs estimation of their ability to address the problem in time with the budgets that they have in fact posted. Any thoughts on those subjects?

BRIAN KEANE: My personal feeling is that the OMP budget estimates are very low, and I can't comment on the methodology that they used to come up with those, if you just do a comparison of the size of some of their applications, the scope of the applications, the range and the technology, compare that to the commercial world where we have a great deal of experience, it's not — it's non sequitur that their budget is as low as it is. You know, how can the government — this would be the first time, perhaps, that the government can do something at a fraction of the cost of what the commercial world can do.

Y2KI: Brian one of the criticisms that is leveled at companies that are seen as Y2K companies is that they may have a business over the next couple of years, but then they're going to hit the Year 2000 and theoretically the problem goes away, and the thought is maybe some of these companies go away. You, on the other hand, are with a company that's been in business for some almost 30 years, and has shown significant growth and this Y2K is a relatively new phenomena for you. My questions are as follows: that the — how much of what Keane Incorporated's business is Y2K related and how big do you expect that to get and what if any segways or advantages you going forward after the problem is theoretically solved?

BRIAN KEANE: Currently our Year 2000 business represents about 15% of Keane's revenues, and that's been growing rather rapidly. We, a year ago, when we had first quarter earnings of 96, it was well less than 1% of our revenue. Today it's 15% and it continues to grow and accelerate. What percentage will it be over the next — in 1997, 1998, 1999 — it will be larger than 15%? Certainly. Will it eventually become the primary part of our business? I doubt it. It may be the single largest component, but we've got a number of large out-sourcing contracts. We continue to develop systems for companies.

There are a lot of firms out there that — that's the beautiful thing about the American economy is that people can start-up a company and be opportunistic when a situation arises. And there are a lot of companies out there that have jumped on the Year 2000 band wagon. And the onus is on them to figure what their business space is going to be — the model is going be after the Year 2000. The way we're looking to leverage it is since last — this is our 32nd year and in that time we have been supporting the CIO. We have been supporting him or her by providing information application systems by developing them by management. Increasingly, we are doing out-sourcing work. We are looking at Year 2000 as an opportunity to increase the amount of out-sourcing work that we're going to be doing for these customers.

Y2KI: Another one of your success stories, in addition to Bank Boston, is Sears and Roebuck. Can you tell us a little bit about how you became involved with them and what role you've played with Sears?

BRIAN KEANE: We've been doing work with Sears for a number of years. In fact, I think some of our early work back maybe I the late 1980s is that we gotten involved and out-sourced some of their applications to Keane and so we were responsible for the ongoing maintenance support, enhancement and development of part of their business. I think based on that relationship and their knowledge that we had an re-engineering practice they invited us into to understand the scope of their Year 2000 problem. That was, I believe, 1995 — 1994, 1995. It was before most companies had really taken a close look into the Year 2000 and Sears was, I think, was one of the first companies to put together a comprehensive plan. The nature of our work was to put together — help them put together an overall plan for addressing the Year 2000.

Y2KI: And is that completed or ongoing, or what's the status of that?

BRIAN KEANE: That project is — Sears continues to work — I don't have in front of me — I don't recall exactly what we are doing with Sears right now — how that project has progressed over the last couple of years. We have over two hundred Year 2000 projects that we've run to date over about 140 different customers and in the beginning I was on top the details of every project.

Y2KI: Right.

BRIAN KEANE: Right now —

Y2KI: — you better have good people.

BRIAN KEANE: Got to have good people, got to have a lot of good people.

Y2KI: Well, that's really my next question is what types of people are you finding necessary to work on these projects and are you having any degree of difficulty in finding these people.

BRIAN KEANE: In terms of the kind of people, we are at an extremely tight labor market. Even if there was no Year 2000 compliance problem out there. We are probably in the tightest labor market our industry has ever seen, you know, for the last 30 years. And you add some of the Year 2000 on top of that, particularly since we are just beginning to get the inflection point of the hockey stick where the staffing is ramping up rapidly, we are in a — it's a problematic situation. It's more and more difficult to hire good people. Right now we have over, for example, over 90 recruiters throughout the United States. We'll be hiring in excess of 3,500 people this year. And we're hiring program managers, project managers, analyst, programmers and in addition, we are putting through about 600 people — we're hiring about 600 entry level people from some of the best colleges in the United States, putting them through a six week intensive program to train them in our methodologies and then putting them out in the field.

Y2KI: The recruiters that you mentioned, are those your own employees? Do you do your own in-house recruiting, or do you use companies like Olston or Robert Haft?

BRIAN KEANE: We have our own recruiters. And generally our business is a branch and we have a number of local branches, for example, we in Rockville, Maryland, that's where our operation is based locally, both our federal systems subsidiary, as well as our commercial branch, and within each branch we generally have two to three recruiters that's focused on that local market place.

Y2KI: Brian, Keane obviously takes a life-cycle approach to application development and coming back into a application that's already been developed to fix a Year 2000 problem, presents special problems. Can you talk a little bit about Keane's methodology and how you deal with complexity?

BRIAN KEANE: Yes. That's a good question, and there certainly are differences between application development and a Year 2000 compliance project. In fact, a Year 2000 compliance project is more similar to a migration effort than new development. In all cases, however, what makes sense is following a methodology. Keane is very methodology driven. We believe that by adhering to a set of processes, by collecting performance metrics, measuring those, you can get improvements, you can go down a learning curve. The nature of Year 2000 is not all that complicated from a technical standpoint. It's just very large, and it's a number of changes over and over and over again. We break our methodology out — our methodology is referred to as "Resolve 2000" — into three phases. The first phase, which we call "Enterprise Planning" really takes an enterprise view of an organization to understand the size and scope of the problem. It also — not only by performing some technical analysis — but also doing some business triage and some environmental analysis. Second phase is some strategy development. How are you going to be addressing the conversion. It also includes some detail analysis of the date fields, and the third phase is the actual conversion and the testing. And the testing, as you know, may represents upwards of 45% to 55% of the overall project.

Y2KI: Yes, let's talk a little bit about that. That's, I think, rapidly emerging as the great unknown. We're seeing the greatest amount of fudge factor being applied to the testing phase. What are you seeing with your clients and what's your approach to testing?

BRIAN KEANE: We've spent a good deal of time looking at this over the last several months and although we have a traditional life cycle and we testing methodologies for new developments for out-sourcing, what we found is no single Year 2000 specific testing methodology out there that's readily available. We — next week will be probably — we expect to be announcing some of Keane's activities and initiatives involving testing methodology that is very comprehensive and is also targeted towards Year 2000 specifically and the unique considerations there.

Y2KI: Now is this something you've developed, or something you're teaming with someone else?

BRIAN KEANE: It's — we — it's something that we've done in conjunction with a couple of other firms and we'll be in a position to talk more about that I expect, next week.

Y2KI: Well, you've intrigued us so we will have to get back to you on word on that. It seems that you've concentrated mostly in the U.S. and Canada. Are you looking to expand worldwide? What type of opportunities do you see worldwide for Year 2000 specifically.

BRIAN KEANE: Well, the United States, it's sort of a — sort of a rolling wave here, where the United States is ahead of the rest of the world with regard to Year 2000 compliance and the commercial part of the United States is the first probably state governments are send, federal government is third. Behind all of those would be Europe and the other parts of the world. As far the IS-related work or IS services worldwide, 85% of the market is made up between the United States and Europe. Right now, Keane's work is limited, or our branch operations are limited to the United States and Canada. We do do work on a case-by-case basis overseas for some of our larger customers on a project basis.

For example some of our Year 2000 projects we've had to be collecting some information, doing some work overseas. We have maintained — in the XX?? services industry company, first and foremost, there are real economies of having a tight focus and being able to share resource of cross-branches. Once you move into a different country, you've got different labor law, you've got different accounting systems, you have currency risks, so that's why we have been slow to move over seas. The way the economy is going, I think it's just a matter of time.

Y2KI: You touched on tools when we spoke about testing earlier, and certainly in this market sector the tool vendors have been one of the hottest sector, also one of the most volatile, Matrydyne certainly has gotten a lot attraction.

BRIAN KEANE: Yes.

Y2KI: But they are also other players like Aladar(sp) and UniCom(sp) who have tools that are specific to certain market segments. What's your philosophy about using tools? Are you using tools provided by these manufacturers? Do you use your own tools? Do you develop them internally?

BRIAN KEANE: Yes. Keane's philosophy on this is that we seek to be tool independent. We're a services company — a solutions company, we're geared towards methodologies and providing solutions. Other companies specialize in the products and tools and there's — it's always that there be a better mouse trap. Our methodologies support multiple tools. We have worked, you know, across the 200-whatever deals that we have — we've worked with most of the tools out there. We're also very progressive, we're proactive in looking to understand what the capabilities are of the different tools, to bench-mark them and bring them to bear, depending upon the client's environment and particular situation.

Y2KI: Do you have experience with Matridigm's products, because one of the, I guess, controversial aspects of Matridigm is that when it initially hit the market, and there were some announcements — it was touted as the silver bullet — something that we talk about a lot here on the show and we try to debunk — what's your experience been with Matridigm?

BRIAN KEANE: Yes, I'm quite familiar with Matridigm, and, in fact, yesterday I was in a meeting in which Jim Brady, their CO was involved with some of their other folks, and I've been out to San Jose and met with their people and looked at their technology. First and foremost, I don't believe there's going to be a silver bullet in this Year 2000 business. If all of us that coded in the past adhere to standard throughout, perhaps there could be, but our industry has been woefully lacking standards for a long time. Therefore, I doubt there's going to be any silver bullet, and I think that that's true with Matridigm. I think it's true with any of the tools out there.

Y2KI: Can they provide significant value?

BRIAN KEANE: Some of these tools, yes. The jury is still out on Matridigm and we are working with them as well as several other firms that have some sort of leading edge technology to try and benchmark and find some pilots to see how they stack up.

Y2KI: Great. You know, one other, I guess, topic within this area might be, how companies work together or compete. The line are somewhat fuzzy, I think, or folks perhaps aren't familiar with the industry, and maybe even some of us who are in it sometimes get confused from time to time as to who's competitor and who's cooperating, and maybe you're doing both at the same time. Do you see yourselves as a competitor of Viasoft(sp) or are you complimentary? How do you interact with them in the market place?

BRIAN KEANE: Well, I — we — I consider ourselves very complimentary with Viasoft and we do have a partnership with Viasoft, and it's been a very successful partnership for the last couple years for both them and for both us. They are not only firm that we work with, but we feel that their technology has a great to offer. Moreover, I think that the Viasoft management has been — is very progressive in understanding where they're going as an organization and how this Year 2000 fits in the hole. Viasoft is not a Year 2000 company, per se, because they started like 13 years ago. Their business is to provided technology, to help better managed applications. Keane's business is to provide the services and the solutions and methodologies to better manage applications. So we've got the services piece, they have the technology piece.

Y2KI: So your people is only complimentary?

BRIAN KEANE: I'm sorry?

Y2KI: You're people intensive, where as they are technology intensive.

BRIAN KEANE: Yes.

Y2KI: Brian, Keane has a real fine website and that's "wwwkeane.com" and there are several very interesting white papers up on that site and I'd like to ask you a couple of questions about those white papers when we come back from the break for our final section. Stay with us folks. You've been listening to the Y2K Investor on Business Radio 730.

Y2KI: Brian, there are several real interesting white papers up on your website. One is called the "Six Deadly Myths of Century Compliance" and briefly their Myth One: It's a simple technical problem; Myth Two: We have plenty of time; Myth Three: All of our systems will be replaced before the Year 2000; Myth Four: We don't have the problem; Myth Five: Someone will invent an automatic solutions; and Myth Six: We will out-source our entire effort to an off-shore vendor, and you go on to describe your point of view on each one of those. The one we have time for or I'd like to get to is the last one: We will out-source our entire effort to an off-shore vendor. We've heard people say that and we've actually talked to some folks who had that capability, but I think there are an awful lot of risks inherent with simply sending code somewhere and I think I forget who it was who had the one hour Photo Mat analogy that drop it or send it in and come an hour and –

TONY KEYES: — Ed?

Y2KI: Yes.

TONY KEYES: Matridigm.

Y2KI: Right, send it in and drop it off and come back in an hour and it will be fixed. What's your experience on something like that, folks using off-shore vendors to fix the problem?

BRIAN KEANE: It's — certainly there is a segment out there market out there that is using some of the off-shore support, and I think the current tightness in labor market is perhaps forcing people to consider as more of an option then they might have otherwise. A couple of things: Ignoring the off-shore, let's talk about off-site. What does it take to move code off-site? Even it's just down the street. And even if it's just moving it off to packaging it up and sending it to a Matridigm or a Parodus(sp) or any of these other tools vendors that work off-site. To package it up, to get the source code, to get all the proper components and you ask any one of those firms, that is considerable more difficult then — it doesn't sound difficult, but it is — then any of them had anticipated. That's where the XX have run into some problems; that's where the Matridigms have run into some problems; certainly, that's where any of the mass change kinds of companies — tools are involved. Compounding that by moving things off-shore, I think that it's potentially somewhat problematic, particularly, if it's a full-life cycle. Keane's position — and we've set up a factory up in Nova Scotia, as opposed to doing it off-shore, it's near-shore. We don't have the language barrier and it's also within similar time zones. But there may be parts of the overall life-cycle, the actual conversion that lend itself to sending off-shore. Full life-cycle, I just don't think it makes sense. The most important part of this project is the up-front planning, and the triage, the environmental analysis — pulling together a plan, and in the back-end, the testing. And none of that can be done off-shore.

Y2KI: You know, this also leads into another aspect, some of the unique dynamic that are involved in Year 2000 problem, one of them being the inability in some environments to work on the code on the primary platform which forces you to move it onto another platform. So there has been a suggestion that companies like Compdisco(sp) might have a big play in the coming years providing resource for companies to use and move the code off to work on alternative platforms. Is that something that is also complicated as your suggesting by moving the code off-shore? Is it also difficult to use an alternative platform?

BRIAN KEANE: Well, we're seeing that as a trend really starting to increase and it's — you've got the Comdisco(sp) and then companies that we're talking with — talking with and/or working with include the Comdiscos and Sunguards(sp), AIGs, the Sabors(sp), the — there's a number of those firms. And I think a year ago they all said act now because all the capacity is going to be run out before you know it. I've never seen — didn't know there were so many firms out there that had data XX capacity until the past year. But most firms — let's take disaster recovery, for example, most firms have or should have a disaster recovery plan, where they take their stuff off-site to a Comdisco or Sunguard or whatever, and run and test their applications probably a couple times a year. So some firms may be accustomed to doing that already. For Year 2000 work, moving it off to say a Sunguard platform, it's not as straight forward as working on the host system, but certainly we're doing it today and it's not a major problem.

Y2KI: Brian, one of the — there are so many questions I want to get to, but what involvements are you seeing in terms of imbedded chips, infrastructure? Are you being brought into those kinds of issues — elevators going to run, things like that? Are you seeing a lot of that?

BRIAN KEANE: There's — yes, one of the things that we do, in some of our up-front phases is take an enterprise view. And some firms say, okay, we just want to look at our applications. Other firms say, hey, we need to at least inventory what our total liability is, and how we utilize dates with our information technology and that goes beyond applications, it means what kind of hardware, what kind of devices, chips, etc. We have the number of projects inventory that stuff for the customers. And provided that — we're not in the business of solving a problem of chips, but we can do is understand where they have a date liability that needs to be addressed.

Y2KI: Well, Brian we've managed to run through a full hour. I want thank you very much for getting up early and being with us.

(END)